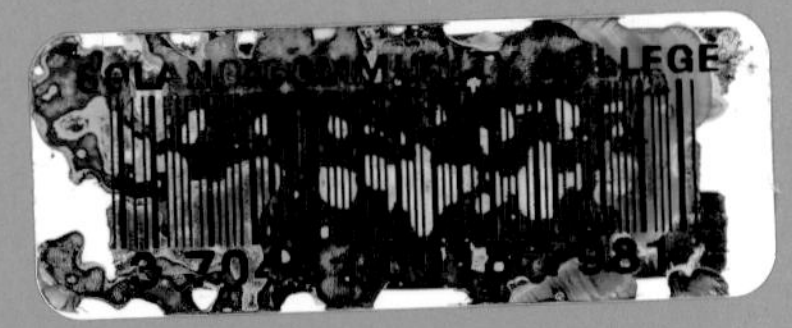

YEATS AND SHELLEY

Shelley's drawing "The Boat, the Dome, the Isle, the Eye of Creative Imagination," MS Shelley e.4. (Courtesy of the Bodleian Library, Oxford)

YEATS AND SHELLEY

George Bornstein

UNIVERSITY OF CHICAGO PRESS
Chicago and London

Standard Book Number: 226–06645–2
Library of Congress Catalog Card Number: 73–92050
THE UNIVERSITY OF CHICAGO PRESS, CHICAGO 60637
THE UNIVERSITY OF CHICAGO PRESS, LTD., LONDON
 Published 1970
Printed in the United States of America

For Christine

CONTENTS

ACKNOWLEDGMENTS

My largest specific debt in writing this book is to Professor Carlos Baker, who played Zonoras to a bumbling Athanase throughout its early stages; his generosity and high standards both as a scholar and as a teacher continue to inspire his former students. Professor A. Walton Litz read and made careful criticisms of an early draft of the whole, and Professor Hugh Witemeyer did the same for several chapters. Professor Eugene Goodheart provided both advice and encouragement during the final stages, and Professors Harold Bloom and Jerome J. McGann preserved me from errors of different kinds. Professors Richard Ellmann and A. Norman Jeffares and Miss Kathleen Raine all took the time to respond to my queries. The staffs of the libraries at Princeton and Harvard, of the British Museum, and of the National Library, Dublin, were unfailingly helpful. The Old Dominion Foundation and M.I.T. granted me a term's leave and a fellowship while I finished this book, and the Research Council of Rutgers University generously provided funds for preparing the final manuscript. Finally, I am grateful to my wife in ways too many and too deep to be enumerated here.

Alspach, editors: "The King's Threshold"; "On Baile's Strand," copyright 1907 by The Macmillan Company renewed 1935 by William Butler Yeats; "The Only Jealousy of Emer," copyright 1921 by The Macmillan Company renewed 1949 by Bertha Georgie Yeats; "A Full Moon in March," copyright 1935 by The Macmillan Company; "The Resurrection," copyright 1934 by The Macmillan Company renewed 1962 by Bertha Georgie Yeats; "The Death of Cuchulain," copyright 1940 by Georgie Yeats renewed 1968 by Bertha Georgie Yeats. *The Variorum Edition of the Poems of W. B. Yeats*, copyright 1903, 1906, 1907, 1912, 1916, 1918, 1919, 1924, 1928, 1931, 1933, 1934, 1935, 1940, 1944, 1945, 1946, 1950, 1956, 1957 by The Macmillan Company. Copyright 1940 by Georgie Yeats. *A Vision*, copyright 1938 by William Butler Yeats.

INTRODUCTION

When Yeats wrote that Shelley shaped his life, he did not exaggerate. In fact, Yeats formed his conception both of the poet and of poetry on Shelley. As a boy he imitated Shelleyan heroes like Athanase and the *Alastor* youth; as a young man he imitated Shelley himself in writing first plays and then poems about Intellectual Beauty; in maturity he reacted against Shelley even while borrowing symbols and ideas from him and while living in Thoor, Ballylee—partly to become Athanase at last; and, after attacking Shelley bitterly, he finally reinstated him as a lesser deity of his poetic pantheon in the late thirties. Besides borrowing lines and symbols from Shelley for his poetry, Yeats used him sometimes as a critical club, sometimes as a rapier in over a hundred literary controversies.

The two parts of this study elaborate related propositions: part 1 argues that the impact of Shelley upon Yeats shaped his art before 1903; and part 2 argues that Yeats's later development can be understood convincingly as a reaction against Shelley. In the nineties, particularly in the Rose poems, his study of Shelley impelled him toward an Intellectual vision of life in which he rejected the flawed, quotidian world for an ideal vision of Intellectual Beauty. Later, he renounced that position, which he identified with Shelley, for an antinomial vision based upon the inclusion of contending opposites, of which Intellectual Beauty and the phenomenal world were one pair. His well-known movement downward upon life rather than upward out of it marks his change from the Shelleyan work of his youth toward his own, independent maturity.

Each part contains four chapters. Chapters 1 and 2 are, in different ways, introductory. The first chapter traces the persistence of Yeats's interest in Shelley from boyhood until shortly before his death. Introduced to Shelley's work by his father when still a child, Yeats took Shelley as his model of the ideal poet, imitated his work, wrote two essays on him, and constantly cited him to illustrate his own thought. The second chapter treats Yeats's work in the eighties. The verse plays of that period are, frankly, bad, and they are read nowadays only because Yeats wrote them. But they have an additional attraction for us: Yeats said that he wrote them "in imitation of Shelley." They adumbrate his later concern with love and magic and show his first, fumbling attempts to assimilate Shelley's style and thought. The chapter concludes with *The Wanderings of Oisin* (1889), which both closes Yeats's early burst of Shelleyan enthusiasm and anticipates his deeper development of Shelleyan themes in the nineties.

Although Yeats had played at being Prince Athanase and "Alastor" (as he insisted on calling the nameless youth of Shelley's poem) in boyhood, in early manhood he used them as idealized self-images in developing his Intellectual vision. Chapter 3 posits Yeats as an "Alastor" seeking Intellectual Beauty; his theory, practice, and defense of poetry in the nineties all derive from Shelley. His own essay on "The Philosophy of Shelley's Poetry" caps the literary manifestoes from which by his own admission he gleaned his poetics—Shelley's *Defence*, Hallam's essay on Tennyson, and Browning's essay on Shelley. The Rose poems conform to the same creed in subject, style, and speaking voice. Chapter 4 posits Yeats as an Athanase seeking wisdom to go with his Intellectual vision. The Platonic and Neoplatonic symbolism he ascribed to Shelley entered his own work as well, particularly in the tower poems, and he willy-nilly found his own doctrines of death and magic shared by Shelley. As the conclusion to part 1, this chapter traces the survival of Shelleyan symbolism in Yeats's poetry long after he repudiated his early Intellectual vision.

I have resisted the lure of imposing an artificial tidiness on this study by imputing a false exactness to Yeats's break with Shelley. In a mind as complex and organic as Yeats's, one cannot state that after, say, May of 1903 he demythologized Shelley and cast down his sometime idol into the street. Rather, the change evolved gradually along with Yeats's entire remaking of his world view between, roughly, the publication of *Ideas of Good and Evil* in 1903 and of *Responsibilities* in 1914. Or perhaps Easter 1916 or his marriage in October 1917 should be the terminal date. In any case, during that period of a dozen or so years Yeats remade his personality and his art. Shelley was so identified with his own self-image in the nineties that Yeats had to attack Shelley violently in order to establish his own independent identity, and he fired away not so much at the actual Shelley as at the Shelley-Yeats hybrid of the nineties.

The four chapters of part 2 examine Yeats's changing evaluation of Shelley and its correspondence to his own work, both in what he rejected and in the few things he continued to praise. The fifth chapter explores the antinomial aesthetic which Yeats created to replace the Shelleyan Intellectual vision of his early career. Long before he broke with Shelley, Yeats had already perceived that "the typical young poet of our day is an aesthete with a surfeit, searching sadly for his lost Philistinism, his heart full of an unsatisfied hunger for the commonplace. He is an Alastor tired of his woods and longing for beer and skittles." By 1903 Yeats had had a surfeit of the Intellectual vision of "Alastor" and turned to developing his own, antinomial vision based on conflicting opposites—Shelley and Dickens, bird and market cart, fair and foul, good and evil. Yet even while casting off most of Shelley, Yeats developed the psychological theories which enabled him to preserve in new form his admiration of "Alastor," Athanase, and Ahasuerus, not as models for the self but as images of the antiself.

The remaining chapters fix the precise nature of Yeats's new "movement downwards upon life" in comparison with Shelley. The sixth chapter traces the early impact of Shelley's concept of the epipsyche on Yeats and his eventual rejection of it for the doctrine of the mask, which precludes knowledge and union of the lovers. The final two chapters examine Yeats's and Shelley's visions of the fair, and Yeats's charge that Shelley's work lacked a counterbalancing vision of the foul and that his own did not. Chapter 7, "History as Revelation," compares Shelley's ideal of Athens with Yeats's of Byzantium and shows that Yeats's antinomial vision led him to rework certain Shelleyan passages to fit them into his new view of history. The final chapter evaluates Yeats's charge that Shelley lacked a Vision of Evil. In Yeats's opinion, Shelley surrendered to a false creativity which led him to present an unrealistic triumph of goodness and a caricature of evil in his verse, and he resolved to avoid Shelley's error.

Ultimately, Yeats and Shelley (as seen by Yeats) offer us two contrasting ways of looking at the world. The first is Intellectual—to see in all things imperfect manifestations of an ideal, to shun whatever cannot be transformed, and to retreat if necessary to private Edens where we can all cultivate our imaginative gardens in peace. When applied to political activism, Intellectual vision creates intolerant self-assertion and its fierce egalitarianism often calls forth the very despotic counterforces which it hates; eventually, having lost that intellectual innocence which Yeats prized so highly, its men and women perch on wagonettes to scream, dupes of their own daimons. The second way is antinomial—to act, but still to accept the continual and unresolved conflict of opposites in the world, whether of good and evil, love and hate, fair and foul, or whatever. Only by accepting them, and not by falsifying our conception of what we oppose or by bleating with shrill hysteria after an impossible victory, can we, like the musicians of "Lapis Lazuli," see with eyes that are gay. As an earlier era would have said, we should be both innocent as the dove and wise as the serpent. To an age with an increasing tendency toward narcissistic polarization, Yeats's message has its merits.

Three points about the method of this book require specific mention. First, as should already be apparent, the actual Shelley and the Shelley seen by Yeats do not always coincide; at times one is almost a parody of the other. I have emphasized Yeats's Shelley in the first part of this study, because that idea of Shelley shaped his early work. In the second part, however, I have tried to redress the balance and to consider also the "actual" Shelley (whoever he is) and the reasons Yeats distorted him. Even though this book is mainly about Yeats, I hope that by comparing him to Shelley the second part says something worthwhile about Shelley as well.

Second, the book focuses on ideas, on the symbols which express them, and on the poetic theory by which Yeats related the two. Yeats's literary achievement suggests that he is right and that those critics who depreciate his ideas or his poetics as silly are themselves wrong. I use the same approach with Yeats that Yeats himself used with Shelley, and believe that that is the best way to understand the relation between the two poets. Yeats, after all, divided his first essay on Shelley into two sections, "His Ruling Ideas" and "His Ruling Symbols," and always emphasized Shelley's metaphysics and symbolism when discussing him. Further, Yeats is capacious enough to subsume other theorists far more easily than they can account for him. I am not against translating Yeats into critical Chinese, but I am willing to leave that job to others.

Finally, this book provides a crucial but not an encyclopedic view of Yeats. He was perhaps the most complex mind of our century, and one cannot fully come to grips with him through any single approach. In emphasizing the impact of Shelley on Yeats, I do not mean to deny the impact of Blake, of Irish writers, of the Italian Renaissance, or of any of the other strands elucidated by other scholars. Yeats's debt to Swinburne and the Pre-Raphaelites, which is beyond the limits of this study, might profitably be examined in detail. Nor should this book be misconstrued as denying Yeats's astonishing originality in any way; for, as he himself continually emphasized, true originality depends in part upon mastery of a tradition, and Shelley was a vital part of the tradition in which Yeats saw himself. I do believe that every stage of Yeats's career—especially the early ones–can be understood better for seeing its relation to Shelley, and that Shelley played a continuing and central role in his development. This work is intended to supplement what is already known, not to throw it out the window, and I am grateful for the prodigious labors of the many Yeats scholars who have erected such a solid foundation for further work.

PART ONE

INTELLECTUAL VISION: THE IMPACT OF SHELLEY ON YEATS

1 The Persistence of Yeats's Interest in Shelley

"Shelley . . . shaped my life."
—*Yeats in his essay* "Prometheus Unbound"

On 28 July 1938, six months before he died, William Butler Yeats visited the Shelley family estate, Field Place, in Sussex. Next day he described his pilgrimage to the literary shrine in a letter to Lady Dorothy Wellesley:

> Yesterday I went to Field Place. The proprietor a Colonel Challenger [*sic*, Charrington] and his guests were at the races but we had arranged beforehand to be shown over the house by the butler. A beautiful old house, one part Tudor, kept in perfect order and full of fine pictures (two Wilsons). We also went to the church where the Shelley tombs are, a great old church defiled by 1870 or thereabouts, stained glass, and pavements not at all as Shelley saw it. Before I leave I shall visit the pond (not that near the house) where Shelley sailed paper boats.[1]

Not a passing interest in Shelley but rather a lifelong fascination with him motivated Yeats's visit. His writings and those of his circle indicate his demonstrably strong interest, at times almost an obsession, for over sixty years. As a boy he imagined himself a Shelleyan hero; as a young man he imagined himself a Shelleyan poet. With middle age he reacted violently against Shelley and asserted his poetic independence. By the end of his life, as the visit to Field Place shows, Yeats reconciled himself to Shelley with a distinct but by no means unqualified admiration. This chapter surveys the biographical facts about Yeats's interest in Shelley, as a support for the remainder of the study.

Like the youthful Shelley, the young Yeats fancied himself a future scientist. As Yeats shifted his interest and began to play at being—in a characteristic association—"a sage, a magician or a

[1] *Letters on Poetry from W. B. Yeats to Dorothy Wellesley*, p. 200.

poet,"[2] he picked such romantic heroes as Manfred and Prince Athanase for his models. Eventually, he tells us in *Reveries over Childhood and Youth*,[3] he "chose Alastor for my chief of men and longed to share his melancholy" and imagined disappearing in a boat drifting down a river. He modeled his women on Cythna in *The Revolt of Islam.* All these characters reappeared in his own work when he began to write seriously.

Yeats's early interest in Shelley did not flourish only in solitary wanderings. His father, John Butler Yeats, a painter with Pre-Raphaelite affinities, repeatedly read the young Willie passages from *Prometheus Unbound.* The elder Yeats prized passion above all in poetry and disliked "generalization or abstraction however impassioned." Thus, his son tells us, "he would read out the first speeches of the *Prometheus Unbound*, but never the ecstatic lyricism of that famous fourth act. . . . All must be an idealisation of speech, and at some moment of passionate action or somnambulistic reverie."[4] John Butler Yeats's enthusiasm had an enduring effect on his impressionable son. A visit to the Pre-Raphaelite paintings in the Tate Gallery in 1913 recalled to Yeats, then almost fifty, the "memories of sketches of my father's on the margins of the first Shelley I had read."[5]

John Butler Yeats introduced his son not only to the works of Shelley but also to the foremost Shelleyan of the time, Professor Edward Dowden of Dublin University. Dowden, who may have unwittingly served as one of the models for Yeats's poem "The Scholars," was then completing his famous biography. Yeats records one visit to Dowden as follows:

> Once after breakfast Dowden read us some chapters of the unpublished *Life of Shelley*, and I who had made the *Prometheus Unbound* my sacred book was delighted with all he read. I was chilled, however, when he explained that he had lost his liking for Shelley and would not have written it but for an old promise to the Shelley family. When it was published, Matthew Arnold made sport of certain conventional-

[2] *Autobiographies*, p. 64. Because, as Joseph Ronsley has reminded us, Yeats changed the title of this work to *The Autobiography* in the last edition published before his death, I have cited it hereafter as *Autobiography* rather than *Autobiographies*. See Ronsley, *Yeats's Autobiography: Life as Symbolic Pattern*, pp. 5, 33.

[3] *Autobiography*, p. 64.

[4] Ibid., p. 65.

[5] *Essays and Introductions*, p. 346. Hereafter cited as *E & I*.

> ities and extravagances that were, my father and I had come to see, the violence or clumsiness of a conscientious man hiding from himself a lack of sympathy.[6]

Yeats noticed Dowden's "lack of sympathy" with Shelley more than once. Eight years later he used the same phrase in a later section of his autobiography, in which he notes that Dowden tried to make Shakespeare into a "British Benthamite" and "flattered Shelley but to hide his own growing lack of sympathy."[7] For Yeats, indiscriminate praise did not signify genuine appreciation. Dowden's *Life of Percy Bysshe Shelley* elicited Matthew Arnold's essay on Shelley, which the young Yeats devoted considerable energy to refuting.

Yeats's own early sympathy for Shelley increased rapidly during his manhood. His enthusiasm both amused and irked his friends. Katharine Tynan combined both feelings in remembering a stormy night in 1886 when the young poet devoted more attention to reciting "The Sensitive Plant" than to sheltering her with an umbrella. She writes in her autobiography:

> I remember one very wet night, after we had been to a meeting of the Protestant Home Rule Association, when we waited in Westmoreland Street for a tram; I in my smart clothes, my high-heeled French shoes, standing in a pool of water; the wind driving the rain as it does only in a seabound city; Willie holding the umbrella at an acute and absent-minded angle which could shelter nobody, pouring the while into my ears *The Sensitive Plant.* It was a moment to try a woman's temper, and mine did not stand the trial well.[8]

Miss Tynan was not always so unresponsive to her friend's enthusiasm, for in 1888 she presented him with the Routledge edition of *The Poetical Works of Percy Bysshe Shelley.*[9]

[6] *Autobiography*, p. 87. [7] Ibid., p. 235.

[8] Katharine Tynan Hinkson, *Twenty-five Years: Reminiscences*, p. 219.

[9] See A. Norman Jeffares, "Thoor, Ballylee," p. 162. Professor Jeffares, who has himself examined the volume of Shelley, has very kindly written me a letter amplifying his brief comment in the article. He writes:

> Mrs. Yeats purchased a copy of Shelley given to WBY by Katharine Tynan—a Routledge Edition—in about 1945–6. I have read this volume and as far as I can recollect there are no marginalia of any significance. Both Mrs. Yeats & I had thought it curious there were no Shelley texts in his library: she bought this volume on a secondbook stall one Saturday morning by chance shortly after we had discussed the Shelley influences. . . . Yeats moved a lot & many of his early books didn't survive" [Letter dated 17 March 1966].

Besides Dowden, Yeats knew six other students of Shelley who published their work before his own essay appeared. Three of them were fellow members of the Rhymers' Club—John Todhunter, who published critical and biographical studies, and T. W. Rolleston and Ernest Rhys, who edited some of Shelley's works. During the eighties Todhunter published a lengthy study of the romantic poet as well as two short monographs. Although Yeats may have approved of the statement that "Shelley . . . was in his loftiest moods a great mytho-poet" and delighted in the phrase "Shelley, the mystic," he would have had little general sympathy with a critic who found the beloved *Prometheus* "immature as compared with *The Triumph of Life*."[10] In a biographical sketch of Todhunter published in 1889, Yeats mentions *A Study of Shelley* without comment.[11]

Other friends who wrote on Shelley included Aubrey de Vere, William Sharp, and Stopford Brooke. De Vere's study, one of many Victorian efforts to divide poetry into two categories, anticipates Yeats in classifying Shelley as a poet of aspiration for the "ideally beautiful" rather than of "vivid sympathy for reality."[12] De Vere's work accords with the essays of Hallam and Browning, for which Yeats showed enthusiasm during the nineties, and may well have influenced his thought.

The affinity between Shelley's poetry and that of Yeats did not escape his friends. Francis Thompson discussed the resemblance prominently in two reviews of Yeats's work in 1890 and 1899. He detected "the evident influence of Shelley" in the poems of the eighties. They were "markedly in the Shelleian

[10] The quotations from Todhunter may be found in the following works, respectively: *A Study of Shelley*, p. 10; *Shelley and the Marriage Question*, p. 18; *Notes on Shelley's Unfinished Poem "The Triumph of Life*," p. 8.

See also Rolleston's editions of the *Address to the Irish People* and *A Philosophical View of Reform* and Rhys' edition of *Essays and Letters of Shelley*.

[11] "John Todhunter," p. 144. The article is conveniently reprinted in *W. B. Yeats: Letters to Katharine Tynan*, ed. Roger McHugh, pp. 152–54.

[12] De Vere, "The Two Chief Schools of English Poetry: Poetic Versatility: Shelley and Keats," in *Essays, Chiefly on Poetry*, 2: 107–8. The discussion of Shelley on pp. 124–32 makes clear that de Vere considers him a poet of the "ideally beautiful."

See also Sharp's *The Life of Percy Bysshe Shelley*, and Stopford Brooke's "Some Thoughts on Shelley" and *Poems from Shelley*.

[*sic*] vein, or rather in one Shelleian vein. Take the Shelley of 'The Witch of Atlas'; imagine him piping on a fairy straw, instead of sweeping the harp of the winds; and you have Mr. Yeats." In a well-meant but ill-chosen phrase Thompson described the author as "a fay hopped out of a corner of Shelley's brain." By 1899 Thompson responded less enthusiastically to Yeats's work but still noted some similarity to Shelley. In his view the poet of *The Wind among the Reeds* belonged "natively to the same order as Coleridge and Spenser and Shelley . . . the Shelley of the songs." Arguing that Yeats lacked Shelley's "large or wide gift," Thompson wrote, "Some of his earlier work, in particular, shows close study of Shelley, and happy affinities with Shelley's lighter fancy; but his most characteristic work is not at all Shelleyan."[13] The next year Yeats published his interpretation of Shelley, which, among other things, showed how astonishingly Shelleyan "his most characteristic work" really was.

Given the strong interest in Shelley both of Yeats himself and of his friends, it is not surprising that he began to work on his own study of the romantic poet. In a letter to his sister Lily on 12 July 1899, Yeats mentioned that besides completing *The Shadowy Waters* he was currently "making notes for an article on the philosophical ideas in Shelley's poetry."[14] That description and the title of the finished essay, "The Philosophy of Shelley's Poetry," reflect Yeats's predominant interest in Shelley's ideas, or in what he called "the system of belief that lay behind" the poems.[15] Even when in later years Yeats strongly criticized Shelley, he did so less on technical than on metaphysical grounds.

Only the first of the two sections of the essay now known as "The Philosophy of Shelley's Poetry" appeared in *The Dome* for July 1900. In that section, subtitled "His Ruling Ideas," Yeats delineates Shelley's vision of life. He finds that the apprehension of Intellectual Beauty underlies all of Shelley's philosophy. Him-

[13] "W. B. Yeats" and "Mr. Yeats's Poems" in *The Real Robert Louis Stevenson*, ed. Terence L. Connolly (New York, 1959), pp. 201–9. The quotations are from pp. 201 and 205. The former essay first appeared in the *Weekly Register*, 27 September 1890, and the latter in the *Academy*, 6 May 1899.

[14] *The Letters of W. B. Yeats*, ed. Allan Wade, p. 323. Hereafter referred to as "*Yeats's Letters*."

[15] "The Philosophy of Shelley's Poetry," *E & I*, p. 66.

self writing poetry partly under the influence of Shelley's conception of Intellectual Beauty, Yeats here defends his model warmly against those who thought him a mere Godwinian revolutionary.

The second section of the essay, "His Ruling Symbols," appeared along with the first in *Ideas of Good and Evil* (1903). Concentrating more on poetical technique, Yeats holds that Shelley adumbrates a coherent symbolical system in which the primary images are the sun, moon, morning star, water, tower, and cave. He admires not the mere technical virtuosity of Shelley's achievement but rather the underlying vision of the world which the symbolism expresses. The concept of using a pattern of recurrent symbols to express a philosophy of life—which he also found in Blake—helped form his own art.

Shelley's vision of Intellectual Beauty helped to sustain the young Yeats in his fight against materialism. Shelley offered both an artistic and a personal example to those who would reject mechanical theories of life. In old age Yeats looked back and recalled "Shelley, whose art and life became so completely identified with romantic contemplation that young men in their late teens, when I was at that age, identified him with poetry itself."[16] By the time of the first essay on Shelley, Yeats associated him not only with "romantic contemplation" but also with mysticism. He begins the essay by recalling his days as a hermetic student, when he hoped to persuade his fellow students to study *Prometheus Unbound* as "a sacred book."[17] Yeats states his belief that whatever of philosophy has been made into poetry is alone permanent (a view which recalls Shelley's reasons for considering Plato a poet). For him, the primary Shelleyan text for mystical study is the *Prometheus*, which he says he has been rereading in the woods of Drim-na-Rod.

Although Yeats moved away from Shelley both aesthetically and philosophically after the nineties, his interest in Shelley and that of his circle continued to be strong. In 1902 he wrote of a visit by Florence Farr: "A friend, who was here a few minutes ago, has sat with a beautiful stringed instrument upon her knee, her fingers passing over the strings, and has spoken to me some

[16] "Introduction" to *Fighting the Waves*, in *Explorations*, p. 375.
[17] *E & I*, p. 65.

verses from Shelley's *Skylark*."[18] Francis Thompson's effusive essay, "Shelley," appeared in *The Dublin Review* for July 1908. In 1909 Arthur Symons, a closer friend of Yeats in the nineties than thereafter, published his survey, *The Romantic Movement in English Poetry*, which included a chapter on Shelley. There Symons quotes from what he calls Yeats's "minute study of the details of Shelley's philosophy," although those details did not dissuade Symons from accusing Shelley of "vagueness."[19] Robert Bridges shrewdly brandished Shelley's name in persuading Yeats to contribute to his wartime anthology, *The Spirit of Man* (1916), and he perceptively juxtaposed passages from Shelley and Yeats in the text itself.[20]

By far the most important influence on Yeats's ideas about Shelley after the turn of the century remained his father. The elder Yeats provided a continuing fund of opinions about Shelley in his correspondence with his son between 1906 and 1917. Although he generally admired Shelley, John Butler Yeats expounded his limitations in detail. In his view those limitations were excessive intellectual abstraction and a lack of "what I call the earthy."[21] On the positive side he found Shelley to be a "true solitary" who possessed "concrete discipline" and a "concrete spirit" and who could in a single line "fill my vision with a wealth of fine things."[22]

John Butler Yeats may have felt obliged to point out the dangers of Shelley as a model because of his awareness of essential similarities between his son and the romantic poet. If so, his warnings were taken seriously by the younger Yeats, who later qualified his admiration of Shelley partly for the same reasons advanced by his father. John Butler Yeats expressed the affinity by the somewhat surprising adjective "benign." He wrote to his son in 1909:

[18] "Speaking to the Psaltery," *E & I*, p. 13.

[19] Arthur Symons, *The Romantic Movement in English Poetry*, p. 280.

[20] See Bridges's letter to Yeats in Joseph Hone, *W. B. Yeats: 1865–1939*, p. 292; cf. Neville Rogers, *Shelley at Work*, pp. 134–35.

[21] *Further Letters of John Butler Yeats*, ed. Lennox Robinson, p. 38. For the charge of abstraction see ibid., p. 9, and *Letters of John Butler Yeats*, ed. Joseph Hone, p. 205.

[22] John Butler Yeats, *Further Letters*, ed. Robinson, pp. 9, 50; *Letters*, ed. Hone, p. 215.

> I think the reason you have the popular gift is because your *talent is benign.* That is its essential quality—[word indecipherable] are *malign;* so are aristocracies and pessimists—it is the whole of *Nietzsche*—so are College Dons and *their retinue;* but so were not Shakespeare or Shelley. Had the latter lived he would have proved it. His "passion to reform the world" which he himself avowed made him quarrelsome, but later on, the quarrels over, he would have been wholly benign. . . . This benign quality you get from me.[23]

Yeats accepted his father's association of himself with Shelley. In both the 1925 and 1937 versions of *A Vision* he assigned Shelley to the same psychological category as himself, although for different reasons. The discussion of Shelley there constitutes a brief essay on the nature of the poet's life and work. By according more closely with Yeats's own work during the nineties than with Shelley's, the statements in *A Vision* suggest the extent to which Yeats had earlier identified himself with his predecessor.

Yeats read Shelley again in the fall of 1924, when he was completing the first version of *A Vision.* By then he had drastically qualified his earlier enthusiasm. Lady Gregory recorded in her journal Yeats's opinion of Shelley at this time. Objecting to a review of Herbert Trench's poems in the *Times Literary Supplement*, Yeats said:

> That man talks nonsense about Shelley. Very little of Shelley will last for, say, forty years. I know for I was reading him the other day. There are about twenty pages of exquisite beauty that will live for ever. . . . I remember my father telling me Keats was a better poet than Shelley. I didn't believe him then but I know what he meant now, though I care more for Shelley.[24]

Yeats read *Prometheus Unbound* again in 1932, when he wrote his second essay on Shelley, this time on the "sacred book" itself. By now Yeats had articulated a world view radically dif-

[23] John Butler Yeats, *Letters,* ed. Hone, p. 217.

[24] *Lady Gregory's Journals,* ed. Lennox Robinson, p. 263. Robinson's dating of this entry as 14 Nov. 1925 seems unlikely. Lady Gregory says the *Times Supplement* containing the review had come "last evening." Since "The Poetry of Herbert Trench" appeared in the *Times Supplement* for 13 November 1924, I have used 1924 rather than 1925 as the year of Yeats's statements. The earlier date is important because it suggests that Yeats read Shelley again in order to treat him in the first version of *A Vision* (1925), rather than afterward.

ferent from the Shelleyan one of his youth; consequently, he adopts a new attitude toward the philosophy of Shelley's poetry. Holding a philosophy of eternal conflict between the ideal and the actual, Yeats now associates Shelley only with a vision of the ideal. For him Shelley represents only half of the various antitheses in his own antinomial system.

Awareness of his break with Shelley did not prevent Yeats from recognizing the immense effect Shelley had had upon his development. In the fourth section of the essay Yeats looks back from old age upon the time of his youth, just as when still a youth he looked forward apprehensively to old age. He recalls the great vogue of Shelley during the period 1885–95 and mentions particularly the Shelley Society, the production and banning of *The Cenci*, and the fashionable pictures of the burning of Shelley's body produced by provincial sketching clubs. Such reminiscences suggest to Yeats a series of speculations which concludes with a surprising revelation: "When in middle life I looked back I found that he and not Blake, whom I had studied more and with more approval, had shaped my life."[25] Presumably, only by breaking away from Shelley did Yeats avoid the fate of several companions in the Rhymers' Club, who, through Shelley's "direct or indirect influence" fell prey to "Jacobin frenzies" and "brown demons."

Yeats's own writings reveal an extensive knowledge of Shelley's work. He either mentions or quotes from all the major poems as well as many of the essays and minor poems. His favorite work was *Prometheus Unbound*. Largely because of the figures of the solitary poet or sage, he also preferred *Alastor*, *Prince Athanase*, and *Hellas*. Besides those, of the major works he knew *Queen Mab*, *The Revolt of Islam*, *Rosalind and Helen*, *Julian and Maddalo*, *The Cenci*, *The Mask of Anarchy*, *The Witch of Atlas*, *Epipsychidion*, *Adonais*, and *The Triumph of Life*. Of the shorter poems he refers to "Hymn to Intellectual Beauty," "Mont Blanc," "Marianne's Dream," "Ode to the West Wind," "The Sensitive Plant," "The Cloud," "To a Skylark," "Ode to Liberty," "Ode to Naples," "The Waning Moon," "The World's Wanderers," "To ———" ("One word is too often profaned"), "Laurels," and *Fragments of an Unfinished Drama*. Of the prose

25 "*Prometheus Unbound*," *E & I*, p. 424.

he mentions the *Defence of Poetry* most often and also quotes from "On Love," "On Life," "Speculations on Metaphysics," and *A Philosophical View of Reform.*[26] Besides writing the two essays on Shelley, Yeats refers to him over a hundred times elsewhere in his works. The strength of his interest in Shelley and the numerous pieces to which he does allude suggest an acquaintance with the whole of Shelley's published work.

Yeats's life and writings, then, provide sound evidence of a thorough knowledge of Shelley. The remainder of this study explores the importance of that knowledge for his own career. Yeats responded to Shelley with boyish enthusiasm in the eighties, understood him more deeply and with even more approval during the nineties, rejected him while forming his own style after the turn of the century, railed against him even while borrowing some of his symbols during the twenties and thirties, and, at last secure in his independence, pardoned and partially reaccepted him toward the end of the thirties. The changing relation between Shelley and Yeats deepens our appreciation of Yeats's work at every stage. "Shelley," he wrote, "shaped my life."

[26] For the reader's convenience in ascertaining that Yeats did indeed refer to or quote from all these works, I have given here the most convenient source for the works he mentions more than once.

The page number on which the following works are mentioned in "The Philosophy of Shelley's Poetry," *E & I*, appears in parentheses following the title of the work: *Prometheus Unbound* (65 ff.), *Alastor* (80), *Prince Athanase* (87), *Hellas* (88), *Queen Mab* (69), *The Revolt of Islam* (*Laon and Cythna*) (68), *Rosalind and Helen* (71–72), *Julian and Maddalo* (70), *The Mask of Anarchy* (69), *The Witch of Atlas* (80 ff.), *Epipsychidion* (81), *Adonais* (72), *The Triumph of Life* (93 ff.), "Mont Blanc" (70), "Marianne's Dream" (79), "The Sensitive Plant" (73), "Ode to Liberty" (88), "Ode to Naples" (68), "The Waning Moon" (92), "The World's Wanderers" (92), "To———" ("One word is too often profaned") (92), "Laurels" (92), *Fragments of an Unfinished Drama* (81), *Defence of Poetry* (67–68), "On Love" (69), "On Life" (84), and *A Philosophical View of Reform* (69).

The number in parentheses after the following works indicates the page on which they are mentioned in *E & I*: *The Cenci* (421), "Ode to the West Wind" (222), "The Cloud" (337), "To a Skylark" (13).

Yeats quotes from "Speculations on Metaphysics" in *Per Amica Silentia Lunae,* in *Mythologies,* p. 352.

Yeats's reference to "that Intellectual Beauty which was to Shelley's mind the central power of the world" on p. 89 of *E & I* prompted me to include the "Hymn to Intellectual Beauty" with the above works.

2 "Imitation of Shelley": Yeats in the 1880s

> "I had as many ideas as I have now, only I did not know how to choose from among them those that belonged to my life."
> —*Yeats,* Autobiography (Reveries over Childhood and Youth)

"I had begun to write poetry in imitation of Shelley and of Edmund Spenser, play after play—for my father exalted dramatic poetry above all other kinds—and I invented fantastic and incoherent plots,"[1] wrote Yeats in *Reveries over Childhood and Youth.* Although he had begun to write poetry as early as 1882, the outpouring of Shelleyan verse dramas between 1884 and 1886 marked Yeats's first sustained literary effort. He later recognized that he had not lisped in numbers and excluded those writings from collected editions of his work. The four published plays from that period—*Vivien and Time*, *Mosada*, *The Island of Statues*, and *The Seeker*—command attention not for their own sake but for what they tell us about the enormous impact of Shelley on Yeats at the beginning of his literary career. Their emphasis on love and magic, like that in the dramatic poem *The Wanderings of Oisin*, demonstrates what "imitation of Shelley" meant to Yeats in the mid-1880s and foreshadows his profounder development of those Shelleyan themes in the 1890s.

Although by the mid-eighties Yeats was probably acquainted with a substantial portion of Shelley's work, the four poems definitely known to him provide the closest analogues to his own wandering lovers and alluring enchantresses. From *Alastor*, *Prince Athanase*, *The Revolt of Islam*, and *Prometheus Unbound*

[1] *Autobiography*, pp. 66–67. Yeats named Shelley and Spenser as the dominant influences on his early work more than once. See also "What Is Popular Poetry?" *E & I*, p. 3, and "A General Introduction for My Work," *E & I*, p. 510. The former essay is dated 1901, the latter 1937.

he extrapolated a world where melancholy lovers seek their ladies with varying success, often in exotic settings presided over by a symbolic star, where esoteric wisdom and magic spells either frustrate or complete the search. Yeats's occasionally idiosyncratic readings of Shelley shaped what he meant by "imitation," for what he found in Shelley did not always coincide with what was there to be found. We may imagine *Prometheus Unbound* hovering over Yeats's juvenilia like a benignant deity sadly puzzled by the antics of its progeny.

I

Yeats followed Shelley in treating love as a continuous quest, ending in death and symbolized by star imagery. Shelley developed that pattern most clearly in *Alastor*, a work which Yeats knew from boyhood, when on the cliffs near Howth[2] he had played at imitating its hero. No wonder, then, that when he began to write he played at being the poem's author, and himself wrote three early works on the search for love—*The Seeker*, *The Island of Statues*, and *Mosada*. Since those dramas are relatively unknown even to the informed reader, brief summaries will illustrate the thematic importance of the quest for love and prepare for later discussion of its relation to death and to star imagery.

Only two scenes totaling eighty-one lines comprise *The Seeker*, by far the shortest of the three plays. The first opens with a conversation about a haunted flute by three shepherds, who conclude that the voice coming from the flute must be an omen. They are interrupted by an old knight, a sort of aged *Alastor* poet, who like his Shelleyan predecessor has been wandering over the earth, especially along "Asian rivers,"[3] led on by a voice he heard in a dream. In the second scene the old knight encounters the "Figure" who has inspired his wandering. Like the maiden in *Alastor*, this Figure has not shown the wanderer her countenance, for he exclaims, "Then let me see thy face before I die."[4] The Figure

[2] *Autobiography*, p. 64.

[3] *The Seeker*, in *The Variorum Edition of the Poems of W. B. Yeats*, ed. Peter Allt and Russell K. Alspach, p. 682. Hereafter cited as *Variorum Poems*.

[4] Ibid., p. 684. The poet in *Alastor* dreams of a "veiled maid"; see *The Works of Percy Bysshe Shelley*, ed. Roger Ingpen and Walter Peck, 1: 181. Hereafter cited as *Works*.

then becomes more like a *belle dame sans merci*, for a "sudden light" reveals that she is really a witch. The knight laments his lost youth and then dies.

The Island of Statues, too, opens with an unyielding lady scorning her would-be suitors. Naschina rejects both Thernot and Colin, two shepherds whose names reveal their Spenserian ancestry,[5] and pretends to reject Almintor, another candidate. To please Naschina, Almintor undertakes to pluck the "flower of joy" from the island of the enchantress. At the island Almintor, like all previous questers, picks the wrong flower and is changed into a stone statue. Naschina, disguised as a man, tricks the enchantress and obtains the flower, which she uses to change all the statues back into human beings. They can then return to the world but choose instead to remain in Arcadia. Yeats uses the word "quest" three times in the play, most prominently in the closing lines, where Naschina declares, "O, my Almintor, noble was thy quest."[6]

Finally, *Mosada* presents the quest for love more ironically in a plot also influenced by Thomas Moore. Agents of the Inquisition arrest the Moorish girl Mosada on charges of black magic. While in prison she yearns for reunion with her lover, Gomez, whom she has not seen for three years. Despairing, she drinks the poison conveniently hidden in her ring. As she is dying, the chief inquisitor Ebremar enters. He turns out to be Gomez, who has entered church and become a powerful officer of the Inquisition. Recognizing Mosada, he suggests that they run away together, but she is already moribund. In this play, the only one with a specific historical and geographical setting, the forces of worldly reality frustrate the quest for ideal love. The Inquisition itself was a favorite target of Shelley's.

Even in this early period Yeats experimented in his own verse

[5] Colin and another shepherd called not Thernot but Thenot appear throughout *The Shephardes Calendar*. In the eclogue for November, one of the four which Yeats liked well enough to include in his edition of Spenser in 1906, Thenot and Colin sing of their love for a maiden called Dido and their sorrow at her death. In the singing match in *The Island of Statues* Thernot and Colin also sing of their love for a maiden, Naschina, and Colin mentions Queen Dido of Troy in his opening song. Although in the November eclogue Spenser handles his characters decorously, Yeats transforms his into comic figures aptly mocked as bumpkins by Naschina.

[6] *Variorum Poems*, p. 679.

by associating love with death in the manner of Shelley. A later essay on William Morris was to praise Shelley for using death as a symbol of the ecstasy of love.[7] The youth in *Alastor* dies because of love; Lionel obligingly likens love's ecstasy to death just before he expires in *Rosalind and Helen;* and the lovers Laon and Cythna perish together on the pyre in *The Revolt of Islam.* Yeats indicated his acceptance of the Shelleyan notion even by the title of a poem published in *The Dublin University Review* for May 1885, "Love and Death."[8] Personifying love and death as "two spirits," the poem maintains that "If one should rise beside thee, / The other is not far."

Yeats's extravagant early plots usually make the quest for love end in death. In them, as later in *The Shadowy Waters,* Yeats's ambivalence about the outcome of the search obscures the exact relation of death to his theme. The old knight in *The Seeker* has scorned the world of human affairs and affection in order to search for his "visionary one."[9] When he finds the Figure he dies. Yeats allows for two contradictory interpretations of the Figure. Her face indicates that she is the bearded witch Infamy, whereas her voice suggests that she is his immortal lady after all. The knight indicates both possibilities in his final lines. Upon seeing her face he cries, "I sought thee not"; but upon hearing her voice, he recognizes that she is the Figure he had sought.[10] The outcome of the quest remains as uncertain as the character of the Figure, for while the knight has found the voice he sought (although possibly not the visionary woman), he does, as the Figure puts it, "die before our lips have met." The uncertainty about the Figure and about the conclusion of the search makes the knight's death ambiguous. On the one hand he could, like the poet of *Alastor,* die because of the failure of his quest; on the other hand, like Keats in *Adonais,* his death may signify entrance into a consuming ecstasy of the spirit.

In *Mosada* and *The Island of Statues* death both accompanies and frustrates the conclusion of the quest for love. Mosada's

7 "The Happiest of the Poets," *E&I,* p. 57.

8 *Variorum Poems,* p. 680. "Love and Death" is also the title of an unpublished play of the same period.

9 *The Seeker,* ibid., p. 684.

10 Ibid., p. 685.

reunion with her beloved Gomez coincides with her own death by poison. Like the knight in *The Seeker* she discovers her beloved, but dies upon finding him. *The Island of Statues* treats the same notion with greater complexity. Having turned the statues back into human beings, Naschina can rejoin Almintor. Yet the final stage direction indicates that their union will not last: "The rising moon casts the shadows of *Almintor* and the Sleepers far across the grass. Close by *Almintor's* side, *Naschina* is standing, shadowless."[11] By displacing the enchantress, Naschina herself has become immortal and no longer casts a shadow. Eventually, Almintor will die with her eyes—like those of the maid in *Alastor*—glimmering at him in the night.

Finally, the unpublished play *Love and Death* presents yet another arabesque on the same notion. Yeats summarized the plot in this way:

> A king's daughter loves a god seen in the luminous sky above her garden in childhood, and to be worthy of him and put away mortality, becomes without pity and commits crimes, and at last, having made her way to the throne by murder, awaits his coming among her courtiers. One by one they become chilly and drop dead, for, unseen by all but her, her god is in the hall. At last he is at her throne's foot and she, her mind in the garden once again, dies babbling like a child.[12]

Like Semele's desire for Zeus, or Yeats's aged knight's for the visionary Figure, such love is suicidal, for the god's power and glory destroy the mortal lover before the moment of union.

By the time of his first essay on Shelley Yeats found that Shelley not only associated love with death but also developed the quest in an image pattern based on the morning and evening star. He noticed that star imagery pervades the opening of *The Revolt of Islam*, that the morning star is "personified as a woman" to Rousseau in *The Triumph of Life*, and that the women in *Hellas* celebrate the morning star as the "beacon of love."[13] He observed, too, Shelley's tendency to move from earthly to heavenly

[11] *The Island of Statues*, ibid., p. 679.

[12] *Autobiography*, pp. 74–75. Cf. Richard Ellmann, *Yeats: The Man and the Masks*, p. 35: "The god at last appears but, since no mortal can behold his glory and live, the queen is destroyed by her own love."

[13] "The Philosophy of Shelley's Poetry," *E & I*, p. 88.

love and was aware that the projected ending of *Prince Athanase* involved the hero's rejection of Pandemos in favor of Venus Urania. Most important of all for his own work, Yeats understood the conjunction of love and death implied by the star, with the lover finding the goal of his quest "as the day finds the Star at evening."[14]

Whether Yeats had grasped all of this by the mid-eighties is doubtful, but both his own work and his devotion to Shelley's suggest that his mind was playing with some of these ideas even then. Thus, although Shelley's star assumes the greatest importance for Yeats during the nineties, it appears in association with love and death as early as the eighties. By 1900 Yeats recognized the intricate connection of the star pattern with other imagery in Shelley's work and, accordingly, adopted such other Shelleyan images as the tower. *Mosada* is the only early work which exemplifies the full Shelleyan cluster. Envisioning life after his reunion with Mosada, Ebremar says:

> We'll fly from this before the morning star.
> Dear heart, there is a secret way that leads
> Its paven length towards the river's marge
> Where lies a shallop in the yellow reeds.
> Awake, awake, and we will sail afar,
> Afar along the fleet white river's face—[15]

The lines unmistakably suggest *Alastor.* Yeats in his youth imagined "maybe at last to disappear from everybody's sight as he [the youth in *Alastor*] disappeared drifting in a boat along some slow-moving river."[16] Furthermore, he uses the unusual term "shallop," which in Shelley appears only in *Alastor.* At the conclusion of the first essay on Shelley Yeats identified the vision

[14] *E & I*, p. 88.

[15] *Variorum Poems*, p. 702. Professor Thomas Parkinson has mentioned the correspondence between this passage and the conclusion of the essay on Shelley in his *W. B. Yeats, Self-Critic*, pp. 22–23. T. R. Henn offers the following lines as examples of how much the verse owes to Shelley:

> There in a dell
> A lily-blanchèd place, she sat and sang
> And in her singing wove around her head
> White lilies, and her song went forth after
> Along the sea.

The Lonely Tower, rev. ed., p. 110.

[16] *Autobiography*, p. 64.

of a boat drifting down a river and following the morning and evening star as the characteristic Shelleyan pattern. Here the image appears concomitantly with the death of Mosada at the completion of her quest. Just as the day finds the star at evening, so has Mosada found her lover at death.

The star image occurs frequently in Yeats's other work during this period. In "The Indian to His Love" the Indian imagines himself and his beloved resting on an island, "While our love grows an Indian star."[17] The star in that poem symbolizes a fully developed romantic love, both eternal and pure. Impelled by the fire within his "most secret spirit," the mad King Goll wanders along the shore by starlight.[18] In a situation of which Shelley in the mood of *The Revolt of Islam* or *The Mask of Anarchy* would have approved, the spirit of the persecuted patriot Ferencz Renyi becomes a star because of the constancy of his love for his country and, more important, for liberty.

Finally, Yeats's use of the star reveals his Shelleyan and Spenserian association of earthly with heavenly love. In *The Seeker* one of the shepherds compares the knight's body to "yon smoke / That from the fire is ever pouring up . . . Star-envious."[19] Just as the smoke emanating from the fire desires to reach the purer fire of the stars overhead, so does the knight's body reveal his desire for a purely spiritual love. The same notion appears in *The Island of Statues*, where the enchantress likens the winds to "moths with broken wings" while the heavens throb with stars.[20] We find here the typical romantic metaphor of the longing of the moth for the star and the impossibility of fulfilling that longing. Earthly love alone does not satisfy either the Shelleyan or the Yeatsian lover, who longs for its ideal completion. Even the fairy-tale world of the early plays (Yeats appended the subtitle "An Arcadian Faery Tale" to *The Island of Statues*) did not lie far enough from reality for Yeats's early heroes.

II

The urge to either escape from mundane reality or transform it led Yeats to "imitate" Shelley in his early work by making

[17] *Variorum Poems*, p. 78.
[18] Ibid., p. 83. [19] Ibid., p. 683. [20] Ibid., p. 671.

magic a major theme. Of course, Yeats did not necessarily come to magic by way of Shelley, and his own esoteric activities gave him a direct knowledge of arcana. What he did find (or thought he found) in Shelley was a justification for taking magic seriously in his own writing, for to him Shelley provided an example of a great poet who regarded magic as a fit poetic theme. To the young Yeats magic and poetry were closely allied: in his 1901 essay on magic he asserted that only a varying degree of consciousness distinguished the magical use of image and symbol from the poetic use. In his view the magician evoked the Great Mind of nature by using consciously the same symbols which the poet used more unconsciously.[21]

The awakening of Yeats's formal interest in magic coincided with the plays of the eighties, although he had imagined himself a Shelleyan magician even as a boy. In the spring of 1885 Yeats read A. P. Sinnett's *Esoteric Buddhism,* which he first heard about in the home of Edward Dowden, the Shelley scholar. From that time on, Yeats participated in esoteric activities, although he did not formally join the London Lodge of Madam Blavatsky's Theosophical Society until 1887. During the years of the early dramas he argued about esotericism with his father and discussed the subject more congenially with George Russell and Charles Johnston. Not surprisingly, a concern with magic and the occult found its way into his first imitations of Shelley.

Although Prince Athanase was Yeats's favorite occult student in literature, the Shelleyan character who most influenced his first plays was Cythna in *The Revolt of Islam.* She attracted Yeats throughout his career but particularly before 1900. In *Reveries over Childhood and Youth* he tells us that in his early teens he "modelled" the women of his romantic fantasies on, among others, "the girl in *The Revolt of Islam.*"[22] At that time he did not associate Cythna with magic but rather with "lawless women without homes and without children," like the childless enchantresses in the plays of the eighties. Yeats's interpretation of Cythna may seem idiosyncratic, since in the poem she is a "purest being" described at one point as an idealized version of Laon's own mind, but Yeats may have considered only her hostility to

21 "Magic," *E & I,* p. 49. 22 *Autobiography,* p. 64.

an unjust social order. Laon himself tells her, "Well with the world art thou unreconciled."[23]

Before 1900 Yeats had extended Cythna's refusal of reconciliation with the world to a general protest against materialism and a consequent avowal of the power of magic. In the essay on Shelley he discusses Cythna not as a lawless woman but as a devotee of "the magical philosophy."[24] To support his argument he refers to Shelley's description of Cythna tracing designs on a sandy beach. The full passage, from the seventh canto, reads as follows:

> And on the sand would I make *signs* to range
> These woofs, as they were woven, of my thought;
> *Clear, elemental shapes, whose smallest change*
> *A subtler language within language* wrought:
> *The key of truths which once were dimly taught*
> *In old Crotona;*—and sweet melodies
> Of love, in that lorn solitude I caught
> From mine own voice in dream, when thy dear eyes
> Shone through my sleep, and did that utterance harmonize.[25]
> [Italics mine]

Yeats quoted the italicized sections of the passage in his discussion of Cythna. Although he wrote his essay on Shelley in 1899, the association of Cythna with magic may have occurred during the period of his greatest involvement with hermetic activities, when he was also composing the early plays. Both his boyish enthusiasm for Cythna and his later remarks about her suggest that she is one likely literary ancestor of the enchantresses of the eighties.

Female magicians appear in all four published plays. The earliest example comes in the one play not yet mentioned, *Time and the Witch Vivien*.[26] From a lengthy version in manuscript Yeats chose only one scene for publication, the defeat of Vivien by Time. The scene opens with her narcissistic speech praising

[23] *The Revolt of Islam*, *Works*, 1: 283–84.

[24] "The Philosophy of Shelley's Poetry," *E & I*, p. 78.

[25] *Works*, 1: 353.

[26] The text here is that in the *Variorum Poems*, pp. 720–22. This is apparently a greatly shortened reworking of the original manuscript, since is has only one scene and does not contain the passage quoted by Ellmann from MS in *The Man and the Masks*, pp. 34–35. Ellmann's passage would apparently precede the scene in the *Variorum*.

her own beauty, which cannot live to comb gray hair any more than can Cythna's. Time enters dressed as an old peddler selling the accoutrements of old age, "crutches and grey hairs." Vivien offers instead to buy his hourglass; he refuses, but accepts her offer to gamble for it. She loses at both dice and chess and dies when he calls checkmate. The pun contained in his final line, "Mate thus," accords well with Yeats's general association of death with magical women; in this case, however, not the lover but the woman herself dies, mated by eternity.

In *The Seeker* and *The Island of Statues* Yeats associates the enchantress with love, just as Shelley did in the stanza of *The Revolt* which caught Yeats's attention. The Figure in *The Seeker* bears a closer resemblance to Keats's belle dame sans merci and to Shelley's *Alastor* maid than to Cythna in possibly leading her mortal lover to his ruin. The old knight calls her a "witch." She does correspond to Cythna, however, by mixing magic and love and by inspiring her devotees to discontent with the world. *The Island of Statues* contains two women who blend magical talent with amorous accomplishment—the enchantress and Naschina. They meet in the third scene, which opens with the songs of the six Voices. These somewhat resemble the four Voices and six Spirits of the first act of *Prometheus Unbound* in their incorporeality and their rapid, choral succession of short speeches. The play associates magic with the eternity of love. The enchantress tells Naschina that on the island "no loves wane and wither."[27] Their ensuing conversation suggests that happiness and peace cannot occur together. Yeats develops that idea in more detail in his later poetry, where he conceives of love as a continuous war rather than a continuous peace between the lovers. Unlike the witch of *The Seeker*, Naschina uses her magical power much as Cythna used hers; she tries to bring about an age of love among mankind. Although Cythna fails to bring love to the human world, Naschina succeeds at least in bringing it to Arcadia. Her success has a limit, however, for by recalling the statues from the immortality of art to the mortality of life, she has in effect introduced death into Arcadia.[28]

[27] *Variorum Poems*, p. 669.

[28] Edward Engleberg has developed the relation between death and Arcadia at length in his essay " 'He Too Was in Arcadia': Yeats and the

Of all Yeats's early heroines Mosada most closely resembles those of Shelley. Her opening speech, like that of Shelley's Indian enchantress in *Fragments of an Unfinished Drama*, expresses a magician's yearning for reunion with her lover. Whereas the Indian enchantress makes only one speech, Cythna dominates a long narrative poem in which her resemblance to Mosada is developed in more detail. Both, in Yeats's view, are imprisoned enchantresses who weave magical spells. Both bear Eastern associations, Cythna by involvement in the affairs of the Golden City and Mosada by her Moorish ancestry. Both are the heroines of the works in which they appear and both overshadow their masculine counterparts (Naschina overshadows Almintor both figuratively and literally). Both are killed by priests and die as martyrs for love. Finally, Mosada forgives Cola for betraying her just as Cythna forgives the populace.

Even at this early stage Yeats did not see how to combine Shelleyan idealism with the life of modern Ireland, but for a time he was content to prefer Prometheus to the Paudeens. For the young poet oscillating from London to Dublin to Sligo and back again, to write on Shelleyan themes was to create an alternate world to the material one and to people it with lovers and magicians in exotic adventures. Near the end of his life Yeats remembered with particular regret writing "under [the influence] of Shelley's *Prometheus Unbound* two plays, one staged somewhere in the Caucasus, the other in a crater of the moon; and I knew myself to be vague."[29] Yeats grew less vague as he grew older, and it is to his first major attempt at fusing Shelley with a specific, Irish setting that we now turn.

III

Yeats wove together the two strands of his Shelleyan development of the eighties—love and magic—in *The Wanderings of Oisin* (1889), a poem which both concludes his earlier appreciation of Shelley and anticipates his much deeper understanding of his predecessor during the following decade. Such factors as his

Paradox of the Fortunate Fall," in *In Excited Reverie: A Centenary Tribute to William Butler Yeats 1865–1939*, ed. A. Norman Jeffares and K. G. W. Cross, pp. 69–92.

[29] *E & I*, p. 510.

conscious resolution to write on specifically Irish subjects as a means of raising nationalistic feeling above party cabals and materialistic goals drove him to compose a long poem on the legendary Fenian hero, but Yeats himself maintained that his interest in Shelley still influenced his art in important ways. Both the general conception of the subject and its specific symbolic technique owed something to Shelley as well as to Irish sources.

Yeats aspired to write an Irish *Prometheus Unbound* which would set its Shelleyan beautiful idealisms of moral excellence firmly on Irish soil and legend. Already, Shelley's Englishness and, even more, his generalized settings bothered Yeats, but he still felt that he could unite the essential spirit of Shelley's work with his own nationalist strategies. Recalling the period of *Oisin* in his autobiography, he wrote:

> I could not endure, however, an international art, picking stories and symbols where it pleased. Might I not, with health and good luck to aid me, create some new *Prometheus Unbound;* Patrick or Columcille, Oisin or Finn, in Prometheus' stead; and, instead of Caucasus, Cro-Patrick or Ben Bulben? Have not all races had their first unity from a mythology, that marries them to rock and hill?[30]

In *Oisin* Yeats did substitute Oisin and Patrick for Prometheus and Jupiter, Ben Bulben and Knocknarea for the Caucasus, and, like Shelley, looked back to a Pre-Christian period more congenial for the exercise of his particular heroic virtues. At the same time, he recognized the inadequacy of the vague or alien settings of his earlier imitations of Shelley. However far Oisin's three islands and the beach near Ben Bulben in Patrick's time might seem from O'Connell Street or the bustling port of Sligo at the close of the nineteenth century, at least they were in Ireland and not Arcadia or Spain. Yet the finished product relates not just to *Prometheus Unbound*, whose rhythms hover behind those of *Oisin*, but also to the bulk of Shelley's work, particularly *Alastor* and *The Triumph of Life*.

Yeats's poem presents his favorite Shelleyan theme of a mortal lover-poet's love for an immortal enchantress and the impossibility of satisfying it within the normal human world. The poem opens with Patrick describing Oisin's "dalliance with a demon

[30] *Autobiography*, pp. 193–94.

thing." An earlier version made Oisin's predicament even closer to that of the *Alastor* youth: "Trapped of an amorous demon."[31] The emphasis on wandering in the title of the poem suggests the troubled search of the youth in *Alastor*, and the images of tower, cave, and water accompanying the lovers' search for an isolated paradise recall the difficulties both of Laon and Cythna and of Prometheus and Asia. Niamh the enchantress fills Oisin with a love hopelessly at odds with the given social order and demanding an ideal setting far from the moral and physical degeneration of Patrick's Ireland.

Yeats's interpretation of the traditional name of Oisin's enchantress, Niamh, shows that by 1889 Shelley was influencing his art more profoundly than a few years earlier. The derivation of Niamh's name from the Gaelic word for brightness or beauty would bring Shelley's star image for love to mind in any case, but Yeats himself made the connection explicit in his first essay on Shelley. There the detailed discussion of Shelley's star prompts him to recall "a Galway tale that tells how Niamh, whose name means brightness or beauty, came to Oisin as a deer."[32] By making Oisin pursue an ideal woman named brightness, then, Yeats associated him with the list of Shelleyan lovers ranging from the youth of *Alastor* to Rousseau in *The Triumph of Life* who also destroy themselves by such a quest.

Yeats manipulates the image of a hound pursuing a deer to relate Oisin to that other foiled, circuitous wanderer, Rousseau in Shelley's *Triumph of Life*, who also found that immortal longings gave no protection from life's chariot. Describing the tracks of deer and wolf which Rousseau saw on desert Labrador after the transforming drink from the goblet, Yeats wrote:

> Because the wolf is but a more violent symbol of longing and desire than the hound, his [Rousseau's] wolf and deer remind me of the hound and deer that Oisin saw in the Gaelic poem chasing one another on the water before he saw the young man following the woman with the golden apple."[33]

The sequence of a hound chasing a deer and a man following a woman with a golden apple occurs not only in *The Triumph*

[31] *Variorum Poems*, p. 2. [32] *E & I*, p. 90.

[33] *E & I*, p. 90. The Gaelic poem, which Yeats read in translation, was by Michael Comyn.

of Life and "in the Gaelic poem" about Oisin, but also in the English one published by Yeats in 1889. There Oisin tells Patrick:

> . . . now a hornless deer
> Passed by us, chased by a phantom hound
> All pearly white, save one red ear;
> And now a lady rode like the wind
> With an apple of gold in her tossing hand;
> And a beautiful young man followed behind
> With quenchless gaze and fluttering hair.[34]

The above passage exactly follows the prose version and shows that Yeats thought of Oisin's adventures as a search for the beauty also hunted by Shelley's heroes. *Oisin* is full of other deer and hounds, for Oisin's longing dominates all three sections of the poem. Like Rousseau, however, he is undone by his attraction to mortal life as well as to Immortal Beauty.

Yeats's attempt to make the story of Oisin into an Irish *Prometheus Unbound* was not an unqualified success, even in thematic terms. The poem did not end with the *regeneratio mundi* praised in the ecstatic fourth act of Shelley's work, nor did it demonstrate the triumph of ideal love and beauty in even a single mind. Instead, Oisin, like so many heroes of Shelley's before him, destroyed himself through his own quest. Not even Niamh's magic could save him from contamination by everyday Irish reality. Yeats might follow Shelley in both theme and imagery, but he could not bring himself to share his predecessor's faith in a world transformed by a vision of love and beauty. Shelley himself was considerably more dubious about the possibility of such redemption than Yeats liked to think, but Yeats could not commit even the vision of it to poetry. Accordingly, he continued to admire *Prometheus Unbound* as a "sacred book" but to follow less triumphant works like *Alastor* as his specific literary models.

In the nineties Yeats deepened his understanding of the linked Shelleyan themes of love and magic into a reasonably coherent philosophy based on the pursuit of Intellectual Beauty. There his early concern with Shelleyan love became a philosophic quest for ideal beauty involving his senses, intellect, and emotions. The early concern with Shelleyan magic became a search

[34] *Variorum Poems,* pp. 11–12.

for an imaginative intellectual philosophy to combat "materialistic" systems based on eighteenth-century British empiricism. In neither case, though, could Yeats fuse those drives with everyday Irish reality, and the failure to unite them was to lead ultimately to his partial repudiation of Shelley. The next two chapters treat the elements in Yeats's work from *Oisin* until the early 1900s which profoundly extend the "imitation of Shelley" we have noticed in his earliest writings. We shall see that he tried to imitate the *Alastor* poet in a quest for Intellectual Beauty and Prince Athanase in a search for the "magical" wisdom of a spiritual philosophy.

3 Yeats as "Alastor": The Search for Beauty

> "There is hardly indeed a poem of any length in which one does not find it as a symbol of love, or liberty, or wisdom, or beauty, or some other expression of that Intellectual Beauty which was to Shelley's mind the central power of the world."
> —*Yeats in "The Philosophy of Shelley's Poetry."*

In the 1890s Yeats identified himself with Shelley as a visionary poet willing to sacrifice wide popularity in order to create a "pure" poetry which would apprehend Intellectual Beauty and reveal it to a select group of startled readers. That goal meant looking at the world with Intellectual vision: that is, renouncing the misshapen world of things as they seem for the ideal world of things as they might be, which in his Platonic moods Yeats also claimed meant things as they really are. Only by hating the bustle of the marketplace could a poet hope to find "In all poor foolish things that live a day, / Eternal beauty wandering on her way." Yeats's earlier flight from quotidian reality for the Tir nan Og of Arcadia or legendary Ireland now became the rejection of a flawed and ugly world in favor of a perfect Intellectual Beauty which might manifest itself even in the streets of London, but more often demanded that its devotees sit on green knolls apart or wander alone through the countryside, preferably by lakes or rivers.

Yeats found the archetype of the kind of poet he wanted to be in the nameless youth of Shelley's *Alastor*, whom he mistakenly called Alastor despite Thomas Love Peacock's well-known warning that the title refers not to the hero but to the spirit of solitude which haunts him. Yeats's conflation of hero and demon made the poem's title for him a description of the visionary poet: *Alastor; or, The Spirit of Solitude*. Since Yeats always called the hero Alastor, it is useful for us to refer to him as "Alastor," which reminds us both that Yeats thought the anonymous poet had a name meaning "spirit of solitude" and that Shelley did not. For Yeats, *Alastor* described the solitary quest of a visionary poet for "Intellectual Beauty," and, as he told the National Literary Society in a Friday lecture, "Alastor" was one of the "great symbols of passion and of mood"[1] in world literature.

Yeats derived his poetic principles and practice during the nineties in part from the three essays on poetry which he most admired. All three pertained to Shelley. He wrote of Hallam's essay on Tennyson, "If one set aside Shelley's essay on poetry and Browning's essay on Shelley, one does not know where to turn in modern English criticism for anything so philosophic."[2] The truncated Victorian reprints of Hallam's essay (before the full edition by Yeats's friend Richard Le Gallienne in 1893) made Hallam's analysis of Keats and Shelley almost as important as his discussion of Tennyson. Yeats's own essay on Shelley, begun in 1899 and published in part in 1900 and in full in 1903, built upon these earlier efforts and extended them philosophically. Yeats argued that the pursuit of Intellectual Beauty underlay all Shelley's poetry, and he cited Shelley's prose as further evidence for his interpretation.

This chapter has three purposes: the first part explores the evolution of Yeats's interpretation of Shelley as a poet of Intellectual Beauty and its growing relevance to his own poetic program; the second part investigates the correspondence between his view of Shelley and the Rose poems; and the third part indicates the continuing influence of Shelley's *Defence of Poetry* on Yeats. During the nineties Yeats struggled to attain the Intellectual vision which would reveal ideal beauty to him. Yet his thought and art during his greatest adherence to "Shelleyan" poetry contain the tendencies that later drove him beyond Shelley (as he understood him) and toward his later, antinomial philosophy based upon the inclusion of opposites.

[1] "Nationalism and Literature," MS 12148 of the National Library, Dublin.

[2] "A Bundle of Poets," p. 81.

Shelley as a Poet of Desire: The "Subjective" Interpretations

In the well-known Victorian distinction between "subjective" and "objective" poetry, Shelley's supporters defended him as a chief example of the subjective school. For the three essayists whom Yeats specifically commended, Shelley embodied a desire for the beautiful. Hallam postulated a subjective art based solely on beauty, predicted the subjective artist's estrangement from society, and emphasized his sensitivity and imagination. Browning declared that the isolated, subjective poet was a visionary as well. Finally, Richard Le Gallienne, a Shelleyan *genius loci* of the Rhymers' Club, grafted fin-de-siècle aestheticism onto the subjective tradition. Yeats then elaborated Intellectual Beauty as the center of Shelley's philosophy and, in defending him from the objective strictures of Matthew Arnold, showed that Shelley's poetic imagery bore the full weight of his Intellectual Philosophy.

Hallam's essay shaped both Yeats's view of Shelley and his entire aesthetic. Yeats discussed Hallam's theory in detail four times, always emphasizing the remarks on Shelley, and identified it as his own aesthetic creed before 1900. In "Art and Ideas" (1913) he recounts being reminded of his father's marginal decorations to Shelley by the Pre-Raphaelite paintings of Millais and D. G. Rossetti in the Tate Gallery. Musing on his early artistic theories, he recalls: "When I began to write I avowed for my principles those of Arthur Hallam in his essay upon Tennyson."[3] Because that essay influenced Yeats's thought so radically, it claims our attention in some detail.

Hallam exalted subjective, or emotional, poetry above the objective, or narrowly rational, kind. His theory defended Tennyson's then unpopular poems against Robert Montgomery's inferior but best-selling *Oxford*, just as Yeats was later to defend his own

[3] *E & I*, p. 347. Hallam sensed the limitations of his essay more acutely than did Yeats. His title reflected his double focus—"On Some of the Characteristics of Modern Poetry, and on the Lyrical Poems of Alfred Tennyson." Hallam wrote to Edward Spedding with polite self-depreciation, "You treat what I have written better than it deserves: it was the hasty product of the evenings of one week: I had no time for revision." (*The Writings of Arthur Hallam*, ed. T. H. Vail Motter, p. 182.) Yeats ignored the ad hoc characteristics of the work and concentrated on the theoretical sections.

work against the "dark Rosaleen" school of Irish propagandists. According to Hallam, Montgomery succeeded because his versified morality appealed readily to an unsophisticated public. To prize such "reflective" poetry was a "gross fallacy," for its composition forced the artist to gratify mere opinion instead of his own "desire of beauty."[4] Since the reason could create only objective poetry, the poet should instead follow his emotions and imagination to create subjective poetry involving "the higher feelings."[5]

Although the desire for subjective beauty proved Tennyson's superiority to Montgomery, it also restricted his popularity and isolated him from his society. The subjective poet's sensibility offered him a realm that "most men were not permitted to experience,"[6] and society consequently derided him as a hapless dreamer. The successful poetaster pandered to popular morality and current opinion, while the neglected poet preserved his personal and artistic integrity against public indifference. Although *Cathleen ni Houlihan* showed that Yeats could stir the public when he chose, he more often agreed with Hallam's principles; he maintained with O'Leary that there were some things a man should not do to save a country, and he praised the Rhymers as poets who "kept the Muses' sterner laws" and "never made a poorer song / That you might have a heavier purse."[7]

Hallam hoped that the breach between the artist and society could be closed. In a metaphor which the later Yeats would have liked he remarked, "Art is a lofty tree, and may shoot up far beyond our grasp, but its roots are in daily life and experience."[8] Through rooting his art in daily life the artist could improve the public's sensitivity and thus elevate the quality of national life. During the nineties Yeats ignored Hallam's hint that the beautiful could be grounded in the ordinary and denied that everyday experiences were proper poetic material. He saw the connection

[4] *The Poems of Arthur Henry Hallam*, ed. Richard Le Gallienne, p. 90. Since Yeats read this edition during the composition of the Rose poems, all quotations from Hallam's essay are drawn from this edition, hereafter cited as Hallam.

[5] Hallam, p. 106.

[6] Ibid., p. 97.

[7] "The Grey Rock," *Variorum Poems*, p. 273.

[8] Hallam, p. 98.

between art and national character but purged from his poetry those roots which Hallam deemed necessary to attract a mass audience. Although Yeats later recognized that all ladders to the beautiful begin in the rag-and-bone shop of the heart, now he repudiated the shop in favor of the spirit.

Both Hallam and Yeats saw Shelley as the type of the subjective poet, but they saw him more as the quiveringly sensitive youth of *Alastor* than as the tough and resilient character he was. Hallam used Shelley and Keats as his leading exemplars "of sensation rather than reflection."[9] Their poetry produced "a number of impressions too multiplied, too minute, and too diversified to allow of our tracing them to their causes."[10] But though the audience could not trace the causes, the poet could. Hallam emphasized the emotional subtlety of Shelley to the exclusion of his other powers, but he had the poet's own sanction for that bias. In a letter to Godwin reprinted by Mary Shelley in her note to *The Revolt of Islam*, Shelley wrote:

> I am formed, if for anything not in common with the herd of mankind, to apprehend minute and remote distinctions of feeling, whether relevant to external nature or the living beings which surround us, and to communicate the conceptions which result from considering either the moral or the material universe as a whole.[11]

The artist, argued Hallam, depended upon the imagination to transform his diverse and remote distinctions into poetry. The presence of that faculty marked the highest kind of poetry, for only "the transforming powers of high imagination"[12] could create a "truly poetic organisation" from the artist's disparate impressions—in short, could hammer his thoughts into unity. Fashionable poems contained no trace of imagination, and the most popular of even "the really pure compositions" dealt with the "*usual* passions" in a "simple state."

The image-making power of the imagination enabled it to bypass reason and apprehend beauty directly. Free from the political and monetary snares of the reason, the poet's "love of the beautiful" created images that strengthened the "powerful tend-

[9] Ibid., p. 93. [10] Ibid., p. 97.
[11] Shelley, *Works*, 1: 410. [12] Hallam, pp. 100–101.

ency of the imagination to a life of sympathy with the external universe."[13] Whereas other poets had to hunt for images to embody their conceptions, Keats and Shelley "lived in a world of images" and so never departed from the truths of the imagination.[14] Hallam conceived of Shelley, then, as a sensitive poet bent on beauty, isolated from society, and pursuing his own images of ideal perfection.

Hallam championed *Alastor* against current indifference to it because that poem embodied his image of the subjective poet. Since Yeats shared that view, we may conclude our survey of Hallam's essay with a look at his remarks on *Alastor* in his own "Timbuctoo," an unsuccessful entry for the Chancellor's Medal (1829). For Hallam *Alastor* preached lifelong fidelity to a vision of ideal love and beauty. He explained his view in a footnote to some very Shelleyan lines: "And the 'veiled maid' is vanished, who did feed / By converse high the faith of liberty."[15] Lest the reference go unnoticed, Hallam hastened to add, "These lines allude to the exquisite personification of Ideal Beauty in Mr. Shelley's Alastor."[16]

Fretting that even his public nod toward *Alastor* would be inadequate, Hallam deepened his gesture to a bow. In later editions the little footnote became a little essay in praise of Shelley's poem. The expanded version, included in the volume of Le Gallienne reviewed by Yeats, read in part:

> These lines contain an allusion to that magnificent passage in Mr. Shelley's "Alastor," where he describes "the spirit of sweet Human Love" descending in vision on the slumbers of the wandering poet. . . .

13 Ibid., p. 95.

14 Ibid., p. 94. Hallam's distinction between those poets who seek images and those who habitually live in them mirrors Schiller's famous distinction between *sentimentalisch* and *naiv* poetry: "Der Dichter, sagte ich, *ist* entweder Natur, oder er wird sie *suchen.* Jenes macht den naiven, dieses den sentimentalischen Dichter." (See Friedrich Schiller, *Werke,* ed. F. H. Ehmcke, 2: 659.) Hallam's poem "From Schiller" was included in Le Gallienne's edition, pp. 54–55. Edward Engleberg has explored the importance of Schiller to Yeats's aesthetic in *The Vast Design: Patterns in W. B. Yeats's Aesthetic,* pp. 55–56 and *passim.*

15 Ibid., pp. 21–22.

16 Quoted by T. H. Vail Motter in his edition of *The Writings of Arthur Hallam,* p. 40.

> [I] transfer the "veiled maid" to my own Poem, where she must stand for that embodiment of that love for the unseen, that voluntary concentration of our vague ideas of the Beauty that ought to be.[17]

By unmasking *Alastor*'s veiled maid as Ideal Beauty, Hallam rescued Shelley from sentimentalism for at least an elite minority of Victorian readers and made it easier for Browning and Yeats to see him as a visionary. Shelley himself had sanctioned such a view, for in the preface to *Alastor* he declared that "the vision in which he ["Alastor"] embodies his own imaginations unites all of wonderful, or wise, or beautiful, which the poet, the philosopher, or the lover could depicture."[18] Browning and Yeats saw that the remarks on *Alastor* applied to the rest of Shelley's work as well. By making Shelley a visionary Yeats could defend him against the two most common Victorian attitudes, philistine damnation as an adulterer or sentimental glorification as a martyr. For him, Shelley was neither an angel nor a demon but a poet, which meant that he resembled the youth in *Alastor*.

Browning's "Essay on Shelley,"[19] which Yeats thought equalled Hallam's, stressed the connection between solitude and vision. If the subjective poet wanted to share the *Alastor* poet's vision he would have to share his isolation as well. The Irish aesthete of the nineties who longed for Innisfree found nothing to deny in Browning's assertions:

> The subjective poet, whose study has been himself, appealing through himself to the absolute Divine mind, prefers to dwell upon those external scenic appearances which strike out most abundantly and uninterruptedly his inner light and power, selects that silence of the earth and sea in which he can best

[17] Hallam, pp. 21–23. Hallam concluded his remarks by quoting thirty-two lines from *Alastor*, prefaced by the following panegyric: "I shall, however, be content to have trespassed against the commandments of Art, if I should have called any one's attention to that wonderful Poem, which cannot long remain in its present condition of neglect, but which, when it shall have emerged into the light, its inheritance will produce wonder and enthusiastic delight in thousands, who will learn, as the work, like every perfect one, grows upon them, that the deep harmonies and glorious imagination in which it is clothed, are not more true than the great moral ideal which is its permeating life."

[18] *Works*, 1: 173.

[19] The original title was "Introductory Essay" to Major Ceorge Gordon de Luna Byron's spurious collection of Shelley letters, 1852.

> hear the beating of his individual heart, and leaves the noisy, complex, yet imperfect exhibitions of nature in the manifold experience of man around him, which serve only to distract and suppress the working of his brain.[20]

What does the subjective poet see, once he has forsaken society? Yeats later quoted Browning's answer: "Not what man sees, but what God sees—the *Ideas* of Plato, seeds of creation lying burningly on the Divine Hand—it is toward these that he struggles."[21] In his struggles the Shelleyan poet risked losing his audience. If he left society to compose his poems, society might well leave him when those Platonic visions entered the marketplace as saleable books. In Browning's terms, since the "seer," unlike the "fashioner," did not appeal to "the common eye and apprehension of his fellow men,"[22] he might not appeal to their purses either. Yet Browning approved the seer's stance, for only thus could Shelley achieve the "simultaneous perception of Power and Love in the absolute, and of Beauty and Good in the concrete."[23] Browning's Shelley forsakes society and chances his popularity to follow his own vision of subjective beauty, or of the metaphysical compound Power-Love-Beauty-Good.

The last remarks on Shelley publicly commended by Yeats were those by Richard Le Gallienne in his introduction to *The Poems of Arthur Henry Hallam* (1893), which printed the full text of Hallam's essay for the first time since its original appearance in Moxon's *English Magazine* (1832).[24] Yeats knew both the full

[20] Yeats would, however, have objected to other points, notably Browning's emphasis on morality and his equal valuation of subjective and objective poetry. The text of the essay used here is the Shelley Society reprint, *An Essay On Percy Bysshe Shelley*, ed. W. Tyas Harden, p. 14.

[21] Ibid., p. 13. Yeats slightly misquotes Browning in *Literary Ideals in Ireland*, by John Eglinton [William Magee], W. B. Yeats, AE, and W. Larminie, p. 35: " 'Ideas' that 'lie burningly on the divine hand,' as Browning calls them."

[22] Browning, p. 13.

[23] Ibid., p. 26.

[24] The earlier editions of Hallam, known as the *Remains in Prose and Verse*, omitted both the attack on Montgomery and the detailed application of Hallam's general principles to specific poems of Tennyson. In the likely event that Yeats read the essay before 1893, the omission of the polemical passages would have reinforced his exclusive attention to the theoretical sections. Whatever edition he read would have contained both the general literary principles and the extensive comments on Shelleyan subjective poetry.

text of the essay and Le Gallienne's introduction, for he reviewed the volume in *The Speaker* during July of 1893.[25] A close acquaintance of Yeats's and a fellow member of the Rhymers' Club, Le Gallienne appears frequently in Yeats's letters and reminiscences of the nineties. Yeats once observed, only half facetiously, that Le Gallienne was "the most like Alastor in appearance among the Rhymers."[26] Because Yeats's review of the volume commended the introduction, we may turn to it for an interpretation of Hallam and Shelley of which Yeats approved.

Le Gallienne anticipated Yeats's fuller discussion six years later by associating Shelley with the search for beauty. He noted Hallam's enthusiasm for Shelley and Dante, both of whom Yeats later assigned to the same psychological category as himself in *A Vision.* According to Le Gallienne, Hallam's literary standards enforced "the first law of aesthetics . . . the law of Beauty."[27] He approvingly quoted Hallam's remark that for a poet "the first object is always the beautiful."[28]

While remaining reasonably faithful to Hallam's own statements, Le Gallienne's interpretation of the essay emphasized its relation to the doctrines of aestheticism favored by the Rhymers' Club. He considered it "one of the early examples in England of that aesthetic criticism which is now so generally accepted amongst us."[29] Yeats agreed with Le Gallienne's observation and declared in his review:

> Writing long before the days of Rossetti and Swinburne, Arthur Hallam explained the principles of the aesthetic movement, claimed Tennyson as its living representative, and traced its origin to Keats and Shelley, who, unlike Wordsworth, made beauty the beginning and end of all things in art.[30]

In his own discussion of Hallam's essay Yeats stressed its appli-

[25] "A Bundle of Poets," p. 81.

[26] *Letters to the New Island*, p. 147. The letter is reprinted from *The Boston Pilot*, 23 April 1892.

[27] Hallam, p. xxxi.

[28] Ibid.

[29] Ibid., p. xxxiv.

[30] "A Bundle of Poets," p. 81.

cation to Shelley.[31] For if earlier he "chose Alastor for my chief of men,"[32] now he chose Shelley-as-"Alastor" for his chief of poets. Accordingly, he adopted three cardinal points of Hallam's essay. First, poetry derived from the apprehension of beauty by a delicate sensibility. Secondly, the pure poet relied solely on his sensibility while the impure one mixed elements of popular morality into his work. Finally, the subjective artist would be estranged from his society, since his work appealed only to a small, refined audience. He adduced Shelley as his example, but we may well suspect that his own career was also on his mind when he wrote:

> Keats and Shelley, unlike Wordsworth, intermixed into their poetry no elements from the general thought, but wrote out of the impressions made by the world upon their delicate senses. They were of the aesthetic school . . . and could not be popular because their readers could not understand them without attaining to a like delicacy of sensation and so must needs turn from them to Wordsworth or another, who condescended to moral maxims, or some received philosophy, a multitude of things that even common sense could understand.[33]

Although Yeats in the nineties appeared to abhor popularity, like Shelley he really abhorred didactic poetry. In his review of Le Gallienne's edition he italicized Hallam's maxim: "Hence, whatever is mixed up with art, and appears under its semblance, is always more favourably regarded than art free and unalloyed."[34] Yeats thought that statement "admirable" in its explanation of "the

[31] The citations, which indicate the impact of the essay on his own development, appear twice during the nineties and twice in later reminiscences of the period. Besides "A Bundle of Poets" and *Literary Ideals in Ireland*, see *Autobiography*, pp. 489–90, and *E & I*, p. 347.

[32] *Autobiography*, p. 64.

[33] *E & I*, pp. 347–48. Compare also Yeats's remark in *Autobiography*, p. 490: "Hallam argued that poetry was the impression on the senses of certain very sensitive men. It was such with the pure artists, Keats and Shelley, but not so with the impure artists, who, like Wordsworth, mixed up popular morality with their work."

Characteristic of Yeats's rejection of Victorian rhetoric in this period is his refusal to consider Tennyson an example of Hallam's principles.

[34] Hallam, p. 100. Italicized by Yeats in "A Bundle of Poets," p. 81. Shelley cautioned against "flattery of the gross opinions of the vulgar" in the *Defence*. See *Shelley's Prose*, ed. David Lee Clark, p. 280. Hereafter cited as *Shelley's Prose*.

popularity of the didactic poets." For him, to avoid didacticism was to avoid popularity. The Irish masses might prefer the Young Ireland poets, but the neuropsychical elite who read his own volumes would save the race's soul through their new apprehension of beauty.

Yeats seized upon the visionary quality which Hallam had intimated and Browning had emphasized. In *Literary Ideals in Ireland* he replied to John Eglinton's (William Magee's) contention that poetry should be a criticism of its age by quoting "the words of the younger Hallam, in his essay on Tennyson." Reiterating his opinion that the essay is "one of the most profound criticisms in the English language,"[35] Yeats repeated Hallam's strictures about popular poetry and indicated that the true poet was a "seer" and, hence, "aristocratic."[36] True poetry was a "spiritual force." Yeats quoted both Browning and Poe (another admirer of Shelley) to support his view. In a characteristic metaphor he likened the concerns of popular poetry to "all the lusts of the market place." Yeats later admitted those lusts to his art and thought, but for now he barred them from the virginal world of his verse.

Although Yeats praised the subjectivist defenders of Shelley, he raged at the objectivist ones like Eglinton who insisted that poetry should criticize life. For Yeats the chief objectivist was Matthew Arnold, whose essay on Shelley first appeared as a review of Dowden's *Life of Percy Bysshe Shelley* in 1886. Mainly biographical, Arnold's essay dismissed Shelley's poetry in the last three sentences, which became a *locus classicus* for those who refused to take Shelley's art seriously. Favoring Trelawney's

[35] *Literary Ideals in Ireland*, pp. 33–34.

[36] Ibid., p. 35. All references in this paragraph are to p. 35.

Yeats probably associated Poe with Hallam and Browning not only for enthusiasm for Shelley but also for Poe's Shelleyan attitude toward beauty. In *The Poetic Principle*, for example, Poe writes: "An immortal instinct, deep within the spirit of man, is thus, plainly, a sense of the beautiful. . . . There is still a something in the distance which he has been unable to attain. We have still a thirst unquenchable. . . . This thirst belongs to the immortality of Man. It is at once a consequence and an indication of his perennial existence. It is the desire of the moth for the star. It is no mere appreciation of the Beauty before us—but a wild effort to reach the Beauty above." (*The Complete Works of Edgar Allan Poe*, ed. James A. Harrison, 14: 273.) "The desire of the moth for the star" is a line from Shelley quoted by Yeats.

"Alastor"-like description of Shelley blushing like a girl, Arnold intoned:

> The man Shelley, in very truth, is not entirely sane, and Shelley's poetry is not entirely sane either. The Shelley of actual life is a vision of beauty and radiance, indeed, but availing nothing, effecting nothing. And in poetry, no less than in life, he is "a beautiful *and ineffectual* angel, beating in the void his luminous wings in vain.[37]

If Dowden's insufficient sympathy with Shelley had disappointed Yeats,[38] Arnold's attack drove him to fury. By condemning beauty on grounds of ineffectuality, Arnold indicted the whole subjective school to which Yeats pledged allegiance. Yeats responded by arraigning the entire objective school. He took to the newspapers to deride "the Matthew Arnold tradition" in which merely "accomplished" men versified material reality and ordinary emotions.[39] Instead, he championed the visionary tradition in which "inspired" artists imaged forth ideal beauty and order. For Yeats, the beautiful was supremely effectual in that it revealed a spiritual order behind the natural one. To desire anything else was to surrender to materialism or naturalism. As George Santayana remarked in his own eloquent defense of Shelley against Arnold, "An angel cannot be ineffectual if the standard of efficiency is moral."[40]

Whereas for Arnold "the laws of poetic truth and poetic beauty" fixed the conditions under which poetry was a "criticism of life,"[41] for Yeats they prevented poetry from criticizing life in Arnold's sense at all. In defending Hallam's view of Shelley Yeats drove home the point against Arnold: men will "more and more reject the opinion that poetry is a 'criticism of life' and be more and more convinced that it is a revelation of a hidden life."[42] Since only the subjective tradition revealed that hidden life, its

37 *The Works of Matthew Arnold*, 4: 185.

38 See chapter 1, pp. 4–5.

39 *Letters to the New Island*, p. 205.

40 "Shelley," *The Winds of Doctrine*, p. 70.

41 *The Works of Matthew Arnold*, 4: 4.

42 *Literary Ideals in Ireland*, p. 36. In *The Spirit of Romance*, p. 222, Ezra Pound rejected Arnold's position with typical blunt contempt: "Poetry is about as much a 'criticism of life' as red-hot iron is a criticism of fire."

visionary artists would soon rout Arnold's accomplished men. In saving Shelley and Hallam, Yeats saved himself as well, for as we saw above he "avowed for my principles those of Arthur Hallam."

Entering the lists against Arnold allowed Yeats to rejoin the subjectivist camp with a new weapon, imagistic analysis. Rebutting Arnold led him to see that Shelley's imagery connected his philosophy with his poetic skill:

> Shelley seemed to Matthew Arnold to beat his ineffectual wings in the void, and I only made my pleasure in him contented pleasure by massing in my imagination his recurring images of towers and rivers, and caves with fountains in them, and that one Star of his, till his world had grown solid underfoot and consistent enough for the soul's habitation.[43]

By basing his quest for beauty on a system of ordered images, the subjective poet could escape from vagueness and create a world where the soul would not wander aimlessly but could chart its own course. The poet's counterpart to the scales and measuring rod of the materialist was the precision of verbal symbols.

Uniting the quest for beauty which he had found in the subjectivists with the analysis of imagery he had learned in refuting Arnold, Yeats published his own essay on Shelley in full in *Ideas of Good and Evil* (1903). He had begun work on the essay four years earlier and had published the first section separately in 1900. As though to emphasize Shelley's impact on him during the period covered by the book (1895–1903), Yeats made the essay on Shelley the longest single piece in the volume. Following William Morris and preceding Shakespeare and Blake in Yeats's ordering, Shelley claims more pages for the discussion of his poetry than does any other writer, although separate surveys of Blake's thought and of his illustrations to Dante win Blake slightly more total attention. Allusions to Shelley in the other essays combine with the long analysis of his work to make him a prominent figure throughout Yeats's treatment of his favorite early subjects—beauty, imagination, magic, mysticism, poetry, theater, and the role of art in Ireland.

Yeats called his essay "The Philosophy of Shelley's Poetry" and

[43] *E & I*, p. 294.

divided it into two parts: "His Ruling Ideas" and "His Ruling Symbols." The title is important, for like Shelley Yeats equated poets with philosophers and in his criticism focused on ideas and the images or myths which could best express them rather than on metrics or prosody. He argues that one cannot understand the poems of Shelley "till one has discovered the system of belief that lay behind them,"[44] a remark which applies equally well to his view of Blake or Dante and to his own work. The ruling idea in Shelley's system of belief, as the first part of Yeats's essay makes clear, is "his vision of the divine order, the Intellectual Beauty." This Intellectual order demands reformation "of the hearts of men" but "was so much more than the regeneration many political dreamers have foreseen, that it could not come in its perfection till the Hours bore 'Time to his tomb in eternity.' "[45] Meanwhile, the poet of Intellectual vision keeps the dream of perfect beauty alive. "His Ruling Symbols" identifies two main clusters of images in Shelley, the earthly and the heavenly. The celestial cluster, including sun, moon, and morning and evening star, symbolizes the three major aspects of the beautiful and of our desire for it. The terrestrial group, containing cave, water (including rivers and fountains), and tower, expresses each man's quest for that beauty within himself. Yeats's essay, remarkable for its time by both its profound study of an author's ideas and its systematic exposition of his imagery, towers over the earlier subjectivist interpretations of Shelley but still rests on the foundation they provided.

Yeats's interpretation of Shelley conforms to the creed which he extracted from Hallam and the other subjective interpreters of Shelley: first, that beauty was the subject of poetry; second, that the artist searches for beauty through his own refined sensibility; and third, that the artist would be estranged from his society. We have seen that Yeats also made those axioms the basis of his own poetic geometry in the nineties. For him Shelley's poetry, like his own, was the poetry of desire for Intellectual Beauty, and expounding Shelley's philosophy allowed him to expound indirectly the ideas behind his own poetry. Let us consider in order his ideas of beauty, sensibility, and estrangement.

[44] *E & I*, p. 66.

[45] *E & I*, p. 67. Yeats is quoting from *Prometheus Unbound* act 4, line 14.

Yeats used the symbols of star, moon, and sun to distinguish Shelley's kind of beauty from that of his fellow romantics Keats and Blake. According to him, Keats found beauty in the moon because that "most changeable of symbols" suited his capacity for "drifting hither and thither," presumably in a state of negative capability, before finding specific subjects for his latent "love of embodied things." Likewise, Blake found Intellectual Beauty in the sun, which suggested "belief and joy and pride and energy."[46] The "children of desire" like Shelley succumbed to neither solar nor lunar worship but instead pursued the morning (and evening) star, whose constancy and purity provided a fit object for their boundless desire. Their longing drove them away from ordinary life and toward their own ideal. Yeats distinguished Shelley from Blake in this way:

> In ancient times, it seems to me that Blake, who for all his protest was glad to be alive, and ever spoke of his gladness, would have worshipped in some chapel of the Sun, but that Shelley, who hated life because he sought "more in life than any understood," would have wandered, lost in a ceaseless reverie, in some chapel of the Star of infinite desire.[47]

The poet followed the star by the compass of his own sensibility, particularly the imagination. Yeats began the essay on Shelley by announcing that "the imagination has some way of lighting on the truth that the reason has not." Imaginative lighting on truth made *Prometheus Unbound* a "sacred book"[48] and caused Shelley, in works like *Alastor*, to render "again and again, a vision of a boat drifting down a broad river between high hills where there were caves and towers, and following the light of one Star."[49] Shelley shunned both Blake's world of will and energy and Keats's constantly changing concrete embodiments of beauty to follow his own longing. Yeats approvingly quotes Mary's warning, "It requires a mind as subtle and penetrating as his own to understand the mystic meanings scattered throughout the poem. They elude the ordinary reader by their abstraction and delicacy of sensation."

Shelley's devotion to beauty and his sensitivity to it estranged

[46] "The Philosophy of Shelley's Poetry," *E & I*, pp. 91–93.
[47] *E & I*, p. 94. [48] *E & I*, p. 65. [49] *E & I*, pp. 94–95.

him from society. Minds as subtle and penetrating as his own were hard to come by in Victorian England, with the result that the bourgeoisie branded him "a crude revolutionist." To them he was a versified Godwin insensitive to the glory of empire and the goddess of capitalism, and they mistook *Prometheus Unbound* for *Political Justice* put into rhyme. Cythna on her island, "Alastor" by his river, and Athanase in his tower are projections of Shelley's estrangement from common life.

In the nineties Yeats held a Shelleyan conception of the poet gleaned from Hallam and Browning but leavened by his own originality. *Prometheus Unbound* showed him that Intellectual Beauty could regenerate the world, and *Alastor* and *Prince Athanase* provided a model of the quest for it. Since in his own work Yeats exalted the quest rather than its result, his own poems more often resemble *Alastor* or the "Hymn to Intellectual Beauty" than *Prometheus Unbound*. They picture solitary poets rejecting easy popularity in order to follow their imaginative Intellectual vision. Later Yeats accepted the broad subject matter and audience implied by Hallam's metaphor of the roots and branches of the tree. Now he saw only that everyday subjects would vulgarize his art. As late as 1906 he still believed that art could either go "up" into the subtlety of Shelley or "down" into the soullessness of Burns.[50] His poems about the symbolic Rose form his major effort to rise into Shelleyan subtlety.

Shelley's Intellectual Beauty and Yeats's Rose Poems

Yeats's Rose poems reflect the comprehensive aesthetic program he fashioned from the poetics of the subjectivists and the Intellectual Beauty of Shelley. His essay, "The Philosophy of Shelley's Poetry," was the coda rather than the prelude to his variations on a theme by Shelley. Yeats indicated the change to John Quinn in 1903: "Tomorrow I shall send you my new book, *Ideas of Good and Evil*. I feel that much of it is out of my present mood; that it is true, but no longer true for me."[51] Regrettably, he did not specify the recently revealed False Florimels, but the changes in his own work and thought suggest that adherence to Shelleyan

50 "Personality and the Intellectual Essences," *E & I*, p. 267.
51 *Yeats's Letters*, p. 469.

Intellectual Beauty was one of the chimeras. Although Shelley's imagery of towers and swans, along with his eloquent defense of poetry, lingered in Yeats's work, the period of full enthusiasm for Shelley was near an end. Consequently, to trace the profound impact of Shelley on Yeats we must turn to the dozen or so years preceding the essay on Shelley, to the poems about the Rose.

Yeats's poetry during the nineties shows a consistently Intellectual vision. The flight from reality in his imitations of Shelley in the eighties matured into a flight from the everyday world toward an ideal one of Intellectual Beauty. The "lusts of the market place" were not a fit subject for poetry, and the marketplace itself not a fit setting. The corrupt, oafish, and actual must not impinge on the pure, sensitive, and ideal. His poetry, he later confessed, showed a movement "upwards out of life" rather than "downwards upon life."[52] Shelley's poetry, in Yeats's interpretation, gave both authority and encouragement to his effort. If he could not incarnate Prometheus and single-handedly regenerate the earth in general and Ireland in particular, he could at least follow "Alastor" in his desire for such a perfect beauty. This section of the chapter examines, first, Yeats's understanding of Intellectual Beauty in Spenser and Shelley, and, second, its relevance to his own poetry of Intellectual vision.

Yeats identified his Rose as Intellectual Beauty, but what did he mean by that? Yeats gave no exact definition, for he was characteristically unwilling to destroy the poetic value of his symbol by attaching too exact a discursive tag to it. Most probably, he used "Intellect," as Shelley and others did, as an equivalent of *nous* to signify the divine mind or suprasensible intelligible world. Intellectual Beauty would then be the beauty of that world manifesting itself in ordinary materiality, the spiritual and eternal in the physical and transitory. Hence, in the essay on Shelley Yeats used "the divine order" synonymously with "the Intellectual Beauty."[53]

By a sort of literary Heisenberg uncertainty principle, Yeats did not define "beauty" precisely either. Instead, his notes to the Rose poems create a compound similar to Browning's Power-Love-Beauty-Good. In the preface to the 1895 edition he called

[52] *Yeats's Letters*, p. 469. [53] *E & I*, p. 67.

the Rose poems "the only pathway whereon he can hope to see with his own eyes the Eternal Rose of Beauty and of Peace."[54] The next preface replaced peace by wisdom: "the only pathway from which he may hope to see beauty and wisdom with his own eyes." The 1899 edition also announced, "The Rose has been for many centuries a symbol of spiritual love and supreme beauty." The Rose thus stands for the cluster, Beauty-Wisdom-Love-Peace. He identified a similar cluster, Beauty-Wisdom-Love-Liberty, as the expression of Intellectual Beauty in Shelley's poetry.[55] Yeats's definitions of Intellectual Beauty are not paradigms of logical rigor, but what he means is on the whole tolerably clear.

Yeats was more precise in identifying the main poets of Intellectual Beauty—Spenser and Shelley. According to him, Spenser "began in English poetry, despite a temperament that delighted in sensuous beauty alone with perfect delight, that worship of Intellectual Beauty which Shelley carried to a greater subtlety and applied to the whole of life."[56] Yeats's early association of Spenser and Shelley had now extended to metaphysics, and the correspondence between Spenser's "An Hymne of Heavenly Beautie" (as Yeats called it) and Shelley's "Hymn to Intellectual Beauty" struck him more forcefully than the exotic settings or fantastic plots he had copied in the eighties.

Recognizing Intellectual Beauty in the full corpus of Spenser's work, Yeats found it particularly in his favorite "An Hymne of Heavenly Beautie," the only one of the *Fowre Hymns* he selected for his edition of Spenser. Three aspects of this hymn bear particularly upon Intellectual vision. First, Spenser associates Heavenly Beauty with Plato's Ideas, which occupy a slightly lower sphere of heaven. He writes, "More faire is that, where those Idees on hie / Enraunged be, which Plato so admyred, / And pure

[54] *Variorum Poems*, pp. 846, 811. [55] *E & I*, p. 89.

[56] "Introduction," to *The Poems of Spenser*, ed. W. B. Yeats, p. xxvi. The most readily available reprint is in *E & I*. Although the edition did not appear until four years later, the essay was completed by October 1902. Yeats thus wrote the essays on Spenser and Shelley at about the same time. A. G. Stock describes the circumstances of publication of the Spenser volume in "Yeats on Spenser," *In Excited Reverie*, ed. A. Norman Jeffares and K. G. W. Cross, pp. 93–101.

Intelligences from God inspyred."[57] Second, Spenser's placement of Sapience in the bosom of God, above even the cherubim and the seraphim, seemed to Yeats a glorification of Intellectual Beauty. In the introduction he refers to her as "a woman little known to theology, one that he [Spenser] names Wisdom or Beauty."[58] Finally, while the earthly hymns utilize the familiar Platonic ladder from lowly things to the highest and most beautiful, the "Hymne of Heavenly Beautie" equates the good only with the fair and emphasizes the ugliness of the earthly. The line "For all thats good is beautifull and faire"[59] would win assent from a disciple of Hallam who aspired to the spiritual subtlety of Shelley. The inclusion of this particular hymn reflects Yeats's determination to move upward with Shelley rather than his later desire to find a ladder connecting foul with fair.

The worship begun by Spenser culminated in Shelley. For Yeats, Shelley was the primary poet of Intellectual Beauty in English literature. He found that beauty's power celebrated in *Prometheus Unbound*, *The Witch of Atlas* and "The Sensitive Plant," and the Hymn, and he eulogized the three Shelleyan figures who (in his view) sought for it—Athanase, Ahasuerus, and, above all, "Alastor." Finally, he knew the discussion of beauty in the *Defence of Poetry*, his favorite essay on literary theory. Having examined the general outline of "The Philosophy of Shelley's Poetry" above, we may now turn to its doctrines on Intellectual Beauty before proceeding to Yeats's own doctrines in the text of the Rose poems themselves.

Yeats thought that Intellectual Beauty "was to Shelley's mind the central power of the world."[60] In that belief he followed Hallam and Browning, but Yeats realized its metaphysical implications more fully than his predecessors. Shelley's liberty transcended that of Godwin's *Political Justice* and became one with Intellectual Beauty. That beauty, under its guises of beauty, love, wisdom, and liberty, could effect the total physical and spiritual regeneration of mankind. Shelley was thus a visionary poet, although Yeats duly notes that the vision would not be

[57] *The Poems of Spenser*, p. 4. [58] Ibid., p. xxv.
[59] Ibid., p. 5. [60] *E & I*, p. 89.

realized until, as in *Prometheus Unbound*, the Hours bore Time to his tomb in Eternity.

Love provided the means of the regeneration. Yeats writes that Shelley "cries again and again that love is the perception of beauty in thought and things, and it orders all things by love."[61] The *Alastor* youth's love for the visionary maiden represents his perception of the Intellectual Beauty she symbolizes. By perceiving Intellectual Beauty we perceive our heightened selves. In *Julian and Maddalo* Yeats rightly identifies Julian with Shelley and quotes his question, "Where is the love, beauty, and truth we seek / But in our mind?"[62] Shelley's belief in a spirit of beauty behind the material world showed that he had "reawakened in himself the age of faith."[63]

Shelley symbolized Intellectual Beauty by the morning and evening star. The star formed the center of his complicated symbolism of sun, moon, and star in the sky and cave, tower, and water on earth. Citing throughout his essay supporting passages from *Alastor*, *Prince Athanase*, *Laon and Cythna*, *Prometheus Unbound*, "Ode to Liberty," and *The Triumph of Life*, among others, Yeats maintains:

> The most important, the most precise of all Shelley's symbols, the one he uses with the fullest knowledge of its meaning, is the Morning and Evening Star. . . . There is hardly indeed a poem of any length in which one does not find it as a symbol of love, or liberty, or wisdom, or beauty, or of some other expression of that Intellectual Beauty which was to Shelley's mind the central power of the world.[64]

Yeats shared Shelley's intent to express his vision of Intellectual Beauty through a pattern of symbols. In place of Shelley's star he puts the Rose, with its Christian, hermetic, national, and literary associations. Describing his own technique as well as the one he thought he found in Shelley, he writes:

> It is only by ancient symbols, by symbols that have numberless meanings besides the one or two the writer lays an emphasis upon, or the half-score he knows of, that any highly subjective art can escape from the barrenness and

[61] *E & I*, pp. 68–69. [62] *E & I*, p. 70.
[63] *E & I*, p. 77. [64] *E & I*, pp. 88–89.

> shallowness of a too conscious arrangement into the abundance and depth of Nature.[65]

In the nineties Yeats hoped that the Rose would free his own subjective art from barrenness just as he thought that the star had freed Shelley's. The first lyrics in which roses become operative symbols rather than picturesque decoration were collected in *The Countess Cathleen and Other Poems* (1892). Yeats first identified them as a distinct group in 1895, when he included them under the title "The Rose" as part of the collected *Poems*. A later series of related poems appeared in *The Wind among the Reeds* (1899), in which seven poems use the rose prominently. Yeats extended his symbol to prose works as well. In 1897 he collected some of his stories published in periodicals during the previous five years into a volume called *The Rose*, with his poem "The Secret Rose" as a preface. During the decade preceding his essay on Shelley, then, the Rose dominated Yeats's symbolism.

Yeats owed to Shelley the significance of his symbol (Intellectual Beauty) rather than the symbol itself (the Rose). Yet, althought he derived the Rose from Christian, occult, national, and Continental sources,[66] as well as from the symbolic horticulture of the Pre-Raphaelites, he did find slight symbolic parallels in

[65] *E & I*, p. 87.

[66] He knew that the rose was "sacred to the Virgin Mary" and was aware of the rose in Dante's *Paradiso*, an image which he later compared to Shelley's Venus Urania. The same symbol figured prominently in the hermetic activities of the nineties. In the year in which he first used the title "The Rose" Yeats also wrote an essay on Father Christian Rosencrux, the founder of the Rosicrucians. Further indication of the importance of the magical tradition appears in Yeats's notes to *The Wind among the Reeds*. Other Irish writers had employed the rose as a symbol; Yeats mentions specifically Douglas Hyde, James Clarence Mangan, and Aubrey de Vere. He undoubtedly also knew the "Rosa Mystica" group of Wilde's poems. Our concern here is for the literary tradition. For Yeats the Rose seemed the perfect symbol for the notion of Intellectual Beauty which he had found in the poetry of Spenser and Shelley and the criticism of Hallam. For the Christian background see *A Vision*, p. 141, and *Variorum Poems*, p. 811. The essay on Father Rosencrux is reprinted in *E & I*, pp. 196–97; his name combines Yeats's two favorite symbols of this period, the rose and the cross. Yeats mentions the other Irish writers on pp. 798 and 811 of the *Variorum* notes. See also Barbara Seward, *The Symbolic Rose*, esp. pp. 1–117.

Shelley as well. The idealized heroine of *The Wandering Jew* is named Rosa, as is the heroine in *St. Irvyne*. The subtitle of the latter work would have appealed to Yeats's use of the rose with the cross, and to his occult interests: *St. Irvyne; or, The Rosicrucian*. In the ten appearances of a rose in Shelley's poetry, Yeats would have noticed Shelley's tendency to associate roses with fountains, for in the essay on Shelley he ranked him with those, like Blake, who understood "that the Holy Spirit is 'an intellectual fountain,' and that the kinds and degrees of beauty are the images of its authority."[67] For example, in the sacred *Prometheus Unbound* he found the image of "fountain-gazing roses" associated with Asia's radiant beauty. Finally, the little lyric "Love's Rose" described heavenly beauty and its fleeting manifestations on earth:

> Sweet the rose that breathes in Heaven,
>   Altho' on Earth 'tis planted,
>   Where its honours blow,
> While by the frosts its leaves are riven
>   Which die the while they glow.[68]

Although the Rose symbol itself found only analogues in Shelley, the referent of the symbol derived from him directly. "I prayed to the Red Rose, to Intellectual Beauty," Yeats recalled of "To Ireland in the Coming Times."[69] Surveying the Rose poems from the vantage point of 1925, he could detect only one difference between Shelley and Spenser's treatment of Intellectual Beauty and his own: "the quality symbolised as The Rose differs from the Intellectual Beauty of Shelley and of Spenser in that I have imagined it as suffering with man and not as something pursued and seen from afar."[70] Even that distinction holds true only for some of the poems, for Yeats in the 1890s was much more closely identified with Shelley than he later cared to admit.

Yeats associated his quest for Intellectual Beauty with Shelley's by giving the Rose poems an epigraph from the same source as the epigraph to *Alastor*—the *Confessions* of Augustine. The entire epigraph to *Alastor*, put together from pieces of the *Confessions*, reads as follows:

[67] *E & I*, p. 78. [68] *Works*, 3: 75.
[69] *Autobiography*, p. 254. [70] *Variorum Poems*, p. 842.

> To Carthage I came, where there sang all around me in my ears a cauldron of unholy loves. *I loved not yet, yet I wanted to love*, and out of a deep-seated want. I hated myself for wanting not. *I sought what I might love, in love with loving*, and safety I hated, and a way without snares. For within me was a famine of that inward food, Thyself, my God [italics mine].[71]

Shelley combined the Latin for the italicized parts of the quotation into his epigraph, "Nondum amabam, et amare amabam, quaerebam quid amarem, amans amare." The relevance seems clear. In secular terms the speaker has not loved, and yet wants to; the notion of love possesses his mind, and he embarks upon a search for a fit object for his love. Augustine rejected the concupiscence of the fleshpots of Carthage as a travesty of the divine love he sought. The poet described in *Alastor* wanders in search of the visionary maiden and ultimately dies unsatisfied because of his inability to find her incarnate upon earth. The purity of his Intellectual love for the veiled maid matches that of Augustine's love for God.

Yeats identified the object of "Alastor's" quest as Intellectual Beauty and its symbol as the star. He often mentioned "Alastor" and the star together; in the essay on Spenser, for example, he writes that "Alastor is wandering from lonely river to river finding happiness in nothing but that star where Spenser too had imagined the fountain of perfect things."[72] For Yeats and Shelley the Intellectual Beauty sought by "Alastor" was the same as that sought by Augustine, although divested of its Christian connotations.

Although the first printing of *The Rose* as a separate unit carried an epigraph from Blake, in all subsequent printings Yeats replaced it with one which recalled Shelley and Augustine. Yeats, too, took his epigraph from Augustine's *Confessions:* "Sero te amavi, Pulchritudo tam antiqua et tam nova! Sero te amavi [Late I loved you, Beauty how old and how new! Late I loved you]."[73] Shelley's epigraph, describing the period before Augustine's con-

[71] Augustine, *Confessions*, trans. E. B. Pusey, book 3, p. 32.

[72] *Poems of Spenser*, p. xl. The fountain and star appear together in stanza 38 of *Adonais*.

[73] *Variorum Poems*, p. 100.

version, emphasizes the notion of the quest; Yeats's epigraph, describing the same period but this time from the viewpoint of the already converted Augustine, emphasizes regret for not having loved Intellectual Beauty sooner. Later Yeats was to regret finding *only* Intellectual Beauty. He then reversed Shelley's quest, and searched not to find the ideal, but to rediscover the actual.

Yeats introduced his series of poems with "To the Rose upon the Rood of Time," an Irish variation on Shelley's "Hymn to Intellectual Beauty." Both poets treat beauty as a kind of muse, who both informs the shapes of the external world and stimulates the poet to sing the glory of that immanence. Shelley had pleaded:

> Thus let thy power, which like the truth
> Of nature on my passive youth
> Descended, to my onward life supply
> Its calm, to one who worships thee,
> And every form containing thee.[74]

So, too, does Yeats pray:

> Come near, that no more blinded by man's fate,
> I find under the boughs of love and hate,
> In all poor foolish things that live a day,
> Eternal Beauty wandering on her way.[75]

Both passages follow the recipe for subjective poetry first concocted by Hallam. The pure poets shun society, dedicate themselves to Intellectual Beauty, and rely solely on their own sensibility to detect beauty's fitful flashes through the world of ordinary appearances.

The spiritual autobiography in Shelley's ode applies equally well to Yeats's own career. Shelley wrote:

> While yet a boy I sought for ghosts, and sped
> Through many a listening chamber, cave and ruin,
> And starlight wood. . . .
> I vowed that I would dedicate my powers
> To thee and thine—have I not kept the vow?

Yeats, too, held nocturnal ghost hunts through the Sligo countryside, a habit which continued until at age seventeen he himself

[74] *Works*, 2: 62.

[75] *Variorum Poems*, p. 101. After 1900 Yeats changed "Beauty" to "beauty."

was mistaken for Macrom's ghost on the cliffs at Howth. Likewise, he dedicated himself body and mind to Intellectual Beauty and maintained the purity of both for thirty years. In his poem, however, he declares only that he follows the Rose "all my days," and he reserves the biographical anecdotes for his prose.

Part of Yeats's address to the Rose reflects his incipient development away from Shelley even during this period of greatest influence. In the Hymn Shelley longs for union with beauty and laments his continued separation from it and consequent subjection to the "dark slavery" of the world. Apprehensive that the spirit of beauty has forsaken him, he implores it to return and transfigure him. In contrast, although Yeats, too, wants the Rose to return, he characteristically warns it to keep its distance as well. He wants beauty to return but not to engulf him so completely that he forsakes the world of "common things." "Come near, come near, come near—Ah, leave me still / A little space for the rose-breath to fill." Those lines anticipate the inclusion of opposites in Yeats's later aesthetic thought.

"The common things" he mentions do not contradict his desire to attain to the spirituality of Shelley as described by Hallam, for they include not the common maxims and morality Hallam condemned, but rather the world of nature ("The field mouse running by me in the grass") and the heroic past ("Cuhoolin battling with the bitter tide"). The pastoral and the legendary are equally remote from the Victorian marketplace. If Yeats were to be absorbed by the Rose, he could no longer sing of those subjects, for he would then be using "a tongue, men do not know." In the mood of this poem, at least, he admires the mystic language Cythna traces in the sand but deplores its inadequate circulation.

In "The Secret Rose" Yeats reverts from the Rose which suffers with man to the Spenserian and Shelleyan notion of Intellectual Beauty "pursued and seen from afar." Whereas in "To The Rose upon the Rood of Time" the Rose was "sad" because it shared human suffering, here the Rose is "Far-off, most secret, and inviolate."[76] The only distinction he drew between his conception of Intellectual Beauty and Shelley's has disappeared. So, too, has his divided allegiance to the ideal, for Yeats in this poem

[76] Ibid., p. 169.

has tired of the world he had earlier yearned to enjoy. He no longer cautions the Rose to keep its distance and leave his sensory perceptions intact but instead longs for it to "enfold" him in its power. He will forsake worldly activity and join Conchubar, Cuchulain, and Fergus in the "sleep / Men have named beauty." In a metaphor echoing the close of the "Ode to the West Wind," he concludes his poem:

> I, too, await
> The hour of thy great wind of love and hate,
> When shall the stars be blown about the sky,
> Like the sparks blown out of a smithy, and die?
> Surely thine hour has come, thy great wind blows,
> Far-off, most secret, and inviolate Rose?

Throughout this and other Rose poems Yeats corrects Shelley's cosmopolitan heresy by giving his work a specifically Irish setting. We saw in chapter 2 that in *The Wanderings of Oisin* he hoped to create an Irish Prometheus with more stability than Shelley's hero because more rooted to the earth. Thus, in the Rose poems Yeats imagines Intellectual Beauty in the Erie of Conchubar, Cuchulain, and Fergus. By substituting a concrete setting for the generalized one of Shelley's Hymn, Yeats hoped to intensify his effect. Further, if he could make Shelley's philosophy agree with Irish legend, as he did by identifying Niamh with Shelley's star, he could bolster his Intellectual belief against the materialists by showing its wide acceptance. Irish peasants and English poets could both be mustered against the mechanists.

Besides following Shelley's concept of Intellectual Beauty, Yeats projected his desire for it into Shelleyan personae. Fergus, Aedh, and other named and unnamed speakers of the Rose poems and other lyrics resemble Yeats's favorite Shelleyan characters, "Alastor" and Athanase. He had imitated those seekers in boyhood and he admired them all his life, albeit for shifting reasons. Images of "the lonely reveries of Alastor" and Athanase's "hair blanched with sorrow"[77] combined with Irish legendary heroes to produce the lonely wanderers of Yeats's own verse during the nineties. The older and wiser Ahasuerus and Prometheus provided

[77] *A Vision*, p. 167. Cf. *Autobiography*, pp. 64, 167. Unless otherwise specified, all quotations from *A Vision* refer to the revised edition rather than to the original, 1925 edition.

powerful symbols of ultimate enlightenment, but it is Shelley's younger, would-be visionaries who attracted Yeats's emulation.

Himself a neophyte in hermetic lore, Yeats was most attracted to "Alastor," the least advanced figure of the subjective hierarchy represented by "Alastor," Athanase, and Ahasuerus. The youth in *Alastor* seeks reunion with the vision he once glimpsed; Athanase immerses himself in study to gain wisdom; and Ahasuerus has already achieved final understanding. Yeats's own heroes correspond more to the untutored, questing "Alastor" than to the studious Athanase or the profound but inaccessible Ahasuerus. Like "Alastor," Fergus, Aedh, and the rest fit the image of the subjective poet Yeats derived from Hallam: devoted to beauty, they are estranged from society, given to melancholy, and dependent on their own sensibility (especially the imagination). Let us consider each of those traits in order.

With the exception of Father Gilligan and the Fiddler of Dooney, the speakers of the lyrics in *The Rose* and *The Wind among the Reeds* shun society. Aedh sits on a green knoll apart, Aengus wanders through hazel woods and swamps, and Yeats himself longs for the New Walden of Innisfree. Each seeks, as Yeats believed Shelley did, to disentangle "his soul . . . from unmeaning circumstances and the ebb and flow of the world."[78] Like "Alastor," Athanase, Cythna, and other Shelleyan outcasts cited by Yeats, his solitaries find that they can disentangle their souls best on seashores and the banks of rivers and lakes. "Alastor calls the river that he follows an image of his mind," wrote Yeats.[79] So, too, in "He Hears the Cry of the Sedge" does Aedh "wander by the edge / Of this desolate lake" which is an image of his own mind.[80] The poems also follow Shelley's traditional use of the sea as a symbol of life in generation, so that another reason Aedh's lake is desolate is that generation cannot contain the Immortal Beauty he seeks.

The most striking of the exiles is Fergus, the legendary Red Branch king who forsook his crown to become a wandering visionary. He appears in three poems in *The Rose*, and allusions to him weave in and out of Yeats's other work. In him Yeats dramatized the opposition between Intellectual Beauty and tem-

[78] *E & I*, p. 95. [79] *E & I*, p. 85. [80] *Variorum Poems*, p. 165.

poral affairs. Fergus concedes the isolation of the visionary from society by telling the druid, "I would be no more a king, / But learn the dreaming wisdom that is yours."[81] Like the other outcasts, Fergus has a Shelleyan fondness for water. Just as "Alastor" cried,

> O stream . . . Thou imagest my life

so does Fergus exclaim,

> I see my life go dripping like a stream.[82]

Merging Fergus with "Alastor" helped Yeats both to fashion a unified tradition in support of Intellectual Beauty and to sustain his devotion to the English Shelley along with his allegiance to Ireland.

The double separation from society and from beauty brings melancholy with it. Fergus learns that the gray bag of the druid contains the "great webs of sorrow" in which he is caught. To seek for beauty in the misshapen world is to suffer sorrow from perpetual mutability. The lover of "The White Birds" learns the same lesson as Fergus. He laments to his companion that Eternal Beauty "has awaked in our hearts, my beloved, a sadness that may not die."[83]

The sadness generated by Intellectual Beauty pervades "The Song of Wandering Aengus," which is an Irish *Alastor* in miniature. Like "Alastor," Aengus, the master of love, has a vision of an ideal maiden in a forest by a stream; furthermore, as in Shelley's poem, she then vanishes:

> It had become a glimmering girl
> With apple blossom in her hair
> Who called me by my name and ran
> And faded through the brightening air.[84]

Bewildered by the disappearing act, Aengus grows "old with wandering." By implication he, too, will never find the ideal prototype of his conception. The poem also recalls the romantic

81 Ibid., p. 103.

82 *Works,* 1: 191, and *Variorum Poems,* p. 104. Yeats later exchanged Fergus's "stream" for a "river."

83 *Variorum Poems,* pp. 104, 122.

84 Ibid., pp. 149–50.

lyric which Yeats associated with *Alastor*, Keats's "La Belle Dame sans Merci."

Illustrating Yeats's view that his Rose differs from the Intellectual Beauty of Spenser and Shelley by sharing human suffering, "The Rose of Battle" makes the melancholy of humanity and the Rose mutual. Here the "Rose of all the World" visits "the wharves of sorrow,"[85] again displaying a Shelleyan predilection for water. Yet Yeats emphasizes that the Rose symbolizes beauty rather than coincides with it: "Beauty grown sad with its eternity / Made you of us." The battle is not military but Intellectual, between the ideal form of beauty and the flawed world of appearances. In the essay on Shelley Yeats interprets ugliness as a violation of the divine order. Thus, in this poem, the Rose appears under the guise of beauty rather than of wisdom or peace. It both comforts and suffers with the "sad, the lonely, the insatiable."

Like Hallam and Browning, or Shelley in the *Defence*, Yeats makes the imagination central to the subjective poet's sensibility. "The Lover Tells of the Rose in his Heart" condemns the "wrong of unshapely things" and nominates the imagination to play the deity in a new *Genesis:*

> The wrong of unshapely things is a wrong too great
>   to be told;
> I hunger to build them anew and sit on a green knoll
>   apart,
> With the earth and the sky and the water, remade,
>   like a casket of gold
> For my dreams of your image that blossoms a rose
>   in the deeps of my heart.[86]

Characteristically, although the speaker wants to redesign the unshapely to conform with his Intellectual vision, he sits apart from the rest of mankind. Yeats himself might remake the soul of Ireland in the pit of the Abbey Theatre, but he always composed in strict solitude.

The original titles of the poems in *The Wind among the Reeds* in effect classified them according to types of imaginative activ-

85 Ibid., pp. 113–14.

86 Ibid., p. 143. These lines also suggest Blake's lyric, "The Crystal Cabinet."

ity. Later substitution of the impersonal "He" obscured the specific distinction between the speakers in the 1899 edition, Michael Robartes, Hanrahan, and Aedh. In a note Yeats warned against confusing them with the similarly named characters in the stories comprising *The Secret Rose*, for in the poems he used them "more as principles of the mind than as actual personages." He offered alternate interpretations of the principles of mind they represent, one hermetic and the other psychological. The psychological interpretation concerns the role of imagination in the poet's sensibility:

> To put it a different way, Hanrahan is the simplicity of an imagination too changeable to gather permanent possessions, or the adoration of the shepherds; and Michael Robartes is the pride of imagination brooding upon the greatness of its possessions, or the adoration of the Magi; while Aedh is the myrrh and frankincense that the imagination offers continually before all that it loves.[87]

Intellectual vision includes all three aspects of the imagination but emphasizes that of Aedh, sacrifice to the object of its love. The imagination sacrifices to Intellectual Beauty all devotion to physical reality; its lonely sorrow becomes the incense offered to that goddess. Thus, Aedh signifies the "myrrh and frankincense" also represented by the melancholy of Athanase, of "Alastor," and of Yeats's own persona during the nineties. The worship of Intellectual Beauty becomes quasi-religious, and Yeats borrows metaphors freely from rites of sacrifice and adoration.

"Aedh Hears the Cry of the Sedge" describes the sacrifice. Like the old knight of *The Seeker*, Aedh at first appears to have been lured to destruction by a belle dame sans merci. Echoing Keats, he says, "I wander by the edge / Of this desolate lake / Where the wind cries in the sedge." Lest the reader fail to identify Aedh's beloved with Intellectual Beauty, Yeats begins his note to the poem by explaining that the Rose symbolizes "spiritual love and supreme beauty."[88] Aedh, whether as principle or personage, becomes more like Shelley's wanderers than Keats's by his hope for eventual reunion with his belle dame. The last four lines of the

[87] *Variorum Poems*, p. 803. [88] Ibid., pp. 165, 811.

poem ironically reverse their apparent meaning—the hopelessness of reunion—when one remembers Yeats's early belief in an apocalypse of regeneration and his knowledge that in Shelley, among others, death signifies ecstatic union. Like Adonais in the famous lines quoted by Yeats in his essay, Aedh must die to be one with what he seeks.

Yeats expressed the union with Intellectual Beauty in a Shelleyan phrase—consuming ecstasy—in "To Ireland in the Coming Times," his eloquent plea for the unity of the Irish and the Intellectual traditions. There he describes the "elemental things" circling his table as

> . . . passing on to where may be
> In truth's consuming ecstasy,
> No place for love and dream at all.

The goal of the messengers' dissolution in the ineffable echoes Shelley's line in "To Constantia, Singing":

> I am dissolved in these consuming exstasies.[89]

If, with Yeats, we imagine Shelley's poem addressed to the Constant Rose of Intellectual Beauty rather than to that inconstant, intellectual beauty Claire Clairmont, we see both how Yeats read Shelley and how that reading informs his own poem. Shelley's opening lines then become a plea to Intellectual Beauty: "Thus to be lost and thus to sink and die, / Perchance were death indeed! —Constantia, turn!" The consuming ecstasy of union matches that sought by Aedh, Aengus, and Yeats himself. There will naturally be no place for love and dream, for both love and dream presuppose separation from the beloved. The Yeatsian lover can join his Rose only posthumously, when he has shuffled off the deformed mortal coil.

Solitary, melancholy, and imaginative, Yeats's early personae fit the image of the subjective poet he derived from Shelley and the Victorian commentators. Despite occasional poems in which Intellectual Beauty suffers with man, more often it remains "far-off, most secret, and inviolate" to its seekers. Their desire, like their Intellectual vision and their diction, matches that which

[89] Ibid., p. 139; and *Works*, 3: 155.

Yeats found in Shelley. In the essay he misquotes Shelley by omitting one line from a minor lyric. He quotes:

> The desire of the moth for the star,
> The devotion to something afar
> From the sphere of our sorrow.[90]

The omission of the quatrain's second line ("Of the night for the morrow") does not change the sense of the passage, but it does concentrate the support Yeats found in Shelley for his own poetry of Intellectual desire. He found there, too, not only a model and a theory of poetry but also the arguments for defending them. It is the business of the final section of this chapter to examine those arguments.

Yeats and the Defence of Poetry

Yeats considered the *Defence of Poetry* to be the most "philosophic" and "fundamental" tract in "modern English criticism."[91] He quoted long passages from it with approval, fashioned his own thought in accord with it, and dramatized some of its contentions in works like *The King's Threshold.* Along with *Alastor*, *Athanase*, and *Hellas*, the *Defence* remained a favorite with Yeats long after he had come to distrust the bulk of Shelley's work and had even written an essay attacking the no longer holy *Prometheus Unbound.* He praised the essay most often between 1898 and 1904, when, after his disheartening experience with the Irish Literary Society, he plunged into the more successful and practical work of supervising the Wolfe Tone Centennial and launching the theatrical movement that resulted in the Abbey. Not surprisingly, then, he emphasized the social application of subjective vision more overtly than he had earlier in the Rose period. His use of the *Defence's* principles in his post hoc apologia for the Rose poems and in his manifestoes for the theater foreshadows his later extension of them to a general defense of all genuine art. The poet might write an *Alastor*, he might even in some respects be an "Alastor," but he could benefit society more than Shelley's hapless lover by offering his private vision to the nation.

[90] *Ideas of Good and Evil,* p. 130. The error has been silently corrected in *E & I,* p. 89. Shelley's poem begins, "One word is too often profaned."
[91] *The Speaker,* 8 (22 July 1893): 81.

During the nineties Yeats wanted to be not only a visionary poet but a patriotic Irishman in an age of revolution. "Know that I would accounted be / True brother of that company / That sang to sweeten Ireland's wrong," begins "To Ireland in the Coming Times." If on the one hand he sought to strengthen his Intellectual vision by seeing it on Irish soil, on the other hand he had to show his antagonistic nationalist critics (like F. Hugh O'Donnell) that he had not betrayed his Irish vision for a foreign muse. What, they asked, did Mangan, Davis, or Ferguson lack that Shelley or Spenser had? Yeats's problem in this poem is to absolve himself from such charges by showing that the "red-rose-bordered hem" of Intellectual Beauty is but an alternate costume for the shamrock-bordered gown of Kathleen ni Houlihan.

He solves the problem by arguing that the soul of the Irish race is bent on beauty when it is not bent on revolution. Indeed, for Yeats the goal of Irish nationalism was to free Ireland for the pursuit of beauty and, hence, of Unity of Being. He argues, "The measure of her [Intellectual Beauty's] flying feet / Made Ireland's heart begin to beat / . . . / And may the thoughts of Ireland brood / Upon her holy quietude."[92] Finally he reaches the paroxysm of a Rose-dominated Ireland as "A Druid land, a Druid tune!" The Irish subjective poet justified himself by preserving his Intellectual vision as a pattern for national aspiration.

When Yeats looked to Shelley (among others) for support of his position, he cited the theoretical *Defence* but not Shelley's own career of political action by a subjective poet. Later condemning Shelley for false optimism, he even in the early period ignored Shelley's revolutionary activity in Ireland. He did not proclaim Shelley's revolutionary agitation in Dublin in 1812, nor his two Irish tracts, *An Address to the Irish People* and *Proposals for an Association of Philanthropists*, nor even poems like "To Ireland" or "On Robert Emmet's Grave." Doubtless, he was embarrassed by the spectacle of young Shelley urging the Irish to give up whiskey and Catholicism as the first two steps of their revolt and maintaining—after the government had crushed Tone and the United Irishmen's rebellion in 1798 and Emmet's in 1803,

[92] *Variorum Poems*, p. 138. I quote the wording Yeats used in the nineties, rather than the later emendation of "her holy quietude" to "a measured quietude" (1925).

and had passed the Union Act in 1800—that "we are in a state of continually progressive improvement."[93] Nor would Shelley's being English, a born Protestant and a professed atheist, and a practising advocate of free love have made him any help to Yeats at the turn of the century. Accordingly, he passed over Shelley's early career in silence.

But the *Defence* was another matter, for it offered a complete rationale for the value of a subjective artist to society. Yeats marshaled evidence from it to support both his own aims and his interpretation of its author's. Emphasizing, of the numerous topics treated there, the role of the poet and the function of poetry, he combined the following four passages into a typical pastiche in the essay on Shelley:

> Poets, according to the circumstances of the age and nation in which they appeared, were called in the earliest epoch of the world legislators or prophets, and a poet essentially comprises and unites both these characters. For he not only beholds intensely the present as it is, and discovers those laws, according to which present things are to be ordained, but he beholds the future in the present, and his thoughts are the germs of the flowers and the fruit of latest time.
>
> Language, colour, form, and religious and civil habits of action are all the instruments and materials of poetry.
>
> [Poetry is] the creation of actions according to the unchangeable process of human nature as existing in the mind of the creator, which is itself the image of all other minds.
>
> Poets have been challenged to resign the civic crown to reasoners and merchants [*sic*, error for mechanists]. . . . It is admitted that the exercise of the imagination is the most delightful, but it is alleged that that of reason is the more useful. . . . Whilst the mechanist abridges and the political economist combines labour, let them be sure that their speculations, for want of correspondence with those first principles which belong to the imagination, do not tend, as they have in modern England, to exasperate at once the extremes of luxury and want. . . . The rich have become richer, the poor have become poorer . . . such are the effects which must ever flow from an unmitigated exercise of the calculating faculty.[94]

[93] *Shelley's Prose*, p. 68.

[94] *E & I*, pp. 67–68. I have preserved Yeats's minor errors of quotations. The proper form of the first two quotations may be found on p. 279, the third on p. 281, and the fourth on pp. 291–92 of *Shelley's Prose*.

Yeats quotes the *Defence* prominently one other time, in a letter writ-

These passages defend the ultimate social value of the apparently private poetry of Intellectual vision which Yeats wrote during the nineties. They insist, first, that only the poet has a vision of the ideal order on which society should be patterned; second, that poetry should use "civic" (Yeats would substitute "national") materials; and, finally, that the utility of art surpasses that of economics or business. Yeats appropriately called Shelley's hope for a social order infused with Intellectual Beauty "his vision of the divine order," and he made Shelley's implicit social application of poetic vision one of his own basic tenets, even while—as Shelley did in those of his works Yeats admired—he excluded direct social commentary from his poetry.

Shelley's arguments in the *Defence* so permeate Yeats's thought that the number of corresponding passages in his work is legion. We saw above that he shared Shelley's vision of Intellectual Beauty. For illustration of his debt to the *Defence* here, however, one passage in Yeats's work for each of Shelley's three main points will suffice. First, he imagined an ideal social order and maintained that all his work was written for "that ideal Ireland . . . in whose service I labour."[95] Second, he stressed the connection between art and national language, colors, and institutions, although he was more insistent about the particular nation than Shelley was. He praised the old Fenian leader John O'Leary for having "seen that there is no fine nationality without literature, and seen the converse also, that there is no fine literature without nationality."[96] Although Yeats later attacked Shelley for ignoring "the converse," he praised him for recognizing the primary propo-

---

ten to Mrs. Patrick Campbell in November 1901. Emphasizing the place of poetry not in a rising social order but rather in a declining one, he told her: "Shelley said that when a social order was in decay, the arts attached themselves to the last things people were interested in—imaginatively interested in. Here people look on the world with more and more prosaic eyes, as Shelley said they did in dying Greece. There, as here, nothing kept its beauty but irregular lovemaking. He called the poetry that had irregular love for subject and was called immoral, 'The footsteps of Astrea departing from the world.'" (Mrs. Patrick Campbell, *My Life and Some Letters*, p. 210. Allan Wade reprints the text on p. 361 of *Yeats's Letters*. The passage from the *Defence* may be found on p. 286 of the Clark edition.)

95 *E & I*, p. 246.

96 *Letters to the New Island*, p. 76.

sition. Finally, Yeats shared Shelley's belief in the greater utility of art over more apparently useful social disciplines like economics and business. He wrote of William Morris:

> His vision is true because it is poetical . . . and he knew as Shelley knew, by an act of faith, that the economists should take their measurements not from life as it is, but from the vision of men like him, from the vision of the world made perfect.[97]

Armed with such arguments, Yeats could legitimately take his place beside the national poetic heroes Davis, Mangan, and Ferguson. Heavy artillery defended the position he took in "To Ireland in the Coming Times." For him a subjective poet became a public writer not by treating national issues or dedicating his work to Parnell or Sinn Fein, but by offering his private vision as an ideal for national aspiration. Even if he appeared to differ radically from the propagandist mood of the times, he surpassed the propagandists even in usefulness. Shelley's life as well as his work became the model. "There have never been men more unlike an Englishman's idea of himself than Keats and Shelley," he declared in "First Principles" (1904), a manifesto for the Irish National Theatre issued the year after the expanded essay on Shelley. "We call certain minds creative because they are among the moulders of their nation and are not made upon its mould."[98]

The play *The King's Threshold*, also published in 1904, dramatized the concept of poets moulding the nation. Shelley maintained that poets had early held an honored position in the state by their dual role as legislators and prophets. The repudiation of that role by purely political figures forms Yeats's subject. King Guaire has expelled from his council the poet Seanchan, another of Yeats's subjective artists. In a preface to the play, Yeats pointed out that because Seanchan is continuously on stage, a performance "should not be attempted where the principal player lacks subjectivity."[99] Resorting to the nonviolent tactics of *A Philosophical View of Reform* admired by Yeats, Seanchan mounts a hunger strike to affirm "the ancient right of poets."[100]

Through his Intellectual vision Seanchan serves the state by

[97] *E & I*, p. 63. [98] *Explorations*, p. 158.
[99] *Variorum Plays*, p. 1306. [100] Ibid., p. 291.

providing a model of the ideal social order. As he forces the Oldest Pupil to recognize, "the poets hung / Images of the life that was in Eden / About the child-bed of the world, that it / Looking upon those images might bear / Triumphant children." Loss of artistic images destroys the state by surrendering it to economic or political images: "If the Arts should perish, / The world that lacked them would be like a woman / That, looking on the cloven lips of a hare, / Brings forth a hare-lipped child."[101] Without the poet's imagination, the mere legislator relies solely upon reason and creates only ugliness and disorder. Yeats noted the correspondence between the *Defence* and the thought of Blake, who, he says, "held that the Reason not only created Ugliness, but all other evils."[102]

In revising the conclusion of *The King's Threshold* more than a dozen years after his Shelleyan period had ended, Yeats kept his earlier ideals from the *Defence* but not his faith in their ultimate victory. The year after the essay on Shelley, he made Seanchan triumph and bestow the crown upon the chastened King Guaire, who knelt at his feet in recognition that "There is no power / But his [the poet's] that can withhold the crown or give it."[103] Yeats justified Seanchan's victory and survival on the Shelleyan grounds that "poetry would have been badly served" by presenting its defeat. By 1922, however, Yeats believed that poetry could have martyrs, but not conquering heroes. Accordingly, he changed the ending of the play to show the defeat of poetic idealism in the material world. Seanchan dies cursing "the white of leprosy / And the contagion that afflicts mankind."[104]

Yeats remained loyal to the *Defence* long after he abandoned his Shelleyan Intellectual vision. Its premises underlie even such late poems as "The Statues" or "Under Ben Bulben." When Yeats writes that Greek art "put down / All Asiatic vague immensities, / And not the banks of oars that swam upon / The many-headed foam at Salamis," we can hear Shelley standing in the background murmuring that art is supremely efficacious.[105] Yeats begins his

[101] Ibid., pp. 264–65. [102] *E & I*, p. 68. [103] *Variorum Plays*, p. 308.

[104] Ibid., p. 309. Yeats emphasized the new conclusion by reprinting it separately under the title "A New End for the King's Threshold," in *Seven Poems and a Fragment*.

[105] *Variorum Poems*, p. 610.

defense of his own art in "Under Ben Bulben" by invoking the Witch of Atlas, who was always for him a Shelleyan symbol for poetry and Intellectual Beauty. Like Shelley arguing for beautiful idealisms of moral excellence, Yeats urges Irish poets to "Sing whatever is well made, / Scorn the sort now growing up / All out of shape from toe to top."[106] The *Last Poems* were in many ways antithetical to *Alastor*, but they could be defended in the same terms.

Until after the turn of the century, then, Yeats derived his theory, practice, and defense of poetry in large part from Shelley. He sought to be a subjective poet like "Alastor," devoted to Intellectual Beauty, reliant on his own sensibility and imagination, and, if need be, estranged from society. Like Hallam, Browning, and Shelley himself, Yeats could defend his own subjective art as being more valuable for society than overtly objective poetry. Yet besides "Alastor," another Shelleyan figure offered Yeats a second self-image—the young scholarly recluse, Prince Athanase. Yeats's devotion to the philosophical and mystical studies favored by Athanase forms our next topic.

[106] Ibid., p. 639.

4 Yeats as Athanase: The Search for Wisdom

> "I wanted to feel that any poet I cared for —Shelley let us say—saw more than he told of, had in some sense seen into the mystery. I read more into certain poems than they contained."
> —*Yeats to Olivia Shakespeare, 9 Feb. 1931*

"My mind gave itself to gregarious Shelley's dream of a young man, his hair blanched with sorrow, studying philosophy in some lonely tower," wrote Yeats in the *Four Years: 1887–1891* section of his autobiography.[1] The Shelleyan character in question is Prince Athanase, whose philosophic studies Yeats identified with his own, and who provided an alternate self-image to the "Alastor" persona during the nineties. As a poet of Intellectual vision, Yeats donned the mask of "Alastor" when he pursued his vision as beauty, but imitated Athanase when he sought it as wisdom. Just as the quest for love in the plays of the eighties became the quest for Intellectual Beauty in the nineties, so did the concern with magic wisdom in the earliest plays become a search for a philosophy of ideal wisdom. Yet because Yeats associated Shelleyan wisdom less closely than Shelleyan beauty with his early poetic creed, he preserved his liking for Athanase even after the nineties, when he wrote a very un-Shelleyan sort of poetry.

Yeats recognized that, like himself, Shelley wrote out of a world view which at once informed his poetry and stood independent of it. Yeats held that such a body of thought provided a bulwark against the invidious effects of popular poetry condemned by Hallam and others. Through philosophy the poet could lift his thought above petty, current squabbles and, concomitantly, sprinkle it with the traditional symbols by which philosophic poets avoided the tyranny of narrow rationalism. Citing Shelley's

[1] *Autobiography*, p. 171.

Epipsychidion, Yeats asserted, "Poetry that is not 'popular poetry' presupposes, indeed, more than it says."[2] Not only *Epipsychidion* but nearly the full corpus of Shelley's poetry demanded a knowledge of the poet's thought beyond that contained in any one poem. One could not appreciate Shelley's works, maintained Yeats, until "one has discovered the system of belief that lay behind them."[3]

Although exploring Shelley's concept of beauty led Yeats back to Spenser and Hallam, discovering Shelley's philosophical "system of belief" led him even further from Ireland in 1900. "If some philosophic idea interested me, I tried to trace it back to its earliest use," explained Yeats.[4] He traced Shelley's philosophic ideas about beauty, love, and the human mind back to Plato and the Neoplatonists. Both poets were acquainted with the European tradition of interpreting Plato according to the works of Plotinus, Porphyry, and Proclus. They each found that merging of philosophical tradition in the works of Thomas Taylor, the influential translator of the Greek philosophers into English during the romantic period. Yeats recognized that Shelley's system was broader than any one tradition; accordingly, he expounded other of his ideas—including speculations on the soul, death, and the afterlife—with only incidental reference to their Neoplatonic usage. Yet he identified an idealist philosophy in the broadest sense as a main characteristic of romanticism and, hence, of Shelley. In the essay on Bishop Berkeley he declared: "The romantic movement seems related to the idealist philosophy . . . and when I speak of the romantic movement I think . . . of Shelley's Prometheus."[5] For Yeats, as the essay on Berkeley makes clear, an idealist philosophy emphasizes mind and the Intellectual rather than the "naturalist movement" and "Locke's mechanical philosophy."

[2] *E & I*, pp. 6–7. [3] *E & I*, p. 66. [4] *Autobiography*, p. 265.

[5] *E & I*, pp. 404–5. Professor Donald Torchiana has recently shown that, strictly speaking, Yeats did not assign Berkeley to either the "naturalist" or the "idealist" philosophies but to a sort of intermediate golden mean. See his helpful essay, "God-Appointed Berkeley," in *W. B. Yeats and Georgian Ireland*, pp. 222–65. Although Shelley, too, was a great admirer of Berkeley, I have not discussed his enthusiasm in relation to Yeats in detail, since Yeats came to Berkeley only in the 1920s and independently of his interest in Shelley.

To Yeats, the system of belief underlying Shelley's work was subtle, metaphysical, and mystical. For support he referred to Mary Shelley's note to *Prometheus Unbound*, from which he approvingly quoted the following passage twice, once entirely and once in part:

> It requires a mind as subtle and penetrating as his own to understand the mystic meanings scattered throughout the poem. They elude the ordinary reader by their abstraction and delicacy of distinction, but they are far from vague. It was his design to write prose metaphysical essays on the nature of Man, which would have served to explain much of what is obscure in his poetry; a few scattered fragments of observations and remarks alone remain. He considered these philosophical views of Mind and Nature to be instinct with the intensest spirit of poetry.[6]

Although zeal to make Shelley into a metaphysical mirror of himself sometimes misled Yeats to "read more into certain poems than they contained," he apprehended their informing spirit brilliantly. The purpose of this chapter is to demonstrate how Yeats understood Shelley's place in a philosophical tradition and how that understanding shaped his own thought and symbolism.

Plato and Athanase

The Intellectual vision of the Rose period led easily to Plato. The drive from the actual to the ideal world and the habit of seeing mutable things as types of immutable beauty found support in the psychological theories accompanying Plato's doctrine of forms. Plato's notion of the two Venuses and of the mind's interplay with the objects of its contemplation struck Yeats forcefully. Emphasizing *Prince Athanase*, he delighted in proving Shelley a pupil of Plato's school. The same teachings on love and the mind found their way into Yeats's own work during the nineties, and Shelley's Platonic use of cave and tower symbols helped mold his own symbolism in later poems. Exploration of these problems need not entangle us in the much-vexed question

[6] Mary Shelley's note to *Prometheus Unbound*, *Works*, 2: 270. Quoted in full by Yeats in *E & I*, p. 66, and in part (slightly incorrectly) in *A Vision*, p. 211. The quotation of this remark both early and late in Yeats's career shows its continuing importance to his view of Shelley.

of the "Platonism" of Shelley or Yeats, since our aim is simply to understand the aspects of Shelley which Yeats judged to be Platonic and to note their impact on his own art.

Himself fresh from reading Plato at the instigation of Lionel Johnson, the early Yeats found that the Platonic love for beauty would give philosophic respectability to his own Shelleyan poetics. Shelley and Plato formed a grand alliance against the materialists. Such association did not detract from the claims of poetry; Shelley himself had asserted that "Plato was essentially a poet."[7] Being a poet, Plato could apprehend the ideals of truth, beauty, and goodness which were the objects of Intellectual vision. That apprehension may underlie Yeats's explication of Intellectual Beauty in Shelley, for there he refers to Shelley as "so good a Platonist."[8] Interest in tracing the history of ideas heightened Yeats's awareness of philosophic traditions. Discussing the world soul (anima mundi) in the works of the seventeenth-century Cambridge Platonist Henry More, he did not hesitate to compare More's notions to those of both Plato and "Shelley, a good Platonist."[9] The subjective aesthetics of Hallam could be shown to have a venerable ancestry.

Allegiance to an idealist philosophy like Plato's provided an alternative to the materialism which Yeats deplored. Although Shelley experimented with materialistic determinism during the period of *Queen Mab*, he rejected it comparatively early and grew closer to Plato and Berkeley. In his essay "On Life," probably written the same year as *Alastor* (1815), he observed that "materialism is a seducing system to young and superficial minds."[10] More mature minds would repudiate materialism and strip "the painted curtain from the scene of things." On the other side of the painted curtain lay Intellectual Beauty.

If Yeats ever passed through a materialistic period, he outgrew it quickly. Even his youthful interest in geology served to cast down orthodox theologians like Ussher rather than to honor

[7] *Defence of Poetry*, *Shelley's Prose*, p. 280. [8] *E & I*, p. 81.

[9] *Mythologies*, p. 351.

[10] *Shelley's Prose*, p. 173. Faced with Adele B. Ballmann and James A. Notopoulos's arguments for a later dating and David Lee Clark's equally persuasive reasons for an earlier dating, I have followed the mean of Rossetti's date, 1815. The exact date of the essay does not affect the argument here.

mechanists like Locke.[11] At the same age at which the Shelley of *Queen Mab* praised the achievement of Newton, Yeats was already attacking astronomers for being "dead" to "human truth."[12] By the nineties his early antimaterialism had become an articulate philosophy. In the dedication to *The Secret Rose* he indicated that the book had "but one subject, the war of the spiritual with the natural order" and was therefore "visionary."[13]

Prince Athanase furnished Yeats the link between Shelley's Platonism and his own interest in the conflict between spiritual and natural. He cites Athanase throughout his writings, always as the student of arcane wisdom and sometimes, more specifically, of Platonic lore. Even in boyhood Athanase stood second only to "Alastor" in Yeats's pantheon of heroes, for "I had many idols, and as I climbed along the narrow ledge I was now . . . Prince Athanase with his solitary lamp."[14] At the turn of the century Athanase figured prominently in the essay "The Philosophy of Shelley's Poetry" as one of Shelley's most characteristic and attractive creations. In "The Phases of the Moon" (1919), the first explicit mention of Shelley in Yeats's poetry, Robartes describes Yeats himself reading blear-eyed in his tower. He has

> chosen this place to live in
> Because, it may be, of the candle-light
> From the far tower where Milton's Platonist
> Sat late, or Shelley's visionary prince.[15]

[11] See *Autobiography*, pp. 59–60.

[12] "Song of the Happy Shepherd," *Variorum Poems*, p. 66. Cf. *Queen Mab* in *Works*, 1: 102 (Section 5).

[13] *The Secret Rose*, p. viii.

[14] *Autobiography*, p. 64.

[15] *Variorum Poems*, p. 373. See commentary by A. Norman Jeffares in "Thoor, Ballylee," pp. 161–68. The following lines are usually cited as analogue:

> His soul had wedded Wisdom, and her dower
> Is love and justice, clothed in which he sate
> Apart from men, as in a lonely tower.

But given the political situation in Ireland during the Troubles, the following lines seem equally appropriate:

> [The Balearic fisher] saw their lamp from Laian's
>   turret gleam,
> Piercing the stormy darkness, like a star
> Which pours beyond the sea one steadfast beam,
> Whilst all the constellations of the sky
> Seemed reeling through the storm.

The late essay "A General Introduction for my Work" makes clear Yeats's attribution of Platonism to Prince Athanase as well as to Il Penseroso. He writes: "I commit my emotion to shepherds, herdsmen, camel drivers, learned men, Milton's or Shelley's Platonist."[16] At Thoor, Ballylee, Yeats could play at being Prince Athanase with both a better stage set and a greater understanding than he had had as a boy.

Shelley expressed the conflict between Intellectual and naturalistic vision by the Platonic concept of the two Venuses, Urania and Pandemos, whose rivalry was to govern Prince Athanase. By her nature each goddess symbolizes her lover's attitude toward the world around him. The naturalist worships Venus Pandemos and finds an ordinary rose a fit object for his love. In contrast, the Intellectualist worships Venus Urania, and finds the natural rose only a symbol for the ideal Rose, for Intellectual Beauty. Mary Shelley herself explained the importance of the concept in the poem:

> The idea Shelley had formed of Prince Athanase was a good deal modelled on *Alastor*. In the first sketch of the poem he named it *Pandemos* and *Urania*. Athanase seeks through the world the One whom he may love. He meets, in the ship in which he is embarked, a lady who appears to him to embody his ideal of love and beauty. But she proves to be Pandemos, or the earthly and unworthy Venus; who, after disappointing his cherished dreams and hopes, deserts him. Athanase, crushed by sorrow, pines and dies. "On his deathbed, the lady who can really reply to his soul comes and kisses his lips." (*The Deathbed of Athanase*). The poet describes her. This slender note is all we have to aid our imagination in shaping out the form of the poem, such as its author imagined.[17]

Yeats knew the description of the two Venuses by Mary. He wrote, "We know too that had *Prince Athanase* been finished it would have described the finding of Pandemos, the Star's lower genius, and growing weary of her, and the coming of its true genius Urania at the coming of death, as the day finds the Star at evening."[18] Since Yeats construed Shelley's star as Intellectual Beauty, he identified it with Venus Urania and associated more mutable objects with Venus Pandemos. Pandemos cheats her

[16] *E & I*, p. 522. [17] *Works*, 3: 146. [18] *E & I*, p. 88.

devotees, offering them only an illusory bower of bliss, while Urania rewards hers properly. As the Christianizing mythographers of the Middle Ages knew so well, Pandemos—or, as they called her, cupiditas—deceives because in loving physical objects the soul really loves itself, and egotism can never be satisfied. Their Urania, or caritas, instead leads the soul to love of other spirits and so beyond the confines of egotism and into satisfaction in what they called God, the Platonists called the anima mundi, and the early Yeats called the Rose. Yeats aligned Shelley with these beliefs, for in his analogy between the Platonism of Shelley and Henry More he argued that Shelley in his early work set the anima mundi in the place of God.[19]

The story of Athanase, trapped between his two Venuses and unable to find the true one except on his deathbed, resembles the plots of Yeats's early plays and the predicament of the "Alastor" figures in his Rose poetry. The knight in *The Seeker*, for example, oscillates between his ideal lady and the foul witch and even at death cannot tell if he has followed Pandemos or Urania. Likewise, *The Island of Statues* contrasts two enchantresses who lead their lovers into either joy or destruction, symbolized, respectively, by petrification and animation. Mary's remark that Prince Athanase was "a good deal modelled on *Alastor*" marked Yeats's own early association of the two solitaries as sound. Both were young, sensitive, secluded from society, and full of love and desire for the ideal. He merged the deaths of "Alastor" and Athanase into a single model for the fate of his own wanderers like Aedh, who can lie by the breast of their beloved only posthumously.

We can see Yeats adapting the ideas of *Prince Athanase* in more detail by looking at Shelley's source for the two Venuses, *The Symposium* of Plato, which Shelley translated into English in July 1818 and which Zonoras describes in two tercets of the poem. Yeats may well have known Shelley's translation; it was readily available to him in Victorian editions of Shelley's prose like those of H. B. Forman (1880) and R. H. Shepherd (1888). The relevant passage, from Pausanias's speech, reads:

> If Love were one, it would be well. But since Love is not one, I will endeavour to distinguish which is the Love whom it

[19] *Mythologies,* p. 351.

> becomes us to praise . . . if Venus were one, Love would be one; but since there are two Venuses, of necessity also must there be two Loves. For assuredly are there two Venuses; one, the elder, the daughter of Uranus, born without a mother, whom we call the Uranian; the other younger, the daughter of Jupiter and Dione, whom we call the Pandemian;—of necessity must there also be two Loves, the Uranian and the Pandemian companions of these Goddesses. . . . The Love, therefore, which attends upon Venus Pandemos is, in truth, common to the vulgar, and presides over transient and fortuitous connexions, and is worshipped by the least excellent of mankind . . . disdaining all that is honourable and lovely . . . the other, the Uranian . . . exempts us from all wantonness and libertinism.[20]

The Yeats of the Rose poems agrees with that philosophy. According to Pausanias the lover should eschew the Pandemian Venus and instead worship the Uranian goddess. He will then despise "transient and fortuitous connexions" and love only the eternally beautiful. The derivation of Athanase's name, from the Greek word for "eternal," emphasizes the eternal aspect of heavenly love. Yeats adopts the same position in "To the Rose upon the Rood of Time," which he significantly places first in the group "The Rose." Like Shelley, Yeats wants to lift the veil of the transient and the material in order to follow his Intellectual vision. He will then find "In all poor foolish things that live a day, / Eternal Beauty wandering on her way."[21] The chasteness, horror of the mob, and constancy of Yeats's wanderers place them, like Athanase, in private chapels of Venus Urania. Yet if Urania never enters those chapels in the flesh, she does inspire her devotees with an Intellectual vision sublimating the lust of the carnal eye.

Through love for Venus Urania the mind itself becomes Intellectual and, consequently, akin to that which it worships. Shelley expresses that idea explicitly in *Prince Athanase*. In the description of Athanase's philosophic studies with his mentor Zonoras, Shelley quotes the line, "The mind becomes that which it contemplates."[22] James Notopoulos has identified the source of the quotation as Thomas Paine's *The Rights of Man* but has

[20] Shelley's translation, in James A. Notopoulos, *The Platonism of Shelley*, pp. 421–22.

[21] *Variorum Poems*, p. 101. [22] *Works*, 3: 139.

also noted the agreement of the idea with Platonic philosophy.[23] Athanase and Zonoras read Plato together and Zonoras invokes the *Symposium* to soothe Athanase's despair. The correspondence between the mind and its objects of contemplation pervades Plato's thought. An extended treatment of the subject appears in the third book of *The Republic*, in which Socrates expounds to Glaucon the importance of the study of art to moral virtue. When a youth "praises and rejoices over and receives into his soul the good" he then "becomes noble and good."[24]

The Platonic interplay between the perceiver and the perceived permeates the *Defence of Poetry*. "It is impossible to feel" the spell of Provençal poetry, contends Shelley, "without becoming a portion of that beauty which we contemplate."[25] Shelley advocates the fullest possible union between the poet and Intellectual Beauty. Poetry is "the interpenetration of a diviner nature through our own" and the poet participates "in the eternal, the infinite, and the one." The greater the poet's imaginative union with the One, the more his images "participate in the life of truth."

The participation of the mind in the Intellectual Beauty which it contemplates makes possible the Intellectual vision of the Rose poems. In "The Rose upon the Rood of Time"[26] Yeats invokes the Rose as a kind of muse who not only inspires him but also allows him to see life *sub specie aeternitatis*. He can detect Intellectual Beauty even in the world of flux. Such contemplation poses a problem for the poet: if he really becomes one with Intellectual Beauty he will be unable to participate in life; yet if he ignores the Rose he will lose its beauty altogether. Yeats compromises between the two poles of total identification and total rejection; the Rose is to "come near," but still to leave him a "little space." His mind will then assume some of the attributes of the Rose but still remain imperfect enough to live in the world of "common things." Although even during the nineties Yeats resisted the annihilation of the self in the Intellectual world de-

[23] Notopoulos, *The Platonism of Shelley*, p. 227.

[24] *The Republic*, trans. Benjamin Jowett, p. 105.

[25] *Shelley's Prose*, p. 289. (See also *Adonais*, 42–43.) Other quotations, pp. 294, 279.

[26] *Poems* (1895), p. 19.

sired by Shelley, the poem does depend upon the same notion that *Athanase* states more baldly. The change within the lover's mind may be all that he will ever know of his beloved; when the lady is Intellectual Beauty, however, to become Intellectual oneself is to unite with her. Yeats had early declared that "there is no truth / Saving in thine own heart"[27] and later liked to remark that man can embody truth but he cannot know it (as an external object). Yeatsian Intellectuality belonged to the brooding Athanase rather than to the convivial scholars of, say, Trinity College Dublin, for in Yeats's work, even if not always in his life, the maverick came closest to getting the girl.

The natural metaphor for the impact of Intellectual vision on the mind is emergence from a cave, when we move from darkness to light. Habitually tracing philosophic ideas back to their sources, Yeats detected in Plato the origin of Shelley's cave symbolism. In the essay on Shelley he takes a census of references to caves in eight poems—*Alastor*, *The Witch of Atlas*, *The Triumph of Life*, *Epipsychidion*, *The Revolt of Islam*, *Prometheus Unbound*, *Rosalind and Helen*, and *Fragments of an Unfinished Drama*.[28] "So good a Platonist as Shelley," he concludes, "could hardly have thought of any cave as a symbol without thinking of Plato's cave that was the world."

Like the other references to Plato, the parable of the cave in *The Republic* affects Shelley and Yeats through their treatment of Intellectual Beauty. As Socrates remarks, "You will not misapprehend me if you interpret the journey upwards to be the ascent of the soul into the intellectual world."[29] For Socrates the Intellectual world is that of the Good, which is the "author" of "all things beautiful and right." While Shelley and Yeats also relate goodness to beauty, they emphasize beauty. Shelley addresses his hymn to Intellectual Beauty and Yeats identifies his Rose with the same quality. They affirm the ethical implications of their doctrine, but for them the "intellectual world" is best characterized by beauty. They do stand in a Platonic tradition, however, and Browning was not engaging in hyperbole when he declared the proper theme of the subjective poet to be "the

[27] *Variorum Poems*, p. 66. [28] *E & I*, pp. 81–82.
[29] *The Republic*, book 4, p. 257.

Ideas of Plato, seeds of creation lying burningly on the Divine Hand."[30]

When Yeats expounded Shelley's use of caves and towers in *Prince Athanase* and elsewhere, he had behind him a tradition of idealist philosophy going back to Plato. The Platonic doctrines of the two Venuses and the mind's relation to the objects it contemplates bolstered his own early belief in Intellectual vision and preserved his images from idiosyncracy by attaching them to a traditional framework. Yet Yeats so intertwined Platonism and Neoplatonism that one cannot understand either his view of Shelley or its effects on his own symbolism without looking at Porphyry as well.

Neoplatonism: Looking at the Witch's Cave from Athanase's Tower

When Yeats sought, like Athanase, "Mysterious wisdom won from toil," he traced Shelley's ideas and symbols not only to Plato but also to the Neoplatonists of Alexandria in the third century, chiefly Porphyry. Deriving Shelley's use of the cave from Plato, Yeats argued that, in addition, "so good a scholar may well have had Porphyry on 'the Cave of the Nymphs' in his mind."[31] So esoteric a scholar as Yeats certainly had Porphyry on his mind when he read Shelley in 1900, for he devoted a dozen pages of "The Philosophy of Shelley's Poetry" to showing the Neoplatonic significance of Shelley's caves, rivers, and towers. The cave of the Witch of Atlas formed Yeats's chief example, and he compared it in detail to Homer's Cave of the Nymphs as explicated by Porphyry in Thomas Taylor's translation of *De antro nympharum.* Shelley and Yeats both read Taylor's translations and commentaries, and their common knowledge of his blend of Platonism and Neoplatonism links the two poets in an important way. Shelley's work had such a strong impact on Yeats's thought and his own symbolic caves and towers partly because Yeats saw an ancient philosophic tradition behind it. Since Taylor remains relatively unknown even to scholars, we can begin our inquiry by answering twin questions: Who was Thomas Taylor, and how did he affect Shelley and Yeats?

30 *An Essay on Percy Bysshe Shelley*, p. 13. 31 *E & I*, p. 82.

Thomas Taylor (1758–1835) was a leader in the English revival of interest in Plato and the Neoplatonists during the late eighteenth and early nineteenth centuries. Largely self-taught, he turned from such early eccentricities as his book on squaring the circle and an abortive experiment with a phosphoric lamp to the translations and commentaries upon which his reputation rests.[32] His many volumes between 1780 and 1834 include Pausanias's *Description of Greece* and most of the works of Plotinus, Porphyry, and Proclus. The extensive commentaries reveal Taylor's fervent identification of Neoplatonism with Platonism; along with Proclus's commentary on the first book of Euclid's *Elements*, Taylor appends his own "History of the Restoration of Platonic Theology by the later Platonists.[33] His major achievement is *The Works of Plato* in five volumes (1804), the first complete translation of Plato's works into English.

Taylor's volumes achieved a wide currency during the romantic period. Among the English romantics acquainted with his work were Wordsworth, Coleridge, Southey, De Quincey, Peacock, Blake, and Shelley. Coleridge, for example, wrote to John Thelwall on 19 November 1796, that "Accounts of all the strange phantasms that ever possessed your philosophy dreamers from Tauth [Toth], the Egyptian to Taylor, the English Pagan" were his "darling studies."[34] Robert Southey and Mary Wollstonecraft were personally acquainted with Taylor. Attach-

[32] For a colorful contemporary account of Taylor, including the experiment with the lamp, see "Mr. Taylor, the Platonist," *British and Irish Public Characters of 1798* (Dublin, 1799), pp. 72–90.

[33] Proclus, *The Philosophical and Mathematical Commentaries: On the First Book of Euclid's Elements, and his Life by Marinus*, ed. and trans. Thomas Taylor.

[34] *Collected Letters of Samuel Taylor Coleridge*, ed. Earl Leslie Griggs, 1: 155. Coleridge did not maintain his high opinion of Taylor. On 21 January 1810, he wrote to Lady Beaumont that Taylor's *Philosophical and Mathematical Commentaries of Proclus* was "so translated that difficult Greek is transmuted into incomprehensible English." (3: 279.)

For Taylor's relations with the romantics see Frank B. Evans III, "Thomas Taylor, Platonist," pp. 1060–79; and Kathleen Raine, "Thomas Taylor, Plato, and the English Romantic Movement," pp. 99–123; and for Shelley in particular see James A. Notopoulos, "Shelley and Thomas Taylor," pp. 502–17. The best modern edition and introductions to Taylor appeared after this book was written; see Kathleen Raine and George Mills Harper, *Thomas Taylor the Platonist.*

ing the popular epithet of the times to the translator's name, Southey wrote to his wife, "On Saturday I am going with Mary Hays to see Barry's Pictures, which Taylor the Pagan is to show us."[35] Mary Wollstonecraft lived nearly three months in Taylor's house, probably in 1783. Taylor found her "a very modest, sensible, and agreeable young lady" but was later surprised to be served wine in a teacup when visiting her in George Street.[36] But it is Taylor's impact on Yeats's two favorite romantics, Blake and Shelley, that interests us most.

Blake seems to have known Taylor's work and possibly Taylor himself from the beginning of both their careers in the late 1780s or early 1790s. At about that time, at the house of Blake's good friend John Flaxman, Taylor delivered a series of lectures on Platonism to a large number of invited guests which probably included the then obscure Blake. The vogue of the Barberini vase and the Eleusinian mysteries in the early 1790s caught up both men. Blake made a set of engravings of the vase to accompany Erasmus Darwin's Eleusinian explication of them in his *Botanic Garden*, and Taylor published his own *Dissertation on the Mysteries of Eleusis and Dionysus* at the same time. Taylor's work between 1787 and 1804 coincided with Blake's most fervent period of enthusiasm for Platonic philosophy, and Kathleen Raine maintains that "it was during those years that each successive publication by Taylor was to find its immediate echo in Blake's writings."[37] Finally, Blake's painting "The Sea of Time and Space" is a detailed and exact rendering of Porphyry's explication of the Cave of the Nymphs, the same work upon which Yeats founded his comparison of Shelley and Porphyry.[38]

Shelley's friend Thomas Love Peacock knew Taylor well and may have introduced Shelley to him. Recalling visitors to Peacock's house in 1819, his cousin Harriet Love remembered "a very remarkable man 'Taylor' (half-mad!) who always addressed your Grandpapa as 'Greeky-Peaky.'—I suppose from his know-

35 *New Letters of Robert Southey*, ed. Kenneth Curry, 1: 188. Southey may have known Taylor personally; in a letter dated April 1802, he mentions *The Works of Plato* two years before its publication: *Selections from the Letters of Robert Southey*, ed. John Wood Warter, 1: 192.

36 *Public Characters*, p. 81.

37 *British Journal of Aesthetics*, p. 107.

38 See Kathleen Raine, "The Sea of Time and Space," pp. 318–37.

ing so much Greek."[39] Harriet's statement that Peacock's friends were not strangers to her at that time suggests that Peacock knew Taylor before then and could have brought him together with Shelley. In his novel *Melincourt* Peacock's Mr. Forester (Shelley) remarks, "When I was in London last winter, I became acquainted with a learned mythologist, who has long laboured to rebuild the fallen temple of Jupiter."[40] The ensuing description of the "learned mythologist" accords with the popular opinion of Taylor at the time. Newman Ivey White has suggested Peacock as a possible author of a description of a dinner of vegetarians in *The London Magazine and Theatrical Inquisitor* for July 1821. "Mr. P. [ercy] B. [ysshe] S. [helley] was vice-president" at the dinner, which was also attended by "Mr. T. [aylor] the Pythagorean philosopher."[41] The evidence indicates that a meeting between Taylor and Shelley is possible but far from certain.

Even if Shelley did not know the English Pagan personally, he did know some of his translations. His copy of *The Cratylus, Phaedo, Parmenides and Timaeus of Plato* in Taylor's translation of 1793 is now in the Bodleian Library.[42] He asked his publisher Charles Ollier to "Be so good as to send me [Byron's] 'Tasso's Lament' a poem just published; & Taylors Translation of *Pausanias*."[43] Besides those two works, Shelley probably read more of Taylor's volumes. Describing his and Shelley's reading while at Oxford, Thomas Jefferson Hogg wrote, "We had several of the publications of the learned and eccentric Platonist, Thomas Taylor."[44] Hogg carefully distinguished the special view

[39] *Works of Thomas Love Peacock*, ed. H. F. B. Brett-Smith and C. E. Jones, 1: xcviii.

[40] Ibid., 2: 65.

[41] "Dinner by the Amateurs of Vegetable Diet (Extracted from an Old Paper)," *The London Magazine and Theatrical Inquisitor*, 4 (July 1821): 31–35, reprinted by Newman Ivey White in *The Unextinguished Hearth*, pp. 263–69; quoted from p. 266.

[42] *The Shelley Correspondence in the Bodleian Library*, ed. R. H. Hill, p. 47.

[43] *The Letters of Percy Bysshe Shelley*, ed. Frederick L. Jones, 1: 548 (24 July 1817). Shelley repeated his request for Taylor's book in his next letter to Ollier, p. 549.

[44] Hogg, *The Life of Percy Bysshe Shelley*, 1: 192. Hogg was not wholly consistent about the translations of Plato read by himself and Shelley. On p. 103 of the same volume he writes, "It seems laughable, but it is true, that our knowledge of Plato was derived solely from Dacier's translation

of Plato to be derived from such translations as Taylor's from Shelley's later, more considered understanding based upon extensive reading in the original. In Hogg's opinion, "It would be absurd to affirm that a profound, accurate, critical knowledge of the author may be acquired through the medium of translations, and at second-hand by abstracts and abridgements."[45] Shelley definitely knew two of Taylor's translations and may well have known more, although his knowledge of Plato before he left for Italy did not match his later and fuller comprehension.

Yeats's knowledge of Taylor constitutes one of the many links between him and the English romantics of the early nineteenth century. He read Taylor's "The Homeric Cave of the Nymphs," quoted it in his essay on Shelley, and cited it again in *A Vision* and the note to "Among School Children." Yeats's enthusiasm for the Cave of the Nymphs in Taylor's rendering suggests that he may have read other works by the English Pagan, although his frequent references to ancient philosophers do not always suggest the translations (or even the exact works) he was reading.[46] Taylor offered Yeats another lance to break against the materialists under the banner of philosophic idealism. His blast against Lockean mechanists supported the early Yeats's Intellectual vision: "According to Mr. Locke, the soul is a mere rasa tabula, an empty recipient, a mechanical blank. According to Plato she is an ever-written tablet, a plenitude of forms, a vital intellectual energy."[47]

Although Shelley and Yeats may have read the same volumes of Taylor, each found that translator's identification of Platonism with Neoplatonism in the works he definitely did read. In the

---

of a few of the dialogues, and from an English version of that French translation."

Evans, "Thomas Taylor, Platonist," suggests that Shelley and Taylor may have met while Shelley was at Oxford (p. 1076).

[45] Hogg, 1: 191–92. The two phases of Shelley's Platonism have received exhaustive scholarly consideration in James Notopoulos's *The Platonism of Shelley*.

[46] Yeats knew at least the following works by Plato: *Phaedrus*, *Republic*, *Symposium*, *Timaeus*, *Parmenides*, and *Theatetus*. See, respectively, *Irish Fairy and Folk Tales* (1888), pp. xvi–xvii; *E & I*, p. 82; *Autobiography*, p. 237; *Explorations*, p. 39f.; and *Yeats's Letters*, p. 724.

[47] *The Philosophical and Mathematical Commentaries*, 1: xxxi.

preface to his copy of the *Cratylus, Phaedo, Parmenides and Timaeus* Shelley not only learned of "the invaluable commentaries of the latter Platonists on Plato's dialogues" but also read that "the present volume was composed with an eye to" those commentaries.[48] Like Athanase, Taylor describes his arduous quest for philosophic wisdom; he has fathomed Plato's "secret doctrine." Taylor's rendering of the *Description of Greece* offered Shelley a footnote describing Porphyry's view of Egyptian daemons in the Cave of the Nymphs.[49]

Yeats found a similar view of Platonic tradition in *The Select Works of Porphyry*. In the introduction Taylor asserts that Porphyry "maintains a very distinguished rank among those great geniuses who contributed to the development of the genuine dogmas of Plato, after they had been lost for upwards of five hundred years."[50] He prominently mentions his own *History of the Restoration of the Platonic Theology*, a much more detailed exposition. It is possible that Yeats read the *Parmenides* and *Timaeus* in the same translation as Shelley, or that Shelley read the same Porphyry as Yeats. (Peacock had a copy of the 1817 edition in his library.)[51] Even if they did not, however, each knew Taylor's Neoplatonic interpretation of Plato.[52]

Full of the philosophic tradition popularized by Taylor, Yeats judged Shelley a part of it. The second half of his essay on Shelley argues at length "how close his thought was to Porphyry's."[53] The similarity between the philosopher's and the poet's attitude toward mind, with the accompanying symbols of cave and water, dominates the discussion of Shelley's symbolism. Porphyry's commentary on Homer's Cave of the Nymphs paralleled Shelley's description of the cave of the Witch of Atlas in detail. Arguing that the Neoplatonic interpretation of Homer's cave also applies

[48] Trans. Thomas Taylor (London, 1793), pp. iv–v. The "secret doctrine" is on pp. vi–vii.

[49] (London, 1794), 3: 330–31.

[50] (London, 1823), p. vii.

[51] F. A. C. Wilson, *W. B. Yeats and Tradition* (New York, 1958), p. 255.

[52] Taylor's merging of Platonism and Neoplatonism drew attention from the first. For an early account see the review of his Plato in *The Edinburgh Review*, 14 (1809): esp. 192ff.

[53] *E & I*, p. 84. See esp. pp. 82–86 for the comparison of Shelley with Porphyry.

to Shelley's, Yeats tells the reader, "I quote Taylor's translation" of Porphyry.[54]

Homer describes the Cave of the Nymphs in the thirteenth book of the *Odyssey*, in which Odysseus returns to Ithaca. Yeats uses the Butcher and Lang *Odyssey* of 1879:

> Now at the harbour's head is a long-leaved olive-tree, and hard by is a pleasant cave and shadowy, sacred to the nymphs, that are the Naiads. And therein are mixing bowls and jars of stone, and there moreover do bees hive. And there are great looms of stone, whereon the nymphs weave raiment of purple stain, a marvel to behold; and there are waters welling evermore. Two gates there are to the cave, the one set toward the North wind, whereby men may go down, but the portals towards the South pertain rather to the gods, whereby men may not enter: it is the way of the immortals.[55]

Relying on Porphyry's commentary, Yeats quotes extensively from the Neoplatonist to explicate the symbols of Homer's cave and the system of belief lying behind them. His conclusions may be summarized quickly. The cave is the world, and the flowing waters and "obscurity of the cavern" symbolize the contents of the world. Yeats characteristically points out Porphyry's designation of "all invisible power" as "occult." Since fountains and rivers symbolize life in generation, the nymphs represent souls that descend into generation. One of Homer's two gates leads to generation, the other, "ascent through death," to the gods; the former pertains to cold and moisture, the latter to heat and fire. The stone looms also symbolize souls that descend into generation. Just as the human body is a garment of the soul, so are the heavens a "veil" of the gods. Besides the Naiads and looms, the bees, too, represent the soul, and their honey the pleasure arising from generation. Those souls that live properly will again return to their native abode, the heavens, just as the bee returns to the place of its birth. In general, the symbolism posits the ordinary world (generation) as a flawed prototype of the Intellectual world and helps the mind to see nature as a storehouse of symbols for a reality beyond natural appearances.

After the description of the Cave of the Nymphs Yeats concisely summarizes the parallels to the witch's cave. His somewhat in-

[54] *E & I*, p. 82. [55] *E & I*, p. 82.

genious comparisons manifest both his desire to interpret previous writers in a manner helpful to his own art and his real insight into the intellectual affinity of two other antimaterialists:

> I find all these details [from Homer] in the cave of the Witch of Atlas, the most elaborately described of Shelley's caves, except the two gates, and these have a far-off echo in her summer journeys on her cavern river and in her winter sleep in "an inextinguishable well of crimson fire." We have for the mixing-bowls, and jars of stone full of honey, those delights of the senses, "sounds of air" "folded in cells of crystal silence," "liquors clear and sweet" "in crystal vials;" and for the bees, visions "each in its thin sheath like a chrysalis;" and for "the looms of stone" and "raiments of purple stain" the Witch's spinning and embroidering; and the Witch herself is a Naiad, and was born from one of the Atlantides, who lay in a "chamber of grey rock" until she was changed by the sun's embrace into a cloud.[56]

For Yeats *The Witch of Atlas* was another *Odyssey*—the odyssey of the immortal soul through mortal life. So long as the witch remains in her cave, she symbolizes the soul. When she leaves the cave she becomes the Spirit of Intellectual Beauty; her journey through the world represents the passage of the Intellectual through the material, causing "moral reformation." For Yeats the poem contains two main symbolic patterns: the witch as

[56] *E & I*, p. 84, with two of Yeats's commas changed to semicolons to facilitate comprehension. F. A. C. Wilson suggests that Yeats would have read *The Witch of Atlas* in the following manner: "The Witch of Atlas, who is a 'sea-nymph and was born from one of the Atlantides,' is a personification of beauty. She is shown dwelling in a cave, by which Shelley symbolizes the descent of absolute beauty into the material world. While there she is wooed by the dryads and hamadryads, symbols for the creatures of time and space, but rejects their love with the words 'I know I cannot die'; for absolute beauty is essentially something outside time, a property of reality. Then she creates her own lover by breathing life into a 'repugnant mass' of 'fire and snow'; that is, the love of beauty instils intellectual life into humanity, previously a mere battle-ground of the opposites, and the lover (who lives in a trance-state) becomes sensible of the visionary world. With her purified, 'sexless' lover, like Asia in her enchanted boat, she sails everywhere over the sea of life, playing practical jokes on solemnity and redressing wrongs; for those who die after lives of great purity, she unwinds 'the woven imagery' of 'second childhood's swaddling bands': a clear symbol for the return to the intellectual condition. Some of this symbolism is so clearly traditional that it must have been part of Shelley's purpose. . . ." (*W. B. Yeats and Tradition,* pp. 21ff.)

the soul and the cave as the world, and the witch as beauty and the river as the world. He expounds the first pattern by reference to Porphyry. Earlier in the essay he reveals the other pattern: the witch "is one of his [Shelley's] personifications of beauty" and "she moves over the enchanted river that is an image of all life."[57] Both patterns express the journey of the immortal through the mortal. Like a medieval commentator on the Bible, Yeats finds his multiple interpretations not inconsistent but simultaneously correct, since each expresses proper doctrine.

The gloss provided by Porphyry to *The Witch of Atlas* did not make such symbols as the cave into fixed signs with only one meaning, for a cave is traditionally a symbol for the human mind. Hence, in Shelley's poetry, continued Yeats, "Again and again one finds some passing allusion to the cave of man's mind . . . for to Shelley as to Porphyry it [the cave] is more than an image of life in the world."[58] By construing the cave as the mind Yeats returned to the parable of the cave narrated by Socrates in *The Republic*, but with an elaborate Neoplatonic afflatus to expound the distinction between Intellectual reality and phenomenal appearances. The problem he returns to again and again is how to look at the world in a nonmaterialistic and nonmechanical way.

A river flowing through a cave became the symbol for events (or ideas of them) passing through the mind. Yeats found that water was Shelley's "great symbol of existence" and that the poet continually meditated over its "mysterious source." He quoted Shelley's own essay on metaphysics to illustrate the double metaphor:

> thought can with difficulty visit the intricate and winding chambers which it inhabits. It is like a river, whose rapid and perpetual stream flows outward. . . . The caverns of the mind are obscure and shadowy.[59]

What is the point of Yeats's tracing Shelley's symbolism back to such ancient sources? By associating Shelley with Porphyry Yeats is not interested in determining influence or imitation. For him the importance of the parallels lies in the demonstration of Shelley's use of traditional symbols. Such poetic materials freed the subjective artist from the limitations of his own consciousness

[57] *E & I*, p. 68. [58] *E & I*, p. 86. [59] *E & I*, pp. 84–85.

and his own time. Yeats declares, "It is only by ancient symbols . . . that any highly subjective art can escape from the barrenness and shallowness of a too conscious arrangement, into the abundance and depth of Nature."[60] The age of the symbols guarantees that the artist does not slavishly follow the modes of his own era, and their strong bond to the unconscious mind (other periods might have called it the soul) protects him from a narrow rationalism. Through Plato and Porphyry Yeats linked Shelley to the mystical Platonic tradition of the classical world which surged up in Ficino's circle in fifteenth-century Florence and in More's in seventeenth-century Cambridge, and which contemporary scholars like George Mills Harper, Kathleen Raine, and F. A. C. Wilson argue shaped English romanticism and some modern poetry. The validity of their argument does not occupy our attention here, although they have clearly shown Neoplatonism to be at least one of the many factors in the romantic and modern periods; what does concern us is that Yeats thought it affected Shelley and interpreted his work accordingly.

Unlike the Shelleyan symbolism of Intellectual Beauty upon which Yeats based his work in the Rose period, Shelley's specifically Neoplatonic cave and tower figure prominently in Yeats's work only after *Responsibilities*. By then Yeats saw that he had identified himself so closely with Shelley that to reject his own Intellectual vision of the nineties he would have to reject Shelley as well, at least temporarily; the *Defence of Poetry* and the Neoplatonic symbols, nevertheless, continued to attract him. The interrelated pattern of symbols which Yeats invoked to defend Shelley against Arnold in the early nineties and to expound Shelley in his own essay of 1899 remained in Yeats's mind. "I remember Shelley's continually repeated fountain and cave, his broad stream and solitary star," wrote Yeats in 1916; "they have made possible a hundred lovely intricacies."[61] Some of the hundred intricacies were Neoplatonic, and the ones which affected Yeats's poetry are the river of life, the honey of generation, the cave of the mind, and, above all, the tower. These symbols, which Yeats interpreted with the help of Porphyry and Thomas Tay-

[60] *E & I*, p. 87. [61] *E & I*, p. 235.

lor, occupy our attention to the extent that they specifically relate to Shelley.

The double significance of the river as both life and mind led Yeats to interchange the two meanings in discussing *Alastor*. In the essay on Shelley, he wrote that "Alastor calls the river that he follows an image of his own mind."[62] In fact, "Alastor" calls the river an image of his life, not his mind. We noted in chapter 3 the correspondence between the line from *Alastor* and one from "Fergus and the Druid":

> O stream . . . Thou imagest my life
> [*Alastor*]
> I see my life go dripping like a stream
> ["Fergus and the Druid"].

Given the premises of his Neoplatonic interpretation of Shelley's symbols, Yeats does not really misread *Alastor*, for there he makes the river alternately life and mind. Since water is Shelley's "great symbol of existence" and since Yeats agrees with his predecessor that all things exist as they are perceived, at least in relation to the percipient, the river is mind as well as life or existence; for only by flowing through the mind as thoughts can the world be said to exist. Such is Yeats's position.

Yeats imported into his "Among School Children" the honey of the bees from the Cave of the Nymphs, which he also found in the crystal vials of the witch's cave. There he asks:

> What youthful mother, a shape upon her lap
> Honey of generation had betrayed

would think her son's old age a "compensation for the pang of his birth?" For the reader new to Neoplatonism Yeats courteously appended an explanatory note: "I have taken the 'honey of generation' from Porphyry's essay on 'The Cave of the Nymphs.' "[63] The reader industrious enough to turn either to Porphyry or to Yeats's essay on Shelley will discover the meaning of the symbol: "honey was the symbol adopted by the ancients for 'pleasure

62 *E & I*, p. 85.

63 *Variorum Poems*, p. 828. In *A Vision* Yeats wondered whether Porphyry's essay also influenced Botticelli's *Nativity* in the National Gallery (p. 292).

arising from generation.' "[64] Porphyry's thought reinforces the likening of sperm to the honey of generation, but, simultaneously, it carries us beyond the purely sexual meaning of the metaphor. As the pleasure of the parents, honey of generation has betrayed the child's soul by summoning it from the ineffable down into the world of generation; but as the child's own future pleasure, the honey will betray him by substituting natural for Intellectual delight. The result in either event is betrayal of the soul to the body and, hence, to the decay of the body. Yet the child should not betray his body to his soul either, for in creating the famous image of the "great-rooted blossomer" Yeats repudiates the "blear-eyed wisdom out of midnight oil" which he had earlier seemed to crave. Consequently he can, in this poem at least, reject Plato along with Aristotle and Pythagoras: "Plato thought nature but a spume that plays / Upon a ghostly paradigm of things." By this time (1927) Yeats had moved far enough from his early Intellectual vision to cast off both Shelley and Plato, but he still uses the "honey of generation" in the sense which he had found in Porphyry and explicated in Shelley almost thirty years before.

The Neoplatonic association of cave and mind appears in a very late poem, "Those Images," in a phrase from Shelley's "Speculations on Metaphysics," which Yeats had quoted in his early essay on Shelley:

> What if I bade you leave
> The cavern of the mind?[65]

The mind is a cavern, first, because the sources of thought are obscure; second, because it is enclosed and linked to the outer world through the openings of the eyes; third, because it contains the depths of the unconscious; and, fourth, because it is a storehouse of correspondences for Neoplatonic images. Those images flow through much of Yeats's poetry, for example, "The Delphic Oracle upon Plotinus,"[66] but Yeats's attraction to Neoplatonism in general, which has received considerable attention, lies outside the scope of our inquiry. The relation of some of them

[64] *E & I*, p. 83. [65] *Variorum Poems*, p. 600.

[66] See F. A. C. Wilson's detailed application of Porphyry's essay to this poem and to "News for the Delphic Oracle," in his *W. B. Yeats and Tradition*, pp. 211–23.

to Shelley has been passed over in a few phrases, however, and it is to the chief of them, the tower, that we now turn.

In his essay on Shelley Yeats assigned the tower to the same image cluster as the cave and water. Making one of his few biographical allusions, he quotes from the preface to *The Revolt of Islam* and later remarks, "As Shelley sailed along those great rivers and saw or imagined the cave that associated itself with rivers in his mind, he saw half-ruined towers upon the hill-tops."[67] Keenly aware of the connection between a poet's life and his art, Yeats quickly extended the chance biographical merging of images to the texture of Shelley's poetry. He collected four of the references to towers—one each from *The Revolt of Islam*, *Prometheus Unbound*, *Rosalind and Helen*, and *Prince Athanase*. Using the hermit's tower in *The Revolt* as his chief example, Yeats argues that towers often represent the mind turning outward upon the world, and caves the mind looking inward upon itself. To him that was the lesson of Laon's rescue by the hermit: "Cythna's lover is brought through the cave where there is a polluted fountain to a higher tower, for being man's far-seeing mind, when the world has cast him out he must to the 'towers of thought's crowned powers.' "[68] In any subjective man, like Laon, the solitude necessary to Intellectual vision can become a perversion instead of a virtue. The hermit guides Laon's mind, in which the fountain of the Intellectual has been corrupted by excessive introversion, back to the world beyond itself. The tower completes the triad begun by the cave and water by affording the mind an escape hatch to ordinary reality.

Shelley need not have intended the meanings of such a patristic exegesis, for in Yeats's theory a subjective writer's ignorance of the traditional meaning of his symbols serves to protect him from the shallowness of overly rational expression. Accordingly, although to Yeats the contrast between tower and cave in *The Revolt* "suggests a contrast between the mind looking outwards upon men and things and the mind looking inward upon itself,"

[67] *E & I*, p. 86. On p. 80 Yeats quotes the following sentence from the *Revolt's* preface: "I have sailed down mighty rivers, and seen the sun rise and set, and the stars come forth, whilst I have sailed night and day down a rapid stream among mountains."

[68] *E & I*, p. 86. Shelley capitalized "Thought's."

he readily admits that such a meaning "may not have been in Shelley's mind." With an ingenuous slyness he adds that in any case his interpretation "certainly helps, with one knows not how many dim meanings, to give the poem mystery and shadow." The art of a "poet of essences and pure ideas" mixes mystery and shadow with "the half-lights that glimmer from symbol to symbol."[69]

The light from Athanase's tower certainly glimmers on Yeats's own tower symbol. We saw above that in "The Phases of the Moon" he confessed that the tower of Athanase, "Shelley's visionary prince," helped prompt his choice of Thoor, Ballylee, as a home. Shelley's visionary figure lay behind the mask of the solitary student which provided Yeats with one image of his antiself. In fact, the situation of Thoor, Ballylee, matches the picture of stream, cave, and tower which Yeats, through Shelley, framed in his mind's eye. A brook, its water symbolic of generation, does flow past Thoor, Ballylee, and for the cave we have either the low arches of the adjacent bridge or the hole where the stream dips underground to reappear in the lake of Coole—another Platonic image of a river flowing through a cavern. Always hoping to make all the world a stage, Yeats at least succeeded in making his own home a backdrop for playing Shelley's Platonist.

Practicing the same interaction of art and life which he ascribed to Shelley, Yeats carried the Shelleyan tower over into his poetry as well. In a note to *The Winding Stair*, a book which, like *The Tower*, suggests the importance of the symbol even in its title, he related his symbol back to Shelley's:

> In this book and elsewhere I have used towers, and one tower in particular, as symbols and have compared their winding stairs to the philosophical gyres, but it is hardly necessary to interpret what comes from the main track of thought and expression. Shelley uses towers constantly as symbols.[70]

Although Yeats mentions towers in twenty-seven of his poems and uses them as early as *The Wanderings of Oisin* (1889), they do not assume important symbolic value until after "Ego Dominus Tuus" (1917). Only that poem and "Blood and the Moon,"

[69] *E & I*, p. 87. [70] *Variorum Poems*, p. 831.

in addition to the ones already mentioned, need detain us here, for they suffice to demonstrate the roles of the lonely student and the meditator on worldly affairs which, together with the overriding importance of Athanase, comprise the specifically Shelleyan pertinence of the symbol.

The solitary student in his tower first appears prominently in the dialogue between Hic and Ille of "Ego Dominus Tuus." The poem opens with a typical description of Yeats's Athanase persona combined with echoes of *The Revolt of Islam:*

> HIC. On the grey sand beside the shallow stream
> Under your old wind-beaten tower, where still
> A lamp burns on beside the open book
> That Michael Robartes left, you walk in the moon,
> And, though you have passed the best of life, still trace,
> Enthralled by the unconquerable delusion,
> Magical shapes.[71]

That description of the isolated visionary tracing magic shapes on the sands derives from the lines describing Cythna in *The Revolt* which influenced Yeats's plays about enchantresses in the eighties and from which he quoted in "The Philosophy of Shelley's Poetry":

> And on the sand would I make signs to range
> Those woofs, as they were woven, of my thought;
> Clear, elemental shapes, whose smallest change
> A subtler language within language wrought:
> The key of truths which once were dimly taught
> In old Crotona.[72]

While Yeats's own lines make the correspondence between his poetic symbols and the Neoplatonic explanation of them in his prose quite clear, the reference to Crotona in his source alerts us to the relevance of ancient philosophies here; for Crotona was the main center of the Pythagoreans, who used many of the same symbols as the Neoplatonists. Yeats himself compared the description of Cythna to that of another figure in a tower, her lover Laon. He described Laon imprisoned in a tower "wherein the sea, here doubtless as to Cythna, 'the one mind,' threw 'spangled sands' and 'rarest sea shells.' "[73] Just as Cythna traced magical wisdom in "elemental shapes" upon the sand by the

71 Ibid., p. 367. 72 *Works,* 1: 353. 73 *E & I,* p. 87.

sea, so does Yeats's figure "trace . . . magical shapes" on the sand beside a stream. The setting carries two of the meanings by which Yeats explicated Shelley's images. First, the water represents the one mind and the tower the individual mind; the visionary traces his symbols on the sand between the two because the symbols mediate between the one mind and the individual consciousness and link the two together. Second, the water represents generation and the tower the Intellect; the visionary then traces his shapes on the neutral ground between the tower of Intellect and the waters of generation because only there can he both apprehend the Intellectual and still belong to the generative world enough to write poetry about his experience. He is like Yeats in "To the Rose upon the Rood of Time," urging the Rose to come near but not too near.

The implicit Neoplatonism of the Shelleyan relevance to Yeats's tower becomes explicit in "Blood and the Moon." There Yeats writes:

> Alexandria's was a beacon tower, and Babylon's
> An image of the moving heavens, a log-book of the sun's
> journey and the moon's;
> And Shelley had his towers, thought's crowned powers
> he called them once.[74]

By comparing Shelley's towers to the Pharos of Alexandria Yeats links them to Porphyry, for Alexandria was the great center of Neoplatonic studies in the third century, home of Plotinus, Porphyry, and a host of others. For Yeats the great Pharos became a symbol of the safeguarding function of Intellect in the generative world; just as the lighthouse warned ships from wreck on the coast and guided them safely into harbor, so does the Intellectual visionary save men's souls from wreck and guide them safely through the second opening of the Cave of the Nymphs. The parallel to Athanase's tower is obvious, for the light of Intellect shines in both. It is that tower, whose Neoplatonic and Shelleyan meaning reinforces the social and Irish ones, which Yeats declares his symbol. He sings it in mockery of an age where Locke and Paine triumph over Berkeley and Burke.

The phrase "towers of thought's crowned powers" comes from

[74] *Variorum Poems*, p. 480.

the fourth act of *Prometheus Unbound,* where the Chorus of Spirits celebrates the moral regeneration effected by Prometheus. Yeats's allusion thus drastically inverts the thrust of Shelley's words, for Yeats applies them ironically to mock the failure of the epoch as a whole. The chorus's speech exploits the full image cluster of cave, water, and tower which Yeats praised in Shelley. The spirits begin by hymning the purification of the human mind. Previously "dusk, obscene, and blind" the mind is now "an ocean of clear emotion." The cleansing of the waters corresponds to Laon's forsaking the "polluted fountain" of the Intellectual for the hermit's tower. Both the inward and the outward gazing mind have been purified; the "caverns are crystal palaces" and "thought's crowned powers" now inhabit "those skiey towers."[75] The reversal of the process in Ireland during the Troubles, when hatred defiled the Intellectual fountains and darkened the mind's cave, impels Yeats to fury. The tower now becomes the last retreat of the spiritual guerrilla who, far from riding in triumph through Persepolis, fights a desperate rear-guard action on behalf of an ancient tradition now threatened with extinction.

Yeats summoned Shelley and the Neoplatonists to defend his creed for the last time in the testamentary "Under Ben Bulben," which begins,

> Swear by what the sages spoke
> Round the Mareotic Lake
> That the Witch of Atlas knew,
> Spoke and set the cocks a-crow.[76]

Since the Mareotic Lake is the lake of Alexandria, which lies on the narrow strip of land between the lake and the sea, the sages must include the Neoplatonists like Porphyry who flourished there. The nonchalance of Yeats's reminder that the Witch of Atlas also knew the Mareotic Lake lulls us into casually accepting the third line, but jolts us when we remember that he has jumped a millennium and a half, from ancient philosophy to romantic poetry. Yeats was fond of such pranks: in "Coole Park and Ballylee, 1931" he asks, "What's water but the generated soul?" That surely must be the last definition that would occur to an ordinary reader, but Yeats's presumption in supplying it intensifies the effect for the initiated. Similarly, the open-

[75] *Works,* 2: 246–47. [76] *Variorum Poems,* pp. 636–37.

ing allusions of "Under Ben Bulben" depend upon the connections he made forty years earlier in "The Philosophy of Shelley's Poetry."

For Yeats, the Witch of Atlas symbolized both the soul and beauty. He interpreted her according to Porphyry's essay on the Cave of the Nymphs in the translation of Thomas Taylor, and related her back to an ancient philosophical tradition stemming from Plato and the Neoplatonists. She provided a fit opening allusion to "Under Ben Bulben" because she related to the exploration of death and artistic power which dominatès the poem thematically. To Yeats those ideas invariably suggested magic and the afterlife. The Witch of Atlas was, after all, a witch, and Shelley had labeled her a "wizard lady" as well.

Mysterious Wisdom: Magic and Death

The idealist army which Yeats fielded against the materialists included recruits from the spirit world and the afterlife. The "elemental creatures" whizzing around his table in "To Ireland in the Coming Times" were certainly not electrons. Tracing Shelley's ideas and symbols of mind back to ancient sources convinced Yeats that a reality existed independent of both materiality and the human mind. Magic allowed that world to flow into the ordinary one during life, and death freed the soul for purgation and ultimate return to its home. Yeats's favorite Shelleyan magicians were Cythna and above all Ahasuerus, the Wandering Jew, particularly as Shelley described him in *Hellas*. Life's dome of many-colored glass became a variegated prison, infiltrated by the occult and splintered finally by death.

The Intellectual vision which Yeats found in Shelley and elaborated himself depended upon an independent spiritual reality. To prove that Shelley "looked upon thought as a condition of life in generation and believed that the reality beyond was something other than thought," Yeats quoted from "On Life":

> That the basis of all things cannot be, as the popular philosophy alleges, mind, is sufficiently evident. Mind, as far as we have an experience of its properties, and beyond that experience how vain is argument! cannot create, it can only perceive.[77]

[77] *E & I*, p. 84 (from *Shelley's Prose*, p. 174).

This system of ideas, which Shelley in his prose called the "Intellectual Philosophy," deprived material reality of any ultimate status by making it dependent on mind, which itself was enslaved to generation except for fitful moments when the veil trembled. At the very most, allegedly real objects had only the same status as, say, dreams. In "Anima Mundi" Yeats cited Shelley's denial of a distinction in essence between the two:

> Shelley was of opinion that the "thoughts which are called real or external objects" differed but in regularity of occurrence from "hallucinations, dreams, and ideas of madmen," and noticed that he had dreamed, therefore lessening the difference, "three several times between intervals of two or more years the same precise dream."[78]

In steering between the Scylla of materialism and the Charybdis of individual consciousness, Yeats headed for the Ithaca he variously called the one mind, the great memory, and the anima mundi of the Platonists. That memory could only be known by means of symbols, and the second half of the essay on Shelley explored the relation between symbolic technique and a theory of mind. Dated 1901, the essay "Magic" conveniently summarizes Yeats's own thought on those topics at approximately the same time as his exposition of Shelley's views. The essay does not deal with magic merely in the normal, limited sense of that word, but instead expounds a comprehensive mental and poetic theory. For Yeats the poet is the successor of the magician in that he uses "half-consciously" the symbols which the "masters of magic" employ consciously.[79] By magicians Yeats means men who create "sounds" which "help their imagination to enchant, to charm, to bind with a spell themselves and the passers-by."[80] Like the visionary poet, the magician affects the minds of human beings by means of symbols and offers them a new reality.

Yeats states his "doctrines" on mind and symbols at the beginning of his essay. They are:

> (1) That the borders of our mind are ever shifting, and that many minds can flow into one another, as it were, and create or reveal a single mind, a single energy.

[78] *Mythologies,* p. 352. The quotations from Shelley are from the "Speculations on Metaphysics," *Shelley's Prose,* pp. 183, 186.
[79] *E & I,* p. 49. [80] *E & I,* p. 43.

> (2) That the borders of our memories are as shifting, and that our memories are a part of one great memory, the memory of Nature herself.
>
> (3) That this great mind and great memory can be evoked by symbols.[81]

The three statements fit Yeats's conception not only of his own poetry but also of Shelley's. By explicating Shelley's caves according to Neoplatonic theory, Yeats was able to find his own mysticism adumbrated in them. Yeats announced with delight, "He seems in his speculations to have lit on that memory of Nature the visionaries claim for the foundation of their knowledge."[82] For Yeats, Shelley was always a visionary poet in that he relied upon symbols to elicit wisdom from intelligences beyond his own—whether from other human beings or from the "memory of nature."

The notion of memory connects the discussion of mind and symbolism to Plato and to the Intellectual Beauty of the Rose poems. "I think that Plato symbolised by the word 'memory' a relation to the timeless," confessed Yeats later in *A Vision.*[83] By stimulating racial and individual memory, poetry of Intellectual vision could put the reader into a direct relation with the timeless, the one mind. Poetic symbols such as Shelley's cave, water, and star, or Yeats's Rose and, later, his tower, raised subjective poetry from neurotic introspection to comprehensive vision. Symbols provided the "half-lights" allowing us both to perceive and to explore those obscure mental caverns of which Shelley spoke. The caverns led to the underground river of the one mind behind the many. "Mont Blanc" was for Yeats "an intricate analogy to affirm that the soul has its sources in 'the secret strength of things which governs thought.' "[84]

Although Yeats could make Shelley's philosophy of mind and symbolism accord with his own, he recognized that Shelley did not share fully his enthusiasm for magic. He did detect some interest, however. Shelley's second novel, *St. Irvyne; or, The Rosicrucian* appealed to the young Irishman who, immersed in hermetic lore, wrote an essay about "The Body of the Father Christian Rosencrux" and called one of his poems "A Song of the

[81] *E & I*, p. 28. [82] *E & I*, p. 74. [83] *A Vision*, p. 54. [84] *E & I*, p. 70.

Rosy Cross." We saw above that as early as 1884 Yeats may have thought of Cythna as a magician. Likewise, he found Ahasuerus a master of the occult. Shelley's "early romances and much throughout his poetry show," said Yeats, "how strong a fascination the traditions of magic and of the magical philosophy had cast over his mind."[85]

The magic of Shelley's enchantress Cythna, which fascinated Yeats in his plays of the eighties, carried over into the nineties as well. Poems like "To Ireland in the Coming Times" tell more than their rhyming because they express the "dim wisdoms old and deep" which, like Cythna's truths taught long ago in old Crotona, stimulate his Intellectual vision. The description of Cythna tracing magic shapes on the sand in *The Revolt of Islam*, which we have already seen influenced Yeats deeply, affected this poem as well, for Yeats's phrase "elemental beings" echoes the "elemental shapes" of Shelley's poem.[86] Yeats's Rose, like Milton's God, has thousands who at her bidding speed. Inspiring and sustaining the poet, they belong to the world of essences and magic joining us to the anima mundi; they are elemental beings and "wizard things" that go "about my table to and fro." After their visit, the ministers return to their origin in the ineffable, which Yeats described in another Shelleyan phrase, truth's "consuming ecstasy."[87]

Not only Yeats's diction but also the function of the elemental messengers derives as much from Shelley as from the Rosicrucian lore to which both are usually attributed. Describing his own belief more faithfully than Shelley's, Yeats wrote in "The Philosophy of Shelley's Poetry" that "Intellectual Beauty has not only the happy dead to do her will, but ministering spirits who correspond to . . . the Elemental Spirits of mediaeval Europe."[88] Because Shelley was ignorant of the "more traditional forms" of such spirits his poetry had "an air of rootless fantasy." Presumably, Yeats avoided that defect by linking his own "elemen-

[85] *E & I*, p. 78. He may well have perceived the parallels between *Alastor* and *St. Irvyne*, which have been examined by F. L. Jones, pp. 969–71.

[86] *Variorum Poems*, p. 138.

[87] The Shelleyan source of this phrase is "To Constantia, Singing," as was shown in chapter 3.

[88] *E & I*, p. 74.

tal beings" to ancient Ireland, but they were still the same beings. To support his conviction of Shelley's mysticism he ransacked his verse, construing every metaphor literally. In one astonishing tour de force he wove together phrases from "Mont Blanc," *The Witch of Atlas*, *Prometheus Unbound*, and, possibly, *The Revolt of Islam:*

> [The elemental Spirits change continuously in Shelley's poetry and] are "gleams of a remoter world which visit us in sleep," spiritual essences whose shadows are the delights of all the senses, sounds "folded in cells of crystal silence," "visions swift, and sweet, and quaint," which lie waiting their moment "each in its thin sheath, like a chrysalis," "odours" among "ever-blooming Eden-trees," "liquors" that can give "happy sleep," or can make tears "all wonder and delight"; "the golden genii who spoke to the poets of Greece in dreams"; "the phantoms" which become the forms of the arts when "the mind arising bright from the embrace of beauty," "casts on them the gathered rays which are reality"; "the guardians" who move in "the atmosphere of human thought," as "the birds within the wind, or the fish within the wave," or man's thought itself through all things . . . [the passage continues with yet more examples].[89]

By reading Shelley literally Yeats very probably read him idiosyncratically. Shelley himself cautioned against just such a literal interpretation of visionary poetry. In the *Essay on Christianity* he declared, "If we would profit by the wisdom of a sublime and poetical mind, we must beware of the vulgar error of interpreting literally every expression which it employs."[90] Even in the *Defence*, which Yeats knew well, Shelley maintained that "the distorted notions of invisible things which Dante and his rival Milton have idealized, are merely the mask and the mantle in which these great poets walk through eternity enveloped and disguised."[91]

The originality with which Yeats interpreted the elemental

[89] *E & I*, p. 75. Except for that concerning the golden genii, which may be a misquotation from *The Revolt of Islam*, 1. 32, the passages are, respectively, from: "Mont Blanc," 49–50; *The Witch of Atlas*, 14. 4; 16; and 15. 2; *Prometheus Unbound*, 3. 3. 51, 53; 1. 676, 683. Yeats held to his opinion. In 1935 he wrote of the "delivered selves" of Indian philosophy, "They are indeed those spirits Shelley imagined in his *Adonais* as visiting the inspired and the innocent." (*E & I*, *p*. 483.)

[90] *Shelley's Prose*, p. 209. [91] Ibid., pp. 289–90.

spirits shows not just a characteristic misreading but, more important, his determination to blend Shelley with his other interests, including his occult ones. As though to prove that Shelley wrote better than he knew, Yeats insisted that poetic expression was literal truth and, accordingly, proposed that the Hermetic Society adopt poetic texts as its gospels. He believed "that whatever the great poets had affirmed in their finest moments was the nearest we could come to an authoritative religion, and that their mythology, their spirits of water and wind, were but literal truth"; and he "had read *Prometheus Unbound* with this thought in mind."[92] Shelley and theosophy coexisted easily in Yeats's mind; indeed, Shelley's description of Ahasuerus in *Hellas* prepared Yeats to read *Esoteric Buddhism* and study theosophy with ready receptivity. "Already in Dublin, I had been attracted to the theosophists because they had affirmed the real existence of the Jew, or of his like," he explained. For a time he even thought that he had found his Ahasuerus, or at least someone who had spoken with him, in the posturing MacGregor Mathers, but he later dismissed MacGregor as a "necessary extravagance" of the nineties.[93]

Ahasuerus ruled the subjective hierarchy in which the wandering "Alastor" and the studious Athanase occupied the lower stations. He became Yeats's ideal image of the sage, and when Yeats wore the masks of "Alastor" and Athanase he hoped eventually to turn into Ahasuerus. Later, when instead of becoming Shelley's solitary mystic he had become a sixty-year-old smiling public man, Ahasuerus became the image most opposed to his natural self which he tried to copy. Even then he thought of Ahasuerus and Athanase together:

> In later years my mind gave itself to gregarious Shelley's dream of a young man, his hair blanched with sorrow, studying philosophy in some lonely tower, or of his old man, master of all human knowledge, hidden from human sight in some shell-strewn cavern on the Mediterranean shore. One passage above all ran perpetually in my ears:—

The remarkably long passage which ran perpetually in Yeats's ears was Hassan's description of Ahasuerus in *Hellas*. Since Yeats

[92] *Autobiography*, p. 90. [93] Ibid., pp. 173, 187.

thought the passage's significance in his life warranted its full inclusion in his autobiography, it deserves our attention here. It is the longest quotation from any writer in the autobiography:

Some feign that he is Enoch: others dream
He was pre-Adamite, and has survived
Cycles of generation and of ruin.
The sage, in truth, by dreadful abstinence,
And conquering penance of the mutinous flesh,
Deep contemplation and unwearied study,
In years outstretched beyond the date of man,
May have attained to sovereignty and science
Over those strong and secret things and thoughts
Which others fear and know not.

MAHMUD

I would talk
With this old Jew.

HASSAN

Thy will is even now
Made known to him where he dwells in a sea-cavern
'Mid the Demonesi, less accessible
Than thou or God! He who would question him
Must sail alone at sunset, where the stream
Of Ocean sleeps around those foamless isles,
When the young moon is westering as now,
And evening airs wander upon the wave;
And, when the pines of that bee-pasturing isle,
Green Erebinthus, quench the fiery shadow
Of his gilt prow within the sapphire water,
Then must the lonely helmsman cry aloud
"Ahasuerus!" and the caverns round
Will answer "Ahasuerus!" If his prayer
Be granted, a faint meteor will arise,
Lighting him over Marmora; and a wind
Will rush out of the sighing pine-forest,
And with the wind a storm of harmony
Unutterably sweet, and pilot him
Through the soft twilight to the Bosphorus:
Thence, at the hour and place and circumstance
Fit for the matter of their conference,
The Jew appears. Few dare, and few who dare
Win the desired communion.[94]

That remarkable passage epitomizes many of the qualities in Shelley's work that most attracted Yeats. There is the image of

[94] *Hellas,* lines 152–85, quoted in *Autobiography*, pp. 172–73.

the omniscient sage, full of the special knowledge he has gathered through patient and obscure study. He conforms closely to Hallam's description of the subjective poet—an isolated visionary, dependent on his own sensibility and preserving it from debilitating social contact. Then, too, Hassan's account of the difficult voyage to the sage matches the pattern of imagery in *Alastor* which Yeats longed to imitate, disappearance in a boat at twilight with a guiding light in the sky. Yeats accepted that pattern as symbolic of approach to Intellectual Beauty. Finally, the passage uses many of Yeats's favorite Neoplatonic images. The voyage over the ocean signifies a voyage through generation, with the soul as boat. Ahasuerus naturally lives in a cave, for that is the symbol both of mind and of the world, and it recalls Porphyry on Homer's Cave of the Nymphs, which also allegorized a successful voyage through generation and arrival home with ultimate wisdom. Finally, the isle is "bee-pasturing" to recall the honey of generation, the pleasures which the visionary must leave behind to return to Intellect.

Hassan's lines also adumbrate much of the discussion in the following chapters. By surviving cycles of generation Ahasuerus testifies to the historical gyres upon which Yeats based his conception of world history. His abstinence inspired Yeats's own early sexual abstinence, which he confessed he had derived from Shelley and the romantic poets. His cavern lies near Byzantium and he is associated with the sages there, for in the lines immediately preceding those quoted by Yeats, Hassan describes Ahasuerus as knowing "The Present, and the Past, and the To-come," just as Yeats himself later longed to become a golden bird singing "of what is past, or passing, or to come."

Besides influencing Yeats's life, Ahasuerus also entered his poetry as the "Old Rocky Face" of "The Gyres," as both A. Norman Jeffares and T. R. Henn have suggested.[95] Shelley's sage merits equal rank with the Delphic Oracle in inspiring Yeats's figure. He presents Rocky Face as the spectator of history, just as

[95] T. R. Henn, *The Lonely Tower*, p. 321; A. Norman Jeffares, *W. B. Yeats: Man and Poet* (corrected ed., London, 1962) p. 289, and idem "Yeats's 'The Gyres': Sources and Symbolism," pp. 87–97. J. R. Mulryne suggests Ben Jonson's "My Picture Left in Scotland" as another possible source in "The 'Last Poems,'" *An Honoured Guest*, ed. Dennis Donoghue and J. R. Mulryne (London, 1965), pp. 125–26.

Hassan presented Ahasuerus as the onlooker of cycles of ruin and decay. Then, too, Rocky Face lives in the cave of the mind, like Ahasuerus, and speaks from the darker passages of that cavern. An early draft of the poem even called him "old cavern man." While on the personal level Ahasuerus and Rocky Face offered Yeats an image of a supremely wise antiself, on the historical level they offer the isolated sage's contemptuous dismissal of an age grown hysterical with its own mechanism.

Even by making Ahasuerus into a magician as well as a sage Yeats could not fully convince himself of Shelley's devotion to magic. "I think . . . of Ahasuerus in *Hellas*, and wisdom, magic, sensation, seem Asiatic," he wrote.[96] Yet for all the esotericism of Cythna and Ahasuerus, or the fascination with magic in the early poems and novellas, Yeats remained unsure of the degree of the fascination which he alleged that the magical philosophy exerted over Shelley. *St. Irvyne*, for example, owes more to literary Gothic traditions than to occult Rosicrucian ones, and Shelley's esoteric studies may have included the Neoplatonists but did not extend to hermetic magicians. Yeats was too shrewd not to perceive that, and he regretfully concluded in his inquiry into Shelley and magic, "I do not find anything to show that he gave it [magic] any deep study."[97]

Yeats found more support in Shelley for his views on death and the afterlife. During the nineties his speculations had not reached the rigorous schematization of the *Vision* period; instead, Yeats sought in poets like Blake and Shelley confirmation of some sort of life of the soul beyond that of the body. Survival of the soul became another means of combatting materialism. To be sure, Shelley in his prose had objected to the standard views of immortality. He detected a "desire to be forever as we are" as the "secret persuasion" of our belief in an afterlife.[98] Yet even in the prose he refused to believe in utter extinction, and in the poetry, particularly *Adonais*, he entertained opinions which Yeats found more congenial. Shelley's symbols for the soul and for aging reappear in Yeats's "Shepherd and Goatherd" and "Nineteen Hundred and Nineteen."

Although Shelley denies our potential of remaining "forever as

[96] *E & I*, pp. 432–33. [97] *E & I*, p. 78. [98] *Shelley's Prose*, p. 178.

we are," he allows for the possibility of our reversion after death to whatever we were before birth. To Shelley, as to Porphyry and Yeats, life in generation differs from any antenatal or post-mortal existence. Shelley makes that point explicit in his essay "On a Future State." His views derive from his philosophy of mind. He maintains that mind's birth is unknown, its action and influence are not susceptible to perception, and its being is eternal. He concludes: "So far as thought and life is concerned, the same will take place with regard to us, individually considered, after death, as had place before our birth."[99]

Although the essay on the future state is a reasonably disinterested speculation, Shelley's other essay on this theme, "On the Punishment of Death," is more an ad hoc political tract against capital punishment. Its ulterior purpose weakens its value as a reflection of Shelley's personal beliefs, and it does not accord with Yeats's understanding of them. Shelley addresses himself to a political situation which he seeks to resolve according to moral considerations. Not without a touch of sophistry, the inveterate foe of established religion in *The Necessity of Atheism* abandons his Lockean principles of evidence to declare here that philosophy "renders probable the affirmative of a proposition, the negative of which it is so difficult to conceive."[100] Materialism, or "the atomic system," is not a counterargument, for it pertains only to the relationship between objects and not to their essence.

Any afterlife will involve our return to a sort of world-soul. Shelley restates the distinction between earthly and nonearthly life: "If we continue to exist, the manner of our existence will be such as no inferences nor conjectures afforded by a consideration of our earthly experience, can elucidate."[101] Instead, the "vital principle" within us will probably become "a unit in the vast sum of action and of thought which disposes and animates the universe, and is called God." Like Adonais, "the pure spirit shall flow / Back to the burning fountain whence it came, / A portion of the Eternal, which must glow / Through time and change, unquenchably the same."[102]

[99] Ibid.
[100] "On the Punishment of Death," ibid., p. 155.
[101] Ibid. [102] *Adonais, Works,* 2: 400 (stanza 38).

The merging of the individual soul into the anima mundi attracted Yeats in "The Philosophy of Shelley's Poetry," for it provided the metaphysical counterpart to his poetic theory. Accepting Shelley's concept of death as a metaphor for the spirit's release from generation, Yeats found the "Eternal" to be the subject of "The Sensitive Plant." Particularly, he quoted the last four stanzas and Mary Shelley's gloss on them. Yeats agrees with Mary that they express the "almost incomprehensible idea not that we die into another state" but rather that

> those who rise above the ordinary nature of man, fade from before our imperfect organs; they remain in their "love, beauty, and delight," in a world congenial to them, and we, clogged by "error, ignorance, and strife," see them not till we are fitted by purification and improvement to their higher state.[103]

Borrowing his last four words directly from *Adonais*, Yeats added, "Not merely happy souls, but all beautiful places and movements and gestures and events, when we think they have ceased to be, have become portions of the Eternal." Yeats continued to think of "The Sensitive Plant," as well as the rest of Shelley, as a vision of the infinite expressed in the finite. In 1930 he described the final stanza of the poem as that type of vision experienced "when some symbol, shaped by the experience itself, has descended to us, and when we ourselves have passed, through a shifting of the threshold consciousness, into a similar state."[104]

One such symbol which Yeats borrowed from Shelley was the swan. Singing only at death, the solitary swan drifting out alone over the sea of generation to die at dusk provided a fit image for the soul of a poet. "The Wild Swans at Coole" owes a great deal to the swans of *Alastor*,[105] but Yeats's clearest Shelleyan use of

[103] *E & I*, p. 73. [104] *Explorations*, p. 330.

[105] The situation in "The Wild Swans at Coole" accords rather closely with that of the poet in *Alastor*, lines 275–90:

> A swan was there
> Beside a sluggish stream among the reeds.
> It rose as he approached, and with strong wings
> Scaling the upward sky, bent its bright course
> High over the immeasurable main.
> His eyes pursued its flight.—"Thou hast a home,
> Beautiful bird! thou voyagest to thine home,
> Where thy sweet mate will twine her downy neck

the symbol appears in "Nineteen Hundred and Nineteen." There he writes:

> Some moralist or mythological poet
> Compares the solitary soul to a swan.

The unnamed mythological poet is, of course, Shelley, and the relevant passage comes from Yeats's sacred book, *Prometheus Unbound*, where Asia, anticipating her return to Prometheus, sings,

> My soul is an enchanted boat,
> Which, like a sleeping swan, doth float.[106]

The swan's death song becomes the song of the poet about to enter the "higher state" symbolized by death. The image fits both the union with Intellectual Beauty of the Rose poems and the union with the anima mundi in some of the later ones.

If death symbolizes union with the eternal, then life, after its midpoint, becomes a process of growing younger rather than older, because one is closer to the transformation symbolized by death. Yeats's later work echoes Shelley's notion of life as a reverse aging. F. A. C. Wilson has suggested an illuminating comparison between a song of Asia's and "Shepherd and Goatherd" in terms of Thomas Taylor's *A Dissertation on the Eleusinian and Bacchic Mysteries*. Discussing Orphic Platonism, Taylor writes, "According to the Orphic theology, souls, while under the government of Saturn, who is pure intellect, advance in retrograde progression from age to youth."[107] In the commentary to his edition of Plato's works Taylor makes a similar observation: man "is no longer seen advancing to old age, but is again

---

> With thine, and welcome thy return with eyes
> Bright in the lustre of their own fond joy.
> And what am I that I should linger here,
> With voice far sweeter than thy dying notes,
> Spirit more vast than thine, frame more attuned
> To beauty, wasting these surpassing powers
> In the deaf air, to the blind earth, and heaven
> That echoes not my thoughts?"
> [*Works*, 1: 184–85].

106 *Variorum Poems*, p. 430, and *Works*, 2: 225.

107 *A Dissertation on Eleusinian and Bacchic Mysteries*, p. 138. See F. A. C. Wilson, pp. 200–205.

changed to the contrary and naturally becomes, as it were, younger and more delicate."[108] Yeats reshapes that idea in terms of the poet and his mask; the young poet adopts a mask of aged sage (Shelley and Ahasuerus), whereas the older poet assumes a mask of youth and vigor. Yeats plays with those ideas gracefully in *The Bounty of Sweden* and develops them more fully in his later poetry.

The idea of progressing backward to an original, diviner state appears in the same song of Asia's at the end of the second act of *Prometheus Unbound*, in which she compares the soul to a swan. She sings:

> We have passed Age's icy caves,
> And Manhood's dark and tossing waves,
> And Youth's smooth ocean, smiling to betray:
> Beyond the glassy gulfs we flee
> Of shadow-peopled Infancy,
> Through Death and Birth to a diviner day.[109]

Yeats expresses a similar idea in "Shepherd and Goatherd," one of his three poems about the death of Major Robert Gregory. Yeats couples the notion of the journey backward with his own terminology of the perne, or gyre. The goatherd declares:

> He grows younger every second
> That were all his birthdays reckoned
> Much too solemn seemed;
> Because of what he had dreamed,
> Or the ambitions that he served,
> Much too solemn and reserved.
> Jaunting, journeying
> To his own dayspring,
> He unpacks the loaded pern
> Of all 'twas pain or joy to learn,
> Of all that he had made . . .
> Knowledge he shall unwind
> Through victories of the mind,
> Till, clambering at the cradle-side,
> He dreams himself his mother's pride,
> All knowledge lost in trance
> Of sweeter ignorance.[110]

[108] *The Works of Plato*, 4: 120.
[109] *Works*, 2: 226 (act 2, scene 5).
[110] *Variorum Poems*, pp. 342–43.

The passages from Taylor, Shelley, and Yeats express a similar idea: man's progression from age in mortal life to an immortal life. A reversal of the normal process of aging signifies the transformation. Whether or not Shelley and Yeats really found the source of that idea in Taylor, the Neoplatonic interpretation still fits their work. For Shelley and for the early Yeats, the immortal realm merges with Taylor's description of the dominion of Saturn or intellect. The poets' Saturn is Intellectual Beauty.

To the poet of Intellectual vision, life becomes a cul-de-sac whose exit is also its entrance. That is the reason both poets think of birth and death in similar terms and describe death as a process of reverse aging or rejuvenation. We progress, in Asia's words, "Through Death and Birth, to a diviner day." Just as the Witch of Atlas could unwind "the woven imagery / Of second childhood's swaddling bands," so does the speaker of "Byzantium" seek to unwind "Hades' bobbin bound in mummy-cloth."[111] Adonais's abode of the eternal and the holy city of Byzantium are both realms of unaging intellect exempt from the world of mutability and generation.

Although Shelley's thought continued to influence Yeats even after the period of greatest affinity, the differences become even more marked. We can see the distinction clearly by comparing the attitudes toward life and death in two elegies, "Adonais" and "In Memory of Major Robert Gregory." Both poets mourn the death of a young man and then deny the finality of his death. The memory of the youth comforts or inspires them. Yet the process works very differently in the two poems. Shelley resolves the problem of Keats's death by imagining his progression to the white radiance on the other side of the many-colored dome of life. Yeats, although aware of the whiteness of eternity (to which Gregory is reborn in "Shepherd and Goatherd") celebrates the varied colors of the dome itself. His poem looks backward over Gregory's mortal life, whereas Shelley's looks forward to Keats's immortal life in the One. Shelley rejects the "dream of life" in favor of "the white radiance of Eternity." Although Keats's works remain immortal, the circumstances of his life on earth are a source of bitterness. Shelley accepts the myth of

111 *Works,* 4: 35 (stanza 70) and *Variorum Poems,* p. 497.

Keats being hounded to death by critics; "herded wolves," "obscene ravens," and "vultures" populate the earth. Consolation comes with the realization that Keats has left mortal ugliness behind and is now "a portion of the loveliness / Which once he made more lovely."[112] The Intellectual world lies on the other side of death. Referring to the fifty-second stanza, Yeats wrote that "in the most famous passage in all his poetry he sings of Death as a mistress."[113] Undoubtedly, he interpreted the passage idiosyncratically. The erotic application of "Die, / If thou wouldst be with that which thou dost seek" fits Yeats's own poetry better than it does Shelley's elegy. Yet Shelley does emphasize the union with eternity as the final achievement of Adonais. He opposes the eternal world to the mutable one and clearly prefers the radiance to its refraction.

In contrast, Yeats celebrates the glory of Robert Gregory's life. Not Gregory's postmortal fate but the manner of his mortal life stimulates the poet's imagination. Comparing the dead Irishman to England's model of the perfect gentleman, Sir Philip Sidney, Yeats recalls the "Soldier, scholar, horseman, he, / As 'twere all life's epitome." In place of the mourners for Adonais, Yeats describes other dead friends, Lionel Johnson, John Synge, and his uncle George Pollexfen. Not what these men are now but what they were then constitutes their triumph over death. Not their works but their lives inspire the poet. Death becomes not a means of reunion with the eternal but rather a "discourtesy" to "Our Sidney and our perfect man." Although Yeats had a great deal to say about life after death in *A Vision* and elsewhere, here he restricts himself to life on earth. He resists his early desire to go "up" into the subtlety of Shelley and insists upon the beauty and value of not only the One but also the "many" that "change and pass." He celebrates Robert Gregory not as a part of white eternity but as a panel of colored glass.

The break with Shelley had not become apparent to Yeats at the time of "The Philosophy of Shelley's Poetry." There, with an admirable grasp of the direction and totality of Shelley's thought, but with numerous idiosyncratic interpretations of details, he expounded his predecessor's poetic techniques and meta-

[112] *Adonais*, lines 344, 462, 243–46, 379–80, respectively.
[113] *E & I*, p. 72.

physical system. Emphasizing Intellectual Beauty, he explored its ramifications poetically in patterns of symbolism and possible personae, and philosophically in terms of mind, the soul, and death. Shelley's thought and symbols had extensive parallels in earlier writers, particularly in Plato and the Neoplatonists. Yeats did not trace Shelley's thought back to his predecessors so much to identify sources as to indicate Shelley's place in the great tradition of antimaterialistic artists. Above all, Yeats sought in such poets as Shelley confirmation of his own philosophy and his own poetic technique. As his philosophy and technique changed, he kept a few of Shelley's symbols but moved ever further from both his own earlier art and his estimation of Shelley's achievement. Those changes, and their effect on Yeats's poetry in comparison to Shelley's, occupy the remainder of this study.

PART TWO

ANTINOMIAL VISION: YEATS'S ALTERNATIVE TO SHELLEY

5 The Aesthetics of Antinomy

"I have myself . . . begun . . . a movement downwards upon life, not upwards out of life."
—*Yeats to Florence Farr, February 1906*

After 1903 Yeats moved from an Intellectual to an antinomial vision of life. He built his new aesthetic upon the tension between balanced contraries rather than upon the intensity of exclusive devotion. Although in the nineties he had forsaken social involvement for Shelleyan purity in his verse, he now wanted to combine both in an art at once popular and profound. "All things fall into a series of antinomies in human experience," he declared in a famous sentence from *A Vision*.[1] To reject any part of experience was to reject the unity of the whole and, hence, to mar the Unity of Being of the individual. The way to "ultimate reality" led not merely upward with the spirit but also downward with the body. For Yeats, Shelley represented the spiritual world of Intellectual Beauty. The more Yeats laced his poetry with the other half of the antinomy—the actual instead of the ideal—the more his enthusiasm for Shelley slackened. For he had earlier identified himself with Shelley so fully that in order to remake his art he had to reject not just his earlier work but also his earlier model. To become Yeats, he had to repudiate Shelley. This chapter opens our inquiry into Yeats's later art and thought by demonstrating, first, the importance of Shelley to the well-known changes in Yeats's aesthetic which crystallized with *Responsibilities* and which may be described as a change from Intellectual to antinomial vision; second, the consequent differences between Shelley's Prometheus and Yeats's Cuchulain; and, finally, the psychological theories by which Yeats retained his fervor for "Alastor," Athanase, and Ahasuerus.

"Alastor" with a Surfeit

"The Philosophy of Shelley's Poetry" (1903) was Yeats's fare-

[1] *A Vision*, p. 193.

well salute to both Shelley and his own youth. By then he was middle-aged, and the "Alastor" face he had worn in the nineties no longer suited either his own widening experience or Ireland in the twentieth century. Shelley seemed just as one-sided as Griffith and Sinn Fein, although each stood for a different side of the question. Even during the nineties Yeats had never been a fully Shelleyan poet: he had, for example, grounded his art firmly on Irish soil in direct opposition to Shelley's internationalism, and even while worshipping the Rose of Intellectual Beauty he had cautioned it to keep its distance from him. After the turn of the century, those tendencies culminated in a total reaction against the Shelleyan style, subject, and attitude of the Rose poems. Antinomial replaced Intellectual vision: mundane reality held equal sway with ideal visions; the joy—at times, the fierce exultation—of acceptance of reality mingled with the sorrow of desire for ideal justice; and the gray of Connemara replaced the red and yellow of Shelley's Italy.

Even in the early nineties Yeats felt the impulses which eventually drove him beyond Shelley, but he did not act upon them for over a decade. He expressed them comically in describing the Rhymers' Club for the *Boston Pilot* in 1892, when he compared the young aesthetes of the Cheshire Cheese to the youth in *Alastor*, whom, as always, he improperly called "Alastor." He wrote, "The typical young poet of our day is an aesthete with a surfeit, searching sadly for his lost Philistinism, his heart full of an unsatisfied hunger for the commonplace. He is an Alastor tired of his woods and longing for beer and skittles."[2] The description of the surfeited "Alastor" fits Yeats himself, who, except for his distinguishing excellence, was certainly a "typical young poet" of the nineties. Yet his Rose poems ignored the aberrant maxim with which he favored the Boston Irish and instead conformed to the Shelleyan positions of the rest of his critical speculations. He shunned the philistines for the select few, hungered not for the commonplace but for an ideal alternative to it, wrote more of the woods than of the city, and worshipped at Shelley's chapel of the morning star rather than roistered at Burns's beerhouse. It took a decade of Intellectual vision for Yeats to feel surfeited with "Alastor."

[2] *Letters to the New Island*, p. 147.

The not yet surfeited aesthete did qualify his Shelleyan poetry in two ways during the nineties. First, he refused the Rose his complete devotion and instead maintained a dual allegiance: to Intellectual Beauty and to the mundane shell of the world. He sought simultaneously to beseech and to rule the Rose:

> Come near, come near, come near—Ah, leave me still
> A little space for the rose-breath to fill!
> Lest I no more hear common things. . . .[3]

Even though the common things of "To the Rose upon the Rood of Time" turn out to be images of the gentleness of nature, the poem clearly resists the full thrust of a Shelleyan desire to lift the painted curtain of life.

Second, Yeats replaced Shelley's international spirit and foreign settings (which he had imitated in the verse plays of the eighties) with nationalism and Irish landscapes. We have seen that he lamented Shelley's eclectic—even cosmopolitan—choice of subject:

> I could not endure, however, an international art, picking stories and symbols where it pleased. Might I not, with health and good luck to aid me, create some new *Prometheus Unbound;* Patrick or Columcille, Oisin or Finn, in Prometheus' stead; and, instead of Caucasus, Cro-Patrick or Ben Bulben? Have not all races had their first unity from a mythology that marries them to rock and hill?[4]

To marry the rock and hill of the Irish west country was to become at least an in-law of common reality. A truly comprehensive world view demanded a full realization of particular environment. "One can only reach out to the universe with a gloved hand," he declared; "that glove is one's nation, the only thing one knows even a little of."[5] Yeats "mourned the richness or reality lost to Shelley's *Prometheus Unbound* because he had not discovered in England or in Ireland his Caucasus."[6] Shelley could then have given "to modern poetry a breadth and stability like that of ancient poetry."[7] The modern reader may boggle at imagining Prometheus suspended from the White Cliffs of Dover, but Yeats did not.

[3] *Variorum Poems,* p. 101. [4] *Autobiography,* pp. 193–94.
[5] *Letters to the New Island,* p. 174.
[6] *E & I,* p. 350. [7] *Autobiography,* p. 150.

Having once mastered "Irishness," Yeats could confidently reach out beyond it with the gloves off. Only after he had developed an antinomial vision, which protected him against internationalism by balancing the foreign with the Irish, did he again include Europe and Asia in his art. By 1912 he could compare (unfavorably) an Irish bourgeois to Duke Ercole. "The Statues" (1938) begins with Pythagoras, mentions Phidias, Hamlet, Grimalkin, and Buddha, and concludes with Pearse and Cuchulain. Not until Yeats could unabashedly compare Robert Gregory to Philip Sidney, or the Dublin Post Office to the Bay of Salamis, would he sail the seas to Byzantium.

Although insistent upon Irishness and occasionally wary of the Rose, Yeats remained reasonably faithful to his Shelleyan principles until about 1903, after which antinomial vision gradually usurped the earlier, Intellectual vision. Two descriptions of his own work in letters to friends, one from 1888 and the other from 1906, illustrate the change:

> 1888: I have noticed some things about my poetry I did not know before . . . it is almost all a flight into fairyland from the real world, and a summons to that flight . . . it is not the poetry of insight and knowledge, but of longing and complaint.
>
> 1906: I have myself . . . begun . . . a movement downwards upon life, not upwards out of life.[8]

Antinomial vision meant an inclusive vision based on the tension between opposites like the ideal and the actual, whereas Intellectual vision is an exclusive focus on the ideal at the expense of "life."[9] Yeats no longer wanted to flee from the actual to the ideal, as he thought that Shelley had, but instead sought to bring the ideal down into the actual for that instant in which a terrible beauty could be born. He would move downward upon life on his own, not upward out of it with Shelley. The downward

[8] *Yeats's Letters*, pp. 63, 469.

[9] After writing this I discovered that Frank Lentricchia has recently used a similar term, antinomic, to describe something different: Yeats's separation from nineteenth century, principally Continental, aesthetics and his "ambiguous and contradictory motivations." See *The Gaiety of Language: An Essay on the Radical Poetics of W. B. Yeats and Wallace Stevens*, p. 42 and passim.

movement required changes in the poet's subject, attitude, and style; let us consider each of them in order.

The pressure of reality eventually crushed the imaginative Arcadia which Yeats constructed under the guidance of Shelley. The Parnell controversy, the *Playboy* riots, the Lane pictures dispute, and the 1913 lockout all dragged him back to the reality of prerevolutionary Ireland. To be sure, in making Shelley the poet of idealized bowers of bliss Yeats distorted his predecessor's work, for Shelley had condemned the Peterloo massacre in *The Masque of Anarchy*, mocked George IV in *Swellfoot the Tyrant*, and castigated most of the injustices of Europe in shorter pieces. But Yeats does not mention those works and instead confines himself to the visionary rhymes. It is his own early work that conforms to the pattern he ascribed to Shelley, and his strictures on the difficulty of combining Shelley with common life reflect his own uneasiness at the products of his youth and at the remaking of his poetry.

Yeats chose Shelley to illustrate these changes in his own thought, particularly in his distinction between bird and market cart. In "Discoveries" (1906) he wrote:

> There are two ways before literature—upward into ever-growing subtlety . . . or downward, taking the soul with us until all is simplified or solidified again. That is the choice of choices—the way of the bird until common eyes have lost us, or to the market carts; but we must see to it that the soul goes with us, for the bird's song is beautiful, and the traditions of modern imagination, growing always more musical, more lyrical, more melancholy, casting up now a Shelley, now a Swinburne. . . . If the carts have hit our fancy we must have the soul tight within our bodies. . . . If it begin to slip away we must go after it, for Shelley's Chapel of the Morning Star is better than Burns's beerhouse . . . and it is always better than that uncomfortable place where there is no beer, the machine-shop of the realists.[10]

By 1906 the carts had clearly hit Yeats's fancy, and his problem became to maintain his soul in the jostling marketplace which he had earlier fled. He now sought just that mass audience which,

[10] *E & I*, pp. 266–67. Yeats's new attraction to the market cart during this period has been admirably elaborated by Edward Engelberg in his *The Vast Design*, chap. 2.

directed by Hallam, he had earlier condemned. The descent to life did not mean abandonment of the ideal, however, for then at best he would become a habitué of Burns's beerhouse and, at worst, of the realists' machine shop. Best of all would be to be a bird perched on a market cart. Yeats's phrasing recalls Shelley's "To a Skylark"—"the way of the bird until common eyes have lost us." Yeats no longer wanted to ascend to the Intellectual with the skylark, but to immerse himself in just that human world, the lusts of the marketplace, which the skylark forsakes. His new symbol would be not a skylark but the man-made golden bird. If the golden bird is out of nature, man, not a Platonic idea, made it so. Shelley writes that the skylark

> of death must deem
> Things more true and deep
> Than we mortals dream.[11]

Yeats located the source of the ideal in just those mortals whom the skylark surpassed. The former exponent of Plato and the Neoplatonists could write by 1927, despite continued attraction to his former masters:

> And I declare my faith:
> I mock Plotinus' thought
> And cry in Plato's teeth,
> Death and life were not
> Till man made up the whole,
> Made lock, stock and barrel
> Out of his bitter soul,
> Aye, sun and moon and star, all,
> And further add to that
> That, being dead, we rise,
> Dream and so create
> Translunar Paradise.[12]

Better than a choice between the ideal and the actual was a reconciliation, or at least a balance. Although he often tried to reconcile spirit and sense, Yeats could at times doubt their meeting and instead imagine only "change upon the instant."[13] Like the

[11] *Works*, 2: 305.

[12] *Variorum Poems*, pp. 414–15. Yeats conceded in a note that these lines were unfair to Plotinus.

[13] *Autobiography*, p. 326.

opposing kings Congal and Aedh in *The Herne's Egg*, the ideal and subtle were locked in a ritual combat with the actual and common from which neither side expected to emerge victorious. Instead, they were united into a whole maintained by the internecine warfare of its parts. Vision consisted in accepting the full dialectic, not merely half of it.

Yeats sometimes chose Dickens to represent the common life of the market cart. Celebrating the Unity of Being of the artist in the age of Homer, Yeats wrote, "A man of that unbroken day could have all the subtlety of Shelley and yet use no image unknown among the common people, and speak no thought that was not a deduction from common thought . . . we may never see again a Shelley and a Dickens in the one body, but be broken to the end."[14] Again, both halves of the antinomy are necessary. Shelley without Dickens ascends into idiosyncratic subtlety, and Dickens without Shelley degenerates into soulless naturalism. The bird must pern around the cart.

Yeats's discussion of Shelley suggests the countertruth to Crazy Jane's famous lines: " 'Fair and foul are near of kin, / And fair needs foul,' I cried." If fair needs foul, foul also needs fair. The fair needs the foul to fasten it to reality and to keep the balloon of the mind from rising out of sight. Likewise, the foul needs the fair to transform it into something beyond mere fury and mire. The artist needs both, for otherwise he risks falsifying his object through failing to present it in tension with its opposite. In "September 1913" Yeats needs both O'Leary and the Paudeens, for each can be understood properly only in relation to the other, and apprehension of that relation guarantees a faithful rendering both of the hostility between bird and market cart in Irish life

[14] *E & I*, p. 296. Yeats expresses the same idea in the preface to *The Unicorn from the Stars and Other Plays* (1908) where he describes the expression in his critical writings of the union of the "rough life of the road" and the "frenzy" of the poets as "a prophecy, as it were, of the time when it will be once again possible for a Dickens and a Shelley to be born in the one body." (*Variorum Plays*, pp. 1295–96.)

John Butler Yeats held a similar view. He wrote, "I have discovered Dickens; yes, here in my single room I have discovered the great romancer and with it made another discovery, the people. . . . I don't think Shelley discovered what I call the earthy. He was too much occupied with the soul and the imaginative reason." (*Further Letters*, ed. Robinson, pp. 37–38.)

and, concomitantly, of the moral universe of which that life is but a part. Vision requires inclusive acceptance rather than exclusive rejection: the artist should condemn the Paudeens, but he should not banish them from his work.

The change in subject meant a change in attitude as well. The joy of antinomial vision replaced the sorrow of Intellectual vision. The unrestrained desire for beauty of Yeats's "Alastor" persona of the nineties led to suffering because of his necessary separation from the Rose. According to Yeats, consciousness of the antithesis of daily life" with the ideal "dream world" led to "intellectual suffering."[15] The melancholy of his solitary wanderers now appeared a morbid indulgence of their own fragmented sensibility. They could only further separate men from the life beyond themselves, whereas the purpose of modern art should be the reunion of mind, soul, and body "to the living world outside us."[16] To do that, to create Unity of Being in the individual and Unity of Culture in the age, meant abandoning the unidirectional quest of *Alastor*, which led only out of life.

To live fully was to accept both halves of the antithesis between the ideal and the actual, which Yeats also viewed as the conflict between reality and justice. In that conflict the ideal always lost, and the poet should simply witness its defeat rather than distort the outcome into a false victory of the good. Hence Yeats's famous aphorism, "We begin to live when we have conceived life as tragedy."[17] The cart would always defeat the skylark, but that tragedy no longer implied sorrow; like Blake, Yeats refused to consider the flowers of spring refuted simply because they were over. To see life Yeats's new way was to see it with antinomial vision and, hence, joyfully. The aged Chinese of "Lapis Lazuli," like the poet who describes them, possess the antinomial vision which the Yeats-"Alastor" of the nineties lacked: "Their eyes mid many wrinkles, their eyes, / Their ancient, glittering eyes, are gay."[18]

To present his new vision of life Yeats needed a new style. The Shelleyan cadences and diction of the Rose poems suited him so long as he wrote the kind of subjective poetry prescribed by Hal-

[15] *Autobiography*, p. 142. [16] "Discoveries: Second Series," p. 299.
[17] *Autobiography*, p. 189. [18] *Variorum Poems*, p. 567.

lam, but they jarred him when he turned to contemporary life for his subjects. He had described Aedh and Oisin in language learned from Shelley but could not do the same for the Easter martyrs, MacDonagh and MacBride, Connolly and Pearse. "It was years before I could rid myself of Shelley's Italian light," he admitted in 1901, "but now I think my style is myself."[19] He elaborated his reaction against Shelley's style in an essay called, significantly, "What is 'Popular Poetry'?" The problem affected him more deeply than his stoical cure—sleeping on a board—might suggest:

> I had a conviction, which indeed I have still, that one's verses should hold, as in a mirror, the colours of one's own climate and scenery in their right proportion; and, when I found my verses too full of the reds and yellows Shelley gathered in Italy, I thought for two days of setting things right, not as I should now by making the rhythms faint and nervous and filling my images with a certain coldness, a certain wintry wildness, but by eating little and sleeping on a board.[20]

Yeats construed his own metaphor for Shelley's style, red and yellow light, as he did Shelley's own images—both literally and symbolically. He repeatedly associated the colors red and yellow with Shelley. A younger friend, Padraic Colum, recalled: "He told me that he was trying to get out of his poems the reds and yellows Shelley had brought back from Italy. Henceforth, he was going to try to put into his poems the greys of the west of Ireland, the stones and clouds that belonged to Galway."[21] Yeats removed "Shelley's Italian light" from his poetry literally by eliminating the words "red" and "yellow," particularly "red." He used the two words eighty-five times before *In the Seven Woods* (1903) and only twenty-seven times after that. Contradicting the metaphor, he also reduced his use of "grey," although after 1903 it does appear about as often as "red" and "yellow" together. The description of Shelley is not entirely accurate, for in fact Shelley uses "grey" more times (124) than either "red" (77) or "yellow" (27).

The change in style meant much more than a change in optical

[19] *E & I*, p. 208. [20] *E & I*, p. 5.
[21] "Reminiscences of Yeats," p. 75.

diction. Besides eliminating the poeticisms and righting the inversions for the *Poems* of 1895 and for *The Wind among the Reeds*, he made the entire texture of his verse more particular and less refined or ornate. He wanted to get the "greys of the west of Ireland" into his poems more deeply than by simply mentioning "cold Clare rock and Galway rock and thorn" in the elegy for Robert Gregory. The new goals were strength and simplicity. In 1905, after the victory over "Shelleyan" diction, he wrote to John Quinn that "I believe more strongly every day that the element of strength in poetic language is common idiom, just as the element of strength in poetic construction is common passion."[22] Yeats now imagined a fisherman in "grey Connemara cloth" and longed to write him "one / Poem maybe as cold / And passionate as the dawn."[23]

It was not only the west of Ireland but also the buildings of Georgian Dublin that were gray. Organizing the Abbey Theatre, castigating William Murphy, fighting for both the Lane pictures and a gallery to put them in, and, later, arguing in the senate of the Irish Free State, Yeats needed a style he could apply to contemporary Irish reality, both urban and rural. Even if he were in London when the Post Office fell in 1916, he could at least describe the loss like an Irishman, not a romantic Englishman. Had he formed his style on, say, *The Masque of Anarchy* instead of *Alastor* and *Prometheus Unbound*, Yeats need not have broken with his predecessor; but in proving Shelley more than "a crude revolutionist"[24] Yeats had proved him something less as well. Now that occasional seeming crudeness had become a poetic virtue, Yeats had no choice but to attack Shelley, and he fired away not so much at the actual Shelley as at his idea of him, which had so closely approximated his idea of himself during the nineties.

In moving from Intellectual to antinomial vision, then, Yeats remade the subject matter, emotional tenor, and style of his work. The actual rivalled the ideal, joy replaced sorrow, and the powerful gray of Ireland overcame the pretty red and yellow of Italy. His earlier art, and his earlier model for it, now appeared to lack

22 *Yeats's Letters*, p. 462.
23 *Variorum Poems*, p. 348.
24 "The Philosophy of Shelley's Poetry," *E & I*, p. 66.

what John Butler Yeats called the earthy. Shelley's use of symbols and his general defense of poetry had impressed Yeats too deeply for him ever to reject them, but he did free himself from the style, emotions, and attitude toward life with which he had emulated his sometime idol.

Cuchulain: Prometheus Rebound

After 1903 Yeats sought to rebind Prometheus to common life through his own major hero, Cuchulain. To him, Shelley's self-proclaimed goal of presenting "visions . . . of the beautiful and the just"[25] had led to the unbinding of Prometheus not merely from the Caucasian cliff, or even from imperfection, but from actual life as well. His own aim, as he implied in his late essay, "*Prometheus Unbound*" (1932), was to "attend, as Shelley would not, to the whole drama of life, simplicities, banalities, intoxications, even lie upon his left side and eat dung."[26] Only in that way could he unite the perfect and ideal with the imperfect and actual. His new movement downward upon life caused him to create a more earthy hero than the divine Prometheus. In striving to unite again Shelley and Dickens, Yeats created in his five Cuchulain plays radically different works from his former sacred book, *Prometheus Unbound*. While keeping Shelley's (and Blake's) habit of creating figures who were simultaneously characters and psychological principles, he projected in Cuchulain qualities antithetical to those of Prometheus. Let us consider first the dual nature of the heroes and then the difference between the Intellectual and antinomial values which each represents.

Like Shelley, Yeats created the dual nature of his hero by grafting his own philosophy and psychology onto traditional mythic tales. Just as the internationally minded Shelley turned to Aeschylus, so did Yeats in his literary nationalism turn to Standish O'Grady and the two books of Lady Gregory for which he wrote the introductions, *Cuchulain of Muirthemne* (1902) and *Gods and Fighting Men* (1904). Impelled by his desire to create an Irish Prometheus, Yeats eventually wrote, besides several poems, five dramas about Cuchulain which he thought of as "a number

[25] *Works*, 2: 67. [26] *E & I*, p. 423.

of connected plays."[27] Although the late figures of Crazy Jane and Tom the Lunatic may loiter usefully in the back of our minds to remind us how far Yeats eventually moved from his early "Alastor," Cuchulain clearly stands as Yeats's central hero. Appearing as early as 1889 and as late as 1939, he dominates the stage between 1905 and 1919, when Yeats forged a new, antinomial vision of life.

Shelley's prefaces to his poems interpret his heroes as principles of mind. He hinted at that view in describing *The Revolt of Islam* as "the growth and progress of individual mind aspiring after excellence, and devoted to the love of mankind."[28] The imagery of *Prometheus Unbound* was "drawn from the operations of the human mind." More important, Shelley wanted to provide the reader with "beautiful idealisms of moral excellence."[29] Prometheus is just such a beautiful idealism; he has less significance as a character than as a symbol of the moral superiority of love and forgiveness.

Yeats was aware of Shelley's tendency to fuse character with abstraction in his heroes. In his first essay on Shelley he called the Witch of Atlas "one of his personifications of beauty."[30] Likewise, he could refer to "Prometheus, or some equal symbol."[31] Shelley's work could not reveal ideal Intellectual Beauty if it created actual characters, for then it would become merely a criticism of life rather than a revelation of a hidden life; on the other hand, eliminating too much verisimilitude could result in vagueness and an air of unreality. Accordingly, after 1903 Yeats's goal was to combine Dickens and Shelley—the world of characters and life and the world of symbols and Life. Although Yeats

[27] *Explorations*, p. 371. Some idea of the scope of the Cuchulain plays may be useful to the reader. Yeats published five Cuchulain plays between 1905 and 1939. Each concentrates on one or two significant actions; the goal, as Yeats expressed it in "The Circus Animals' Desertion" was "Character isolated by a deed." In the order of the events in Cuchulain's life, not the order of Yeats's composition, the plays show: Cuchulain's vain attempt to drink the waters of immortality from the Hawk's Well (*At the Hawk's Well*), his attainment of the Red Man's Helmet at the expense of Laegaire and Conall (*The Green Helmet*), his slaying of his son and subsequent battle with the sea (*On Baile's Strand*), his rescue from death by his wife Emer and his mistress Eithne Inguba (*The Only Jealousy of Emer*), and his second and final death after battle with his former lover Aoife (*The Death of Cuchulain*).

[28] *Works*, 1: 239. [29] *Works*, 2: 172, 174.

[30] *E & I*, p. 68. [31] *Autobiography*, p. 150.

sought to make his Cuchulain more Dickensian, more a novelistic "character," he still wanted him to be Shelleyan—to be a poetic symbol. He always opposed the debased naturalism of the followers of Ibsen and praised stylization, whether in lyric poetry, *No* drama, or Byzantine mosaics.

Even in the nineties Yeats had spoken in his lyrical poems through personae that were more types than individuals. He described the speakers of some of the Rose poems, Aedh, Hanrahan, and Michael Robartes, "more as principles of the mind than as actual personages."[32] There the principles were different aspects of the imagination. Whereas another devotee of Shelley—Browning—used specific historical figures, like Filippo Lippi, in concrete situations, Yeats deliberately generalized both speaker and setting. Personal emotion was to be channeled through traditional poses: "I was about to learn that if a man is to write lyric poetry he must be shaped by nature and art to some one out of half a dozen traditional poses, and be lover or saint, sage or sensualist, or mere mocker of all life."[33] By the time he wrote the Cuchulain plays, Yeats had both experimented with "characters" who were more psychological principles than personages and had evolved a literary theory demanding just such figures.

Cuchulain united Dickensian characterization with Shelleyan personification. Yeats described both qualities in a letter to Frank Fay, who, with his brother William, was preparing to stage *On Baile's Strand.* Yeats sketched Cuchulain's character in detail, even to his approximate age:

> I have also to make the refusal to the son's affection tragic by suggesting in Cuchullain's [*sic*] character a shadow of something a little proud, barren and restless, as if out of sheer strength of heart or from accident he had put affection away. He lives among young men but has himself outlived the illusions of youth. He is probably about 40, not less than 35 or 36 and not more than 45 or 46, certainly not an old man, and one understands from his talk about women that he does not love like a young man. Probably his very strength of character made him put off illusions and dreams (that make young men a woman's servant) and made him become quite early in life a deliberate lover, a man of pleasure who can never really surrender himself.[34]

32 *Variorum Poems,* p. 803. 33 *Autobiography,* p. 87.
34 *Yeats's Letters,* pp. 424–25.

While maintaining Cuchulain's heroic stature, Yeats made him a much more human "character" than the Titan Prometheus. Cuchulain enjoys getting drunk and making love. In *The Green Helmet* he joins—and wins—a tavern boasting contest. He has a wife and at least two mistresses, who continually squabble over him. The First Musician in *The Only Jealousy of Emer* calls him "That amorous, violent man, renowned Cuchulain."[35] One could conceivably call Prometheus "violent" in his defiance of Jupiter, but not "amorous" in his attraction to Asia, at least until act 4.

Characterization counted for nothing without personification and symbolism. Yeats continues the letter to Fay in terms of psychological type and celestial symbol: Cuchulain "is the fool—wandering passive, houseless and almost loveless. Conchobhar [*sic*] is reason that is blind because it can only reason because it is cold. Are they not the cold moon and the hot sun?" The conflict between Cuchulain and Conchubar becomes a conflict between opposing principles of mind and philosophies of life. In the Cuchulain plays Yeats renders dramatic the same technique he used in his lyrics. As much "principles of mind" as "personages," Cuchulain and Conchubar reproduce the same pattern of conflict as Self and Soul in "A Dialogue of Self and Soul," Hic and Ille in "Ego Dominus Tuus," and, less markedly, Robartes and Aherne in "The Phases of the Moon."

The dichotomy between Dickensian and Shelleyan applies even more clearly to the minor figures. Ione and Panthea in *Prometheus Unbound* and the Blind Man and the Fool in *On Baile's Strand* comment on the main action and partially reproduce it on their own, lower level. Yet there is a significant difference, for Ione and Panthea, although inferior to Asia, belong to the same order, whereas the Blind Man and the Fool belong to a totally different order than Cuchulain. Scholars agree that Ione and Panthea represent rising degrees of a hierarchy headed by Asia, whether of "aspects of love," "degrees of love and perceptiveness," or, more recently, "Titanic sexuality."[36] Ione occupies the lowest rung. She does not understand her dream (2.1) and lacks Panthea's

[35] *Variorum Plays*, p. 533.

[36] Carl Grabo, *Prometheus Unbound: An Interpretation*, p. 52; Carlos Baker, *Shelley's Major Poetry: the Fabric of a Vision*, p. 103; Harold Bloom, *Shelley's Mythmaking*, p. 119.

fortitude to watch the Furies torture Prometheus. Panthea holds a higher position: she both explains the action to Ione and accompanies Asia on the visit to Demogorgon. As principles and personages they both belong to the same order as Asia, though not to the same degree; they are lesser angels.

Yeats made his own characters more "earthy" than those of Shelley. He later complained that *Prometheus Unbound*'s Justice was a "vague propagandist emotion" and that "the women that await its coming are but clouds."[37] Yeats's minor figures repeat the main action on a level not only lower but, more importantly, venial. They are both principles of mind—undirected action (Fool) and cunning impotence (Blind Man)—and novelistic characters. Just as Conchubar exploits Cuchulain, so does the Blind Man trick the Fool out of his share of the chicken. The Blind Man is a sort of Irish Rogue Riderhood, outwardly deferential to authority but intent only upon his own ends. Not even Cuchulain's death sways him from gratifying his appetites: "There will be nobody in the houses. Come this way; come quickly! The ovens will be full. We will put our hands into the ovens."[38] Unlike Ione and Panthea, the Fool and the Blind Man represent the antithesis of the main characters, not merely a lesser degree of the same excellence. By 1939, when he had the Blind Man decapitate the wounded Cuchulain for a dozen pennies, Yeats could justifiably claim to have gotten Dickens into his work.

The desire to unite Shelley and Dickens affected not merely characterization but the whole purpose of heroic art. Yeats desires not an apocalyptic metamorphosis of society but rather an infusion of heroic standards into it. In place of the "new world of man" of *Prometheus Unbound* he puts the Easter rising of 1916—a heroic action by specific men. Yeats linked the Irish rising specifically to Cuchulain: "Pearse summoned Cuchulain to his side," he wrote in "The Statues."[39] The Irish patriots may become "a stone / To trouble the living stream,"[40] but they do

[37] *A Vision*, p. 144. [38] *Variorum Plays*, p. 525.

[39] *Variorum Poems*, p. 611.

[40] Ibid., p. 393. William I. Thompson has given a very interesting account of "Easter 1916," and of Yeats's attitude toward Ireland at the time, in *The Imagination of an Insurrection: Dublin, Easter 1916*, chap. 5.

not transform the stream of generation itself. Yeats wants not to transcend the current social order (which in his view is a *donnée*) but rather to ennoble it.

The manipulation of chronology supports the distinction in purpose. Yeats locates Cuchulain firmly in the Irish historical, or at least legendary, past. He describes the actions reputedly performed by Cuchulain, like the fight with the sea. Shelley sets his drama more ambiguously. Although he chooses a myth from the past—Prometheus's struggle with Jupiter—he transfers it to a future which, his work implies, will come into existence if and when mankind wills it. The drama treats a future action in the present tense. It opens with the current situation—Prometheus, whether as the mind of man or of the One—*is* chained and tormented because of its impurities. The action itself, Prometheus's rejection of hatred and attainment of perfect love and forgiveness, occurs in an indefinite (and, Shelley the man would add, possibly unattainable) future: in our world mind has not yet freed itself. Yeats desires to infuse the past into the present; Shelley to transform the present into the future, which is, we read in the *Defence*, "contained within the present as the plant within the seed."[41] Yeats wants to transplant and Shelley to cultivate a garden.

Prometheus and Cuchulain embody radically different values, for *Prometheus Unbound* champions an Intellectual vision of life and the Cuchulain plays champion an antinomial one. In *Prometheus Unbound* Shelley imagines a future of social harmony brought about by universal forgiveness and resulting in peace. Through love, his suffering hero transforms the misshapen world to conform to an ideal Intellectual pattern. The goal is to blend the variegated colors of life back together into the white radiance of eternity. In contrast, Yeats presents in the Cuchulain plays a past order of individual excellence dependent upon vengeance and resulting in struggle. Rejecting the movement out of imperfection toward perfected life, he projects in Cuchulain the antinomial man's heroic defiance of tragedy. If experience falls into a series of antinomies in human consciousness, then the war of

41 *Shelley's Prose*, p. 278.

opposing qualities rather than the rosy peace of heaven and hell is the proper representation of it. Unlike Prometheus, within whose mind the entire drama may be said in one sense to take place, Cuchulain is less comprehensive and himself represents but half an antinomy, of which Conchubar is the other half; nevertheless, his defiant stance captures Yeats's praise. These differences may profitably be examined in some detail.

When Prometheus exorcises hate from his own mind, he exorcises it from society as well; both are reclaimed for love. The chorus of spirits joyfully pledges, "We will take our plan / From the new world of man, / And our work shall be called the Promethean."[42] He is a Titanic Laon, who, in *The Revolt of Islam*, held love to be "the sole law which should govern the moral world" and aimed not so much at specific political reform as at "a change in the spirit which animates the social institutions of mankind."[43] Prometheus, too, serves humanity, providing the gift of fire and also, in Shelley's version, defending mankind against the cosmic incarnation of oppression, Jupiter. He wants to "Be what it is my destiny to be, / The saviour and the strength of suffering man."[44] By forgiving Jupiter and recalling the curse on him, Prometheus dissolves the power of evil. As Shelley indicates in the preface, the champion does not reconcile himself to the oppressor of mankind by making an opportunistic peace with evil; instead, he conquers it through love and thus establishes a universal peace.

The end of Prometheus's separation from Asia symbolizes the dissolution of all the antitheses of life which Shelley longed to overcome and Yeats came to accept. The drama moves from Prometheus's isolated suffering in the Caucasus, attended only by Panthea and Ione, to his joyful reunion with Asia and its effect upon mankind. Shelley remained more dubious about the possibility and the permanence of such a victory than Yeats admitted, but one can at least see what led Yeats to declare in his essay on *Prometheus Unbound* that Shelley shared "our political problems, our conviction that, despite all experience to the contrary, love is enough."[45] For Yeats, as we shall see in the

[42] *Works*, 2: 248. [43] *Works*, 1: 247.
[44] *Works*, 2: 204. [45] *E & I*, p. 424.

remaining chapters, separation was a permanent feature of love, of history, and of metaphysics.

Unlike Prometheus, Cuchulain champions the old order of warfare and violence. Whereas Shelley set *Prometheus Unbound* at that point in future time when love would replace violence, Yeats set *On Baile's Strand* at the past instant when the old, heroic order succumbed to the new, antiheroic one of peace. His enemy, Conchubar, represents the Shelleyan values which Cuchulain himself rejects. Yeats transposes Shelley's view of hero and antagonist, so that Conchubar becomes a mortal Prometheus and Cuchulain a benevolent but equally selfish Jupiter. In *On Baile's Strand* King Conchubar attempts to bind Cuchulain by an oath to uphold the welfare of the kingdom. When Cuchulain asserts, "I'll not be bound," Conchubar replies with a plea for the future welfare of the kingdom: "I would leave / A strong and settled country to my children."[46] The contrast is clear. Cuchulain wishes to keep his spirit unfettered by the bonds of social obligation; Conchubar, the envisioner of a future, benevolent social order, seeks to bind the unwilling hero to it. For all his royal position and nationalism, Conchubar—by envisioning a future state of society superior to that of war and devastation—comes closer to the Shelleyan prototype than Cuchulain, who seeks to retreat to the heroic age of martial glory rather than to lead the way to the coming age of peace and order.

Cuchulain champions not the freedom of social equality but the anarchic, individual liberty to "dance or hunt, or quarrel or make love."[47] Equality gives way to the hierarchy of ability in battle. Like King Fergus, who abjured his political duty in order to revel and write poetry, Cuchulain's virtues pertain only to a small band held together by personal loyalty, not to mankind as a whole. Since he exemplifies Unity of Being, his resistance to the evolving social order is understandable, for the modern age, we read in *A Vision,* makes such unity impossible. Retreat into the heroic past rather than advancement into the coming order befits such a hero.

[46] *Variorum Plays,* pp. 477–79. [47] Ibid., p. 477.

Forgiveness is not a Yeatsian virtue, and Cuchulain does not share his predecessor's ability to forgive his foe. Based upon a system of conflicting opposites, Yeats's antinomial vision calls not for forgiveness but for continuing struggle. When the aged Cuchulain forgives Eithne Inguba's infidelity to him (ironically, since she is innocent), she at once tells him that he is no longer the mighty man he was, for if he "can forgive / It is because you are about to die."[48] Likewise, in the last of the Cuchulain plays, approaching death coincides with his loss of malice toward his old enemy Aoife. An attribute of the Yeatsian hero in decline, forgiveness constitutes a chief virtue of the Shelleyan hero at his moment of greatest triumph.

Finally, Cuchulain does not praise that reign of peace described by the Spirit of the Hour at the close of the third act of *Prometheus Unbound,* but instead sees it only as a source of corruption. The foundation of his world is war, and he reacts violently to the crumbling of it represented by peace. For him a peaceful kingdom is not a moral advance of love but a moral retrogression from the virtue of the battlefield. He argues that peace produces inferior men:

Conchubar,
I do not like your children—they have no pith,
No marrow in their bones, and will lie soft
Where you and I lie hard.[49]

Time and domesticity have watered the high king's spirit, or he would recognize these deficiencies in his children.

Unlike Prometheus, Cuchulain is mortal and his death is inevitable. So, to Yeats, is his defeat. Cuchulain undergoes the unique experience of dying twice, once in *On Baile's Strand* and again in *The Death of Cuchulain.* He is rescued from the first excursion into darkness by the female machinations described in *The Only Jealousy of Emer*. In both instances his death, in context of his own society, lacks the social significance of that of, say, Laon and Cythna. He dies in isolated conflict with enemies who are not evil but simply part of the entire fabric of life, with its interwoven threads. He appeals to the imagination

[48] Ibid., p. 1055. [49] Ibid., p. 481.

of his audience by his uncompromising fulfillment of his own identity and the implicit lesson that they should fulfill theirs. The inspiration is to a heroic attitude toward life, not toward specific social or ethical ideals.

The implications of Cuchulain's first death, his fight with the sea, fascinated Yeats, for he referred to it several other times in his poetry over a period of forty years—in "Cuchulain's Fight with the Sea," "Alternative Song for the Severed Head" (*The King of the Great Clock Tower*), and "The Circus Animals' Desertion"—and alluded to it again in the final play of the Cuchulain cycle. Tricked directly by Conchubar and Conlaoch, and indirectly by fate, into a fight in which he kills his own son, Cuchulain goes mad and attacks the sea itself. The attack on the sea is an implicit attack upon the unavoidable tragic irony of life. The social order, evolving toward the settled state visualized by Conchubar, excludes the fierce warrior; love exists only as a truce in midbattle, and the former lover trains her own son to kill his father. Cuchulain literally takes arms against a sea of troubles, but does not end them, for they are without end. There is not even a hope of ultimate future victory, only continual opposition. Cuchulain dies a martyr to a past social order which there is no hope of redeeming.

Antinomial vision and the desire to bind Shelley to Dickens impelled Yeats to create a hero and an aesthetic theory radically different from his own "Alastor" figures and subjective poetics of the nineties. He rebound Cuchulain to the earth which he thought Prometheus had transcended, and he urged his audience to accept a world view consistent with warring opposites rather than with a millennial resolution of life's antinomies. In that exhortation he obliquely defended the change in his own work even while overtly either attacking Shelley or pressing him into an entente with Dickens. Yet even as the sensuality of Crazy Jane conquered the purity of Aedh, and as *Prometheus Unbound* became a diabolic rather than a sacred book, Yeats preserved in altered form his earlier admiration for *Alastor*, *Prince Athanase*, and *Hellas*. The psychological theories which transformed Yeats's earlier models for the self into models for the antiself form our next subject. Intellectually, Yeats had had a surfeit of "Alastor," but antinomially he could not get enough of him.

Shelley's Antiselves

Perning as much around the market cart as the bird, and wavering in his estimation of Prometheus, Yeats continued to admire "Alastor," Athanase, and Ahasuerus. While a boy he had chosen "Alastor" for his chief of men and in early manhood had imitated the occult and Platonic studies of Prince Athanase. After 1903 he began to cultivate the new psychological theories, later harvested in *A Vision*, which enabled his admiration for the three lonely questers to survive his metaphysical and aesthetic break with Shelley. The antinomies which caused Yeats to reject Shelley—fair and foul, cart and bird, good and evil—pertained mostly to diction, choice of subject, and metaphysics; there was, however, another pair of antinomies which described the artist's complex struggle to achieve Unity of Being—self and antiself. By regarding Shelley's three figures as images of the antiself, as masks, rather than as models for the self, Yeats continued to make use of them both in his thought and in his art.

Although during the nineties Yeats had formed his art and personality by his conception of Shelley, now he reversed the positions and made his sometime model into an example of his independent theory of the antiself. A man's antiself was "a Mask that delineates a being in all things the opposite to [his] natural state."[50] Since the complexities of the twentieth century made the conscious personality fragmented and incomplete, the man bent on regaining a Unity of Being must imagine an ideal self opposite to his normal identity, an antiself. This antiself will be an image out of the anima mundi, which is the storehouse of traditional images of unity. Completeness, however, comes from neither the natural self nor the traditional image, but from the blending of the two through the creative tension of meeting "the greatest obstacle he may confront without despair."[51] The joining of the two selves cannot be permanent, for they are one pair of those antinomies into which life falls in our consciousness; for that reason, death is sometimes the symbol of the completed union.

[50] *Autobiography*, p. 247.

[51] Ibid., p. 272. Yeats's favorite examples of poets who attained Unity of Being in their art were Dante and Villon. See below, chap. 8.

The mature Yeats admired *Alastor*, *Athanase*, and *Hellas* because he thought that in them Shelley had created ideal images of his antiself. In the nineties Yeats had identified himself and Shelley with Athanase or the *Alastor* poet; now he regarded those figures as the *opposites* of himself and Shelley. The creation of an antiself was the proper business of a poet, who must assume a traditional pose or mask in his art and, possibly, in his life as well: "all joyous or creative life is a rebirth as something not oneself."[52] The poet who has found his antiself will then "assume wisdom or beauty as Shelley did, when he masked himself as Ahasuerus, or as Prince Athanase."[53] Free of the political and amorous intrigues of Shelley the man, those figures offered Shelley the poet a chance to complete his personality and thus achieve Unity of Being.

Hunting his own antiself, Yeats turned for help to Shelley's images of isolation. He always thought of himself and Shelley as similar psychological types, and much of the vehemence in his quarrel with Shelley came from his determination to follow Shelley's successes while avoiding his failures. In making isolation the primary characteristic of the lyric poet's antiself Yeats reversed his outlook of the nineties, when he had described the subjective poet as a solitary. Now he thought of himself and Shelley as "gregarious." Consequently, solitude characterized their masks rather than their true selves. He cited Athanase and Ahasuerus in particular as inspiration for his own struggle to create an antiself:

> In later years my mind gave itself to gregarious Shelley's dream of a young man, his hair blanched with sorrow, studying philosophy in some lonely tower, or of his old man, master of all human knowledge, hidden from human sight in some shell-strewn cavern on the Mediterranean shore. One passage above all ran perpetually in my ears.[54]

He followed that admission with the long quotation from Hassan's description of Ahasuerus, of which we noted the Neoplatonic symbolism in the last chapter; here, we are concerned

[52] *Autobiography*, p. 503. [53] Ibid., pp. 247–48.

[54] Ibid., p. 171. Yeats then quotes lines 152–85 of *Hellas*. See also *A Vision*, p. 143. As usual when quoting from memory, he made minor errors.

with its illumination of the antiself. The inaccessibility and isolation of the old Jew dominated Yeats's thought. He quoted one phrase both in the *Autobiography* and in *A Vision:* "Less accessible / Than thou or God!" Ahasuerus's isolation symbolized his antithesis to the gregarious Yeats and Shelley, and the arduousness of the quest to reach him signified the difficulty of finding such an image. "Few dare, and few who dare / Win the desired communion," says Hassan. Those few, argued Yeats, live "as it is natural for a Morris or a Henley or a Shelley to live, hunters and pursuers" of the antiself.[55]

Yeats developed his scattered remarks on the antiself and its application to Shelley more comprehensively in *A Vision.* He assigned himself and Shelley to the same psychological category, phase seventeen, which is also the phase of Dante and Landor. The remarks about Shelley have special application to Yeats, who identified himself with Shelley during the nineties. He condemned in Shelley those tendencies he wanted to avoid in his own work and praised those he wished to develop.

Yeats organized his representation of human psychology into four conflicting "faculties" which combined with each other in twenty-eight different ways, one for each phase of the moon. He called the faculties Will, Mask, Creative Mind, and Body of Fate. Since he defined the four terms metaphorically in the revised version of *A Vision,* we must turn to the first edition for some rough definitions:

> 1. "*Will*" is "feeling that has not become desire because there is no object to desire . . . as yet without result in action."
> 2. "*Mask*" is the antiself: "the image of what we wish to become, or that to which we give our reverence. Under certain circumstances [i.e., when we are united with our antiselves] it is called the *Image* [like the Venus Urania desired by Shelley when he has merged his own self with that of Athanase, his antiself]."
> 3. "*Creative Mind*" is "intellect, as intellect was understood before the close of the seventeenth century—all the mind that is consciously constructive."
> 4. "*Body of Fate*" is "the physical and mental environment,

[55] *Autobiography,* p. 248. Only by such pursuit, says Yeats, can Shelley (unlike George Herbert, Francis Thompson, or George Russell, who are "fugitives" belonging to a different psychological type) find a Uranian rather than a Pandemian Venus.

> the stream of Phenomena as this affects a particular individual, all that is forced upon us from without, Time as it affects sensation."[56]

The four faculties constitute two pairs of conflicting opposites. Will (self) struggles with Mask (antiself); Creative Mind (intellect) struggles with Body of Fate (world).

The concept of Mask bears on Shelley's solitary heroes. The Mask for the phase of Yeats and Shelley comes from phase three. It represents the antithesis of the conscious and normal self. Yeats calls the poet of his and Shelley's phase a "daemonic man"[57] because his personality allows him to harness "daemonic" or unconscious power to create a Mask, or antiself. "Gregarious" Shelley needed a solitary Mask. Yeats describes that Mask abstractly as "simplification through intensity." He holds that Shelley represented this simplified intensity through Ahasuerus, Athanase, and the *Alastor* youth, who "represent intellectual or sexual passion." They unite simplicity and intensity in their passion for an ideal Image. The Mask, that is, seeks its corresponding Image (which, confusingly, Yeats sometimes calls "Mask"). Yeats identifies the Image sought by the Masks of Shelley as Venus Urania, whom Shelley himself had named as the true object of Athanase's quest.

Yeats elaborates his interpretation of Shelley's minor heroes in discussing phase three, from which the Mask comes. He writes:

> Seen by lyrical poets, of whom so many have belonged to the fantastic Phase 17, the man of this phase becomes an Image where simplicity and intensity are united, he seems to move among yellowing corn or overhanging grapes. He gave . . . to Shelley his wandering lovers and sages.[58]

The poet's (internal) Creative Mind can either menace or foster his creation of the Mask. Creative Mind, which for subjective artists is best described as imagination,[59] can take a false form or a true; the false form diverts his energies to improper ends. He then becomes "out of phase" and succumbs to "*automatonism*,"

[56] *A Vision* (1925), pp. 14–15. I have capitalized "Mask" when comparing it with the other three faculties of *A Vision,* but not elsewhere.

[57] All quotations in the discussion of *A Vision* are from pp. 140–45 of the revised (1937) edition unless otherwise identified.

[58] *A Vision,* pp. 108–9. [59] Ibid., p. 142.

or a mechanical creativity in place of an imaginative one. Yeats held that Shelley's hopes for human regeneration represented an abandonment of his personal quest for self-completion. In his opinion "Shelley out of phase writes pamphlets and dreams of converting the world, or of turning man of affairs and upsetting governments." There is little point in marshaling evidence to challenge Yeats's remarks, for they pertain less to Shelley than to himself. At this time Yeats was a senator of the Irish Free State and described himself as a "sixty-year-old smiling public man." He, more than Shelley, faced the possibility of surrendering his creative talent to legislative activity. In condemning Shelley's supposed mistake he cautioned himself against seduction by political affairs and consequent abandonment of aesthetic efforts.

If the poet chooses his true Creative Mind instead of the false one he can continue the quest for the Mask. Creative Mind for phase seventeen is "Creative imagination through *antithetical* [subjective] emotion." By applying his creative imagination to his subjective emotion, the poet can find his Mask. That sometimes happened to Shelley, who "returns again and again to these two images of solitude, a young man whose hair has grown white from the burden of his thoughts, an old man in some shell-strewn cave whom it is possible to call, when speaking to the Sultan, 'as inaccessible as God or thou.' " As in the nineties, Yeats considers Shelley a subjective poet; however, he now understands that term more complexly.

Finally, the Body of Fate, or external events, threatens the poet's Mask. By creating his true Mask (to achieve self-fulfillment) he conquers the world of mutability; by creating a false Mask (to regenerate the world) he succumbs to inevitable failure and compensates for actuality rather than defeats it. He should seek "*by the help of the Creative Mind to deliver the Mask from Body of Fate.*"[60] Yeats expressed the victory over external events in his *Autobiography:*

> Among subjective men (in all those, that is, who must spin a web out of their own bowels) the victory is an intellectual daily re-creation of all that exterior fate snatches away, and so that fate's antithesis; while what I have called "the Mask" is an

60 Ibid., p. 91.

> emotional antithesis to all that comes out of their internal nature.[61]

To Yeats the creation of "Alastor," Athanase, and Ahasuerus signified Shelley's self-completion. Although he objected to ideality defeating actuality in the world, he allowed for it in the individual. The Masks enabled Shelley to achieve temporarily the fulfillment symbolized by the full moon at phase fifteen. Yeats wrote:

> This transformation must have seemed to him [Synge] a discovery of his true self, of his true moral being; whereas Shelley's came at the moment when he first created a passionate image which made him forgetful of himself. It came perhaps when he had passed from the litigious rhetoric of *Queen Mab* to the lonely reveries of *Alastor*.[62]

Yeats may have created a passionate image which made him forgetful of himself first with his tower persona of 1917. "I must choose a traditional stanza, even what I alter must seem traditional," he declared. "I commit my emotion to shepherds, herdsmen, camel-drivers, learned men, Milton's or Shelley's Platonist."[63] The student in the tower of "Ego Dominus Tuus" and "The Phases of the Moon" represents Yeats's antiself in being solitary, constant, and devoted to only one activity. He is one of those images of passionate intensity and (because wholly devoted to one object) simplicity through which Yeats's many-faceted self sought Unity of Being. Profiting from Shelley's mistake, Yeats tried to carry his Mask over from his art to his life, and after 1919 the Irish senator and Nobel Prize winner spent part of every year at Thoor, Ballylee, until bad health forced him to abandon it a decade later.

Yeats preserved his approval of *Alastor*, *Athanase*, and *Hellas*, then, because they provided images of an antiself consistent with his new, antinomial vision. He rejected as much of Shelley as supported only an Intellectual vision and kept the images and ideas which supported his new outlook. Shelley's three wanderers

[61] *Autobiography*, p. 189. Yeats could use the metaphor of the spider's web less favorably—see *E & I*, pp. 510–11. His source for the image was Swift's *Battle of the Books*.

[62] *A Vision*, p. 167.

[63] *E & I*, p. 522.

resemble not so much Cuchulain as the shepherd and poet of *The King of the Great Clock Tower* and *A Full Moon in March.* In the next chapter, which examines Shelley's and Yeats's conceptions of love, we shall see how Yeats followed Shelley in creating the Masks of those two plays even while rejecting his general treatment of love.

6 The Epipsyche and the Mask: The Vicissitudes of Imaginative Love

> "The sage, in truth, by dreadful abstinence
> And conquering penance of the mutinous flesh"
> —*Hassan's description of Ahasuerus in* Hellas,
> *quoted by Yeats in* Autobiography, *p. 172,*
> *and* A Vision *(1925), p. 28.*

> "I am so lecherous with abstinence."
> —*Second Sailor in* The Shadowy Waters

Yeats's antinomial vision transformed the Shelleyan quest for love, which had helped to generate the Intellectual vision of his early work. In accord with his upward movement out of life during the nineties, he imagined a perfect union of lovers in which their separate identities fused into one whole, after which they lived in idyllic retreat from the everyday world. His verses lolled along the trail blazed by Shelley in hunting the epipsyche, the soul within the soul. But after the last revision of *The Shadowy Waters* in 1907, Yeats experimented with the continued separation of the lovers, who thus became one of his famous pairs of antinomies, the lover and the lady. The quest of love now became an alternate form of the struggle to realize mask and Image. The lover joined in conflict with his lady, who was still a soul within his soul but—in Yeatsian terms—the exact contrary rather than the Shelleyan counterpart to his normal self.

The doctrine of the mask enabled Yeats to avoid the Shelleyan conflict between two modes of the imagination, the creative (which both creates the archetypal lady and expresses her in poetry) and the sympathetic (which unites the poet-lover with his ideal archetype). He needed both kinds in the nineties, for his Intellectual vision demanded both creation of the ideal and union with it. But his later antinomial vision kept within the limits of the creative faculty, for it precluded the coalescence of the contraries. This chapter examines, first, the influence of Shelleyan love on Yeats's life; second, Shelley's notion of the epipsyche; third, the adherence to Shelleyan love in Yeats's early work; and, finally, Yeats's creation of an alternative to Shelley in his doctrine of the lovers' masks. For Yeats, making "Alastor" antinomial meant making him an antiself.

"An Idea of Perfect Love": Biographical Backgrounds

"I had gathered from Shelley and the romantic poets an idea of perfect love," wrote Yeats in reaction against the casual morality of the Decadence. "Perhaps I should never marry in church but I would love one woman all my life."[1] Shelley shaped not just Yeats's art but also his attitude toward women. To the young Yeats women were something slightly unreal, to be approached with a romantic asceticism which would raise the unfulfilled passion of a refined sensibility to its greatest intensity. If he were to find any sexual delight, it would be in an ideal union with one woman. He not only wrote prose in the extravagant style he learned from Pater, but he wrote poetry and loved Maud Gonne in the exotic style he learned from Shelley. If he thought of himself as "Alastor," he thought of women as the ideal maiden of that poem. He wrote in an unpublished manuscript that his head was "full of the mysterious women of Rossetti . . . which seem always waiting for some Alastor at the end of a long journey."[2] Our concern here is with Yeats's "Alastor" quest not as the search for Intellectual Beauty or for wisdom, which we have already examined, but as a pattern for love in

[1] MS. "A First Rough Draft of Memories made in 1916–17 and containing much that is not for publication now or ever. Memories come down to 1896 or thereabouts. W.B.Y., March, 1921," p. 34. The exact reading of the quotation, in which "from Shelley" has been crossed out, is: "I had gathered ~~from Shelley~~ from the romantic poets an idea of perfect love." I have followed the reading given by Professor A. Norman Jeffares in *W. B. Yeats: Man and Poet*, p. 58.

In the final version of *Autobiography* the remark became more general: "A romantic, when romanticism was in its final extravagance, I thought one woman, whether wife, mistress, or incitement to platonic love, enough for a lifetime" (p. 431).

[2] "A First Rough Draft," p. 36. Yeats also wrote that "the fiery hand of the Intellectual movement" affected his relation to Maud (ibid., p. 95).

both his life and his work. Both poets reacted against the frustration of their search for love by forming idealized conceptions of the perfect woman. They retreated from amorous reverses to fortresses of philosophic idealism, from which they could love their ladies' spirits while resigning (either temporarily or permanently) claim to their persons. Building the fortresses upon the imagination made them aesthetically useful without lessening their psychological effectiveness.

Shelley's genuine even if adolescent attraction to Harriet Grove set the pattern for his later idealizations. The demise of his hopes for union led first to a questioning of love itself and then to a reaffirmation of love for an ideal woman. The winter of 1810–11 saw the wreck of his own hopes for Harriet and of his plans to marry off his sister Elizabeth to his friend Thomas Jefferson Hogg. Six months after the double debacle he referred to love as an "unstable deceitfull thing" and a "pleasing delusion."[3] His idealization of Harriet could not withstand her susceptibility to custom and prejudice: "she abhors me as a Deist, as what *she* was before." Already Shelley had perceived the disparity between the actual Harriet and the ideal one, yet he persevered in his love for the ideal. He pondered, "The question is What do I love? . . . Do I love the person, the embodied entity . . . No! I love what is superior what is excellent, or what I conceive to be so." He countered his rejection by Harriet with an affirmation of his own love for a paragon among women. Loving not "the person" but rather the incarnated ideality left him free either to continue in his love (Yeats's choice) or to seek the same ideality in another woman (Shelley's own choice).

As Shelley persevered in his quest for *das göttliche weibliche* he put his vision on a pedestal. Earlier, he had desired to liberate and instruct Harriet Grove. Now the beloved became a superior being who could remake and elevate the lover. "I believe I must become in Marys [*sic*] hands what Harriet [Westbrook] was in mine," he declared in 1814.[4] Fear that too great an inequality would preclude union led Shelley to repudiate immediately his

[3] All quotations in this paragraph are from *The Letters of Percy Bysshe Shelley*, ed. Frederick L. Jones, 1: 104, 35, and 44. Hereafter cited as *Shelley's Letters*.

[4] *Shelley's Letters*, 1: 414.

"unjust" simile and to discuss the (spiritual) pleasures of "constituting but one being." Although he is not totally coherent, Shelley evidently conceived of his women as in some way incarnating an ideal which he also incarnated, only less perfectly. These theories of the love quest reached their fullest exfoliation in *Epipsychidion*.

Yeats applied the "idea of perfect love" which he had "gathered from Shelley" to his unsuccessful courtship of Maud Gonne. Suffering continual attraction and frustration and yet remaining firmly attached to the idea of love, Yeats followed Shelley in idealizing certain qualities in his beloved. Having detected those, he could remain firm in his devotion. The scarcity of published autobiographical information forces us to rely on the poetry itself. In "No Second Troy" Yeats rhetorically asks, "Why should I blame her that she filled my days / With misery?" Her apparent faults arise merely from an inadequate outlet for her excellence: "Was there another Troy for her to burn?"[5] His imagination allows him to love her ideal qualities while abjuring the quotidian ones.

To Yeats, as to Shelley, a successful rival represented the unworthy world encroaching upon his imaginative vision. Shelley had exclaimed to Hogg, "She is gone, she is lost to me forever —She is married, married to a clod of earth, she will become as insensible herself, all those fine capabilities will moulder."[6] Yeats, too, despised his successor. "I have just heard a very painful rumour," he told Lady Gregory—"Major MacBride is said to be drinking. It is the last touch of tragedy if it is true."[7] Only MacBride's heroic action in the Easter rising could make Yeats see him as anything but a "drunken, vainglorious lout."

Continued allegiance to Maud Gonne eventually wore out Yeats's patience with the Shelleyan "idea of perfect love." He modeled his early women on "the girl in *The Revolt of Islam*"[8] but received an abrupt shock when he met a real-life Cythna in Maud. Although he emulated Shelley's hero by furnishing instruction to his girl, he could not play Laon to her Cythna in liberating the Golden City of Dublin from the English. Eventu-

[5] *Variorum Poems*, pp. 256–57. [6] *Shelley's Letters*, 1: 41.
[7] *Yeats's Letters*, p. 414. See also "Easter 1916."
[8] *Autobiography*, p. 64.

ally, he abandoned any real hope of Shelleyan union, with its purification and elevation. A quarter of a century was long enough to play "Alastor." He accepted separation from his beloved and desired neither to change her (as Shelley did with Harriet) nor to be changed by her (as Shelley did with Mary). Love "does not desire to change its object," he concluded; "It is a form of the eternal contemplation of what is."[9]

Unsuccessful in early love affairs, both poets wrote about the masculine need for completion by the female. Paradoxically, the more Yeats's ideas resembled Shelley's, the less his life did. Although influenced by Shelley's concept of love as union, he maintained in his life an un-Shelleyan continuing devotion to a single woman. The liaison with "Diana Vernon" in the late nineties foreshadows the coming change; for the first time he could no longer rank himself with "those ascetics of passion" who were "my ideal of those years." Salome's perverted virginity fascinated him as an art work but ever less as a pattern for life.[10] As Yeats adopted a radically different view of love, he married another woman and so illustrated in his life Shelley's continuing quest for love. To understand Yeats's development we must first examine the concept of love embodied in Shelley's works.

The Epipsyche

"I have everywhere sought sympathy and found only repulse and disappointment," wrote Shelley in "On Love."[11] The continual repulse and disappointment only strengthened his belief that the male sought completion through a female principle. That quest forms the subject of much of his poetry and prose. Its goal may be defined as a secluded, loving union of part with counterpart, brought about by the imagination. Shelley treats the quest at length in two works of 1815, "On Love" and *Alastor*, makes an intermediate statement in the essay on the Athenians, and reaches his mature position by 1821, in the *Defence of Poetry* and *Epipsychidion*. Examining the roles of the lady, the imagina-

[9] *Yeats's Letters*, p. 876.

[10] *Autobiography*, p. 335. The short poems "The Lover Mourns for the Loss of Love" (pub. 1898) and "Memory" (pub. 1916) suggest that before Yeats's marriage other women were mainly a distraction from Maud.

[11] *Shelley's Prose*, p. 170. All quotations from "On Love" are from here.

tion, and ultimate union in Shelley's poetic quest will allow us later to establish its point-by-point correspondence with Yeats's early work.

As early as "On Love" Shelley saw that if the lover was ever to unite more than physically with the lady, the two would have to be basically similar. Love was "that powerful attraction" to something beyond ourselves, but that something was still a "likeness" of the "something within us" which impels the love. Specifically, Shelley made the lady a "likeness" of the lover's "soul." She is, in fact, the "soul within our soul," the epipsyche, as Professors Carlos Baker and R. G. Woodman have shown.[12] My interpretation differs from theirs in arguing that the epipsyche is essentially the same as the psyche, only purged of impurities. The lady is a perfected version of a nascent form within the lover himself. Shelley writes:

> We dimly see within our intellectual nature a miniature as it were of our entire self, yet deprived of all that we condemn or despise, the ideal prototype of every thing excellent or lovely that we are capable of conceiving as belonging to the nature of man.

Shelley provides another word for what is loved, the "antitype." Antitype refers to the corresponding (not, as is usually maintained, the opposite) type of our soul: what Shelley calls the "ideal prototype." Through the imagination the antitype can join with us to form "a frame whose nerves, like the chords of two exquisite lyres, strung to the accompaniment of one delightful voice, vibrate with the vibrations of our own . . . in such proportion as the type within demands." That, says Shelley, is "the

[12] Carlos Baker, *Shelley's Major Poetry*, pp. 41–61 and 215–39, see esp. pp. 52–55; and Ross Grieg Woodman, *The Apocalyptic Vision in the Poetry of Shelley*, pp. 55–60 and passim. Woodman's illuminating discussion of the role of the imagination in love and poetry complements mine by emphasizing poetry rather than love, although I dissent from his use solely of "On Love" to show "the impossibility of finding that anti-type in another person" (p. 56). After "On Love" Shelley developed a concept of the imagination which did allow for discovery of the antitype in another person, although not for simultaneously uniting with it and portraying that union in poetry.

Although both Shelley and Yeats merge human love with Intellectual eros, I have here avoided Baker and Woodman's Platonic terminology, having already treated Intellectual Beauty and Plato in chapters 3 and 4.

invisible and unattainable point to which Love tends." The type without corresponds to the type within.

In its accepted meaning the "antitype" resembled the type and differed from it only in representing a higher or purer stage of development. One example from the NED is especially illuminating here: a Victorian theologian compared the relationship of the Old Testament to the New as "that of Type to Antitype, of Porch to Temple, of Dawn to Day."[13] Porch and dawn are not the opposites of temple and day; they are the predecessors, essentially similar, only the second is a higher development of the first. Shelley did not mean, then, that the epipsyche or antitype was the opposite of the psyche or type. To him it represented only the "ideal prototype" of the imperfect self. Like the dawn, the type tended toward the "discovery of its anti-type."

The type does not discover its antitype in *Alastor*, where the anonymous Poet can imagine his epipsyche but cannot find and unite with her. The poem supports our contention of correspondence between lover and lady. Shelley writes in the preface that the Poet's mind "thirsts for intercourse with an intelligence similar to itself" and in the poem that "Her voice was like the voice of his own soul."[14] The Poet images forth his epipsyche in his visionary dream. But, having always lived "in solitude" (60), he lacks the ability to commune with another being. His blood beats "in mystic sympathy / With nature's ebb and flow" (651-52) but not with the maiden's. He embarks on a quest he can never complete.

The "Discourse on the Manners of the Ancient Greeks," written in 1818, shows Shelley groping toward the imaginative means for completing the quest of *Alastor*. In arguing that the absence of suitable women (because of their inferior upbringing) did not impair the Greeks' capability for noble love, Shelley writes, "This object or its archetype for ever exists in the mind which selects among those who resemble it that which most resembles it and instinctively fills up the interstices of the perfect image."[15]

[13] *A New English Dictionary on Historical Principles*, ed. James A. H. Murray, 1: 376. The *NED* defines "antitype" as "That which is shadowed forth or represented by the 'type' or symbol."

[14] *Works*, 1: 173 and 181. Line numbers for other quotations from *Alastor* appear in parentheses within the text.

[15] *Shelley's Prose*, p. 220.

The mind contains within it the archetype of the beloved, which, we have seen, corresponds to the purified image of man's own soul. The mind searches among the women in the world for embodiments of its archetype. After selecting the figure which most resembles the archetype, the creative imagination corrects the deficiencies of the beloved ("fills up the interstices") until she corresponds to the true image of the lovable within the mind. The lover need not, like "Alastor," perish because of the inaccessibility of the visionary maid. Through his imagination he can transform an actual woman into his epipsyche. Shelley has solved the problem of finding the maiden in the world but not that of uniting with her.

By 1821 Shelley had articulated a concept of the sympathetic imagination which allowed for completion of the quest of love. He now believed in two kinds of imagination—the creative, described in the Athenian essay and in the bulk of the *Defence*, and the sympathetic. He described the second kind in a famous passage of the *Defence:*

> The great secret of morals is love, or a going out of our own nature and an identification of ourselves with the beautiful which exists in thought, action, or person, not our own. . . . The great instrument of moral good is the imagination; and poetry administers to the effect by acting upon the cause.[16]

The apparatus absent from *Alastor* has now been completed. The creative imagination allows the lover to select the proper woman and to transmute her into the "ideal prototype" of himself, the epipsyche. Moreover, by that process the creative imagination raises his psyche to the level of his purified antitype and so prepares the lover for union with it. Then, the sympathetic

[16] *Shelley's Prose*, pp. 282–83. I must here dissent from Earl Wasserman's contention in his brilliant article "Shelley's Last Poetics," in *From Sensibility to Romanticism*, ed. Harold Bloom and Frederick W. Hilles, p. 504, that Shelley does not assign a sympathetic function to the imagination in the *Defence*. Shelley may assign the "going out of our own nature" to love, but that is because love depends upon the sympathetic imagination. In the same passage of the *Defence* Shelley uses "imagine intensely" synonymously with "put himself in the place of another" so that the "pains and pleasures of his species must become his own." Meyer Abrams, whom Wasserman is here rebutting, is on firm ground in defining the imagination as "the organ by which the individual identifies himself with other people" in *The Mirror and the Lamp*, p. 331.

imagination allows him to escape his imperfect self and join "the beautiful which exists in . . . person not our own" and which the creative imagination has revealed to him.

Shelley applies his psychology to the fulfillment of the lover's quest in *Epipsychidion*.[17] Two early passages in that poem illuminate our main concern, the poet's concluding vision of love in the island paradise. In line 52 he declares to Emily, "I am not thine, I am a part of *thee*." He again asserts,

> I know
> That Love makes all things equal: I have heard
> By mine own heart this joyous truth averred:
> The spirit of the worm beneath the sod
> In love and worship, blends itself with God.[18]
> [126–29]

These lines exemplify the foregoing discussion. The poet can become a part of his epipsyche, Emily, by uniting with her through a process in which the imagination (creatively) figures forth that which it loves and then (sympathetically) becomes one with it. That is the process by which the spirit of the worm blends with the spirit of God. For all the incongruity of the metaphor, Shelley here describes himself as a worm (his psyche or self) which participates through love in God (his epipsyche or antitype); the worm and God are different levels of divinity; yet even the spirit of the worm contains the archetype of God within its soul. If the worm were as imaginative as Shelley, it could figure forth God's archetype and then merge with it; that is, merge with its highest self, which is the archetype of God present within the self.

Later in the poem the poet exhorts Emily to board ship with him and sail to an amorous paradise, which resembles the secluded bowers of bliss in *The Revolt of Islam*. He describes the island as follows:

[17] All quotations from *Works*, 2: 357–74. Line numbers appear within the text.

[18] Yeats uses a variant of the image of God and the worm in *A Vision*, although not as a metaphor pertaining to imagination: "I knew a man once who, seeking for an image of the absolute, saw one persistent image, a slug, as though it were suggested to him that Being which is beyond human comprehension is mirrored in the least organized forms of life" (p. 284).

And every motion, odour, beam, and tone,
With that deep music is in unison:
Which is a soul within the soul—they seem
Like echoes of an antenatal dream.—
[453–56]

The poet again envisions his epipsyche; only in contrast to his counterpart in *Alastor*, he is now imaginatively fit for his love quest. The beloved comes as "Not mine but me" (392). The poet's fervor grows as he describes the union on the island:

We shall become the same, we shall be one
Spirit within two frames, oh! wherefore two?
One passion in twin-hearts, which grows and grew,
'Till like two meteors of expanding flame,
Those spheres instinct with it become the same,
Touch, mingle, are transfigured.
[573–78]

The description coincides with the psychology of the prose writings. Shelley's passion for union with the purified self led to a conflict between the creative and the sympathetic aspects of the imagination. The creative imagination both molds the epipsyche and expresses it in poetry. The sympathetic imagination moves toward union with the epipsyche and consequent transcendence of the world of the poem. Shelley reveals the dilemma in the concluding lines of his vision:

Woe is me!
The winged words on which my soul would pierce
Into the height of love's rare Universe,
Are chains of lead around its flight of fire.—
I pant, I sink, I tremble, I expire!
[587–91]

The sympathetic imagination of the poet has nearly united his psyche to his epipsyche. In Platonic terms, he seeks to overcome the limiting conditions of his normal self and become, like Adonais, a beacon "from the abode where the Eternal are." Yeats's formulation of that Platonic notion in the first version of *A Vision* serves as an apt gloss: "the Fixed Stars being the least changing things are the acts of whatever in that stream changes least, *and therefore of all souls that have found an almost change-*

less rest"[19] (italics mine). Such a psyche has completed its quest and can view life *sub specie aeternitatis.* But to view life that way is to deny poetic expression to the vision. Words are inadequate; even as they help the soul pierce into Love's universe, they become "chains of lead" which the poet must repudiate or else fail in his quest. "The deep truth," Shelley recognized in *Prometheus Unbound*, "is imageless."[20]

Intellectual vision forces the poet either to forsake the many-colored glass of life and to unite sympathetically with the Eternal or to restrict himself to creatively imaging forth his epipsyche in the poem and to abjure uniting with it. Shelley, like the skylark, could ascend out of sight into a world unknown to men; otherwise, he must break off the vision of *Epipsychidion* and sink down into life again. Yeats faced the same dilemma as early as "To the Rose upon the Rood of Time," when he sought to balance the rival claims of the Rose and of common things. He could free himself later from the limitations of his early, Shelleyan love poetry only by renouncing hope of "an almost changeless rest" and instead accepting the continuing struggle of antinomies. Yet if he was not always willing to travel to Eternity with the lover of Emily, he was willing to travel to death with the youth in *Alastor;* his early works may be read not only as canticles to Intellectual Beauty but also as canzones to earthly love.

The Epipsyche and the Early Yeats

During his period of unqualified admiration for Shelley, Yeats wrote a very Shelleyan sort of love poetry. He knew well Shelley's chief works dealing with that subject. In the essay on Shelley he quoted from "On Love," *Alastor*, the *Defence*, and *Epipsychidion* to illustrate his predecessor's "ruling ideas." In particular, he cited two passages from "On Love" describing the epipsyche: "We are born into the world, and there is something within us which, from the instant that we live, more and more thirsts after its likeness" and "[we have] a soul within our soul that describes a circle around its proper paradise which pain and

19 *A Vision* (1925), p. 158.

20 *Works*, 2: 221 (act 2, scene 4, line 116).

sorrow and evil dare not overleap."[21] Yeats followed Shelley's belief in the creative imagination and made a half-hearted attempt to accept the sympathetic imagination as well, but he never effectively fused the two. This section treats, first, the early lyrics and, second, *The Shadowy Waters* as Yeatsian redactions of Shelleyan love.

Yeats's love poetry of the eighties and nineties is usually likened to that of the Pre-Raphaelites, but it owes at least as much to Shelley. His lyrics follow the Shelleyan formula of secluded, loving union of part with counterpart, brought about by the imagination, and sometimes symbolized by death. Five poems which appeared at intervals of two or three years between 1886 and 1897 offer representative examples: "The Indian to His Love" (1886), "To an Isle in the Water" (1889), "The Lover Tells of the Rose in His Heart" (1892), "The Heart of the Woman" (1894), and "The Travail of Passion" (1897).

The Revolt of Islam and *Prometheus Unbound* served as roadmaps for the amorous strolls of Yeats's successful lovers in the eighties. Laon and Prometheus both describe the pleasures of idyllic wanderings with their beloveds. Laon remembers that Cythna's feet "Wandered with mine where earth and ocean meet" and that the two lovers strolled hand in hand under "boughs of incense." Prometheus, too, remembers walking with Asia through "o'er-shadowing woods" and "drinking life from her loved eyes."[22] The notion of the lover wandering hand in hand with his lady by the shore under heavy branches appealed to Yeats. In "The Indian to His Love" the speaker anticipates how he and his lover will "wander ever with woven hands / . . . / Along the grass, along the sands" beneath "heavy boughs." The poem is brief enough to be quoted in full as a paradigm of Yeats's early handling of Shelleyan love:

> The island dreams under the dawn
> And great boughs drop tranquillity;
> The peahens dance on a smooth lawn,
> A parrot sways upon a tree,
> Raging at his own image in the enamelled sea.
>
> Here we will moor our lonely ship

[21] *E & I*, p. 69.
[22] *Works*, 1: 281 (canto 2 lines, 25–26) and 2: 183 (act 1, line 122–23).

And wander ever with woven hands,
Murmuring softly lip to lip,
Along the grass, along the sands,
Murmuring how far away are the unquiet lands:

How we alone of mortals are
Hid under quiet boughs apart,
While our love grows an Indian star,
A meteor of the burning heart,
One with the tide that gleams, the wings that gleam and dart,

The heavy boughs, the burnished dove
That moans and sighs a hundred days:
How when we die our shades will rove,
When eve has hushed the feathered ways,
With vapoury footsole by the water's drowsy blaze.[23]

Yeats follows Shelley in using geographical separation to suggest the profounder separation of the world of loving union from the normal world of mutability. Yeats's Indian resembles the lover of *Epipsychidion* in envisioning an island paradise of love. Like the retreats of Laon and Prometheus, the island enjoys exemption from the normal cares of humanity. Prometheus describes a landscape "Where we will sit and talk of time and change, / As the world ebbs and flows, ourself unchanged."[24] The speaker of "To an Isle in the Water" longs for just such a retreat. Likewise, the Indian informs his beloved that they will wander "Murmuring how far away are the unquiet lands." He and his lady are counterparts, not antinomies.

Although the notion of secluded union lingers on into the poems of the nineties, the importance of the imagination as the creating and realizing force of love emerges as a more important theme. Those poems, like Shelley's about the epipsyche, maintain that "immortal passion breathes in mortal clay."[25] The imagination, that is, infuses its "immortal" longing for the purified antitype into the lover's ordinary self or "mortal clay." The longing of the Yeatsian lover thus resembles the longing of "Alastor" for the visionary maid or the poet's spiritual desire for Emily. The lyrics imply an imaginative union with the beloved, and in the nineties Yeats experimented with the sympathetic capabilities of

[23] *Variorum Poems*, pp. 77–78.
[24] *Works*, 2: 232 (act 3, scene 3, lines 23–24).
[25] *Variorum Poems*, p. 172 ("The Travail of Passion").

the imagination. Adopting the position of Shelley in the *Defence*, he wrote in an essay on Blake (1897) that the "imagination . . . binds us to each other by opening the secret doors of all hearts."[26]

Yeats prefigures his later rejection of sympathetic union by stressing the creative power of the imagination. In "The Lover Tells of the Rose in His Heart" the lover considers that the "wrong of unshapely things" transgresses against his ideal image of the beloved.[27] That image coincides with what Shelley called the "something within us" that inspires our love; that something, he maintained in the essay on the Athenians, was the "archetype" which "forever exists in the mind." Yeats's lover cannot bear the disparity between the archetypal image and the world. Looking at the components of the everyday world, he longs "to build them anew." As in the *Defence*, the creative imagination constructs its own world. Since such imaginative activity implies seclusion from the normal world, the lover contemplates his vision while sitting "apart" on a green knoll.

To Shelley's formula of love Yeats adds an ingredient which Shelley had treated less prominently—death as a symbol of union. In *Alastor*, for example, Shelley hints that death may bring the union denied the feckless Poet in life. Immediately after the vision of the dream maiden Shelley asks, "Does the dark gate of death / Conduct to thy mysterious paradise, / O Sleep?"[28] Yeats ignored the poem's insistence that separation from the epipsyche brings death and instead emphasized the suggestion that death symbolizes union by freeing the mortal soul from the travail of generation. In his own poetry Yeats sought to resolve the Shelleyan conflict between sympathetic and creative imagination by symbolizing the union (through death) rather than by actually presenting it.

Although Yeats could have found the similarity of death and sleep, and even the association of death with final union, throughout most of Western literature, he in fact consistently ascribes it to Shelley. A prominent instance occurs in the essay on William Morris, "The Happiest of the Poets," which—as though to emphasize its relevance to Shelley—Yeats placed immediately before the essay on Shelley in arranging *Ideas of Good and Evil*. In argu-

[26] *E & I*, p. 112. [27] *Variorum Poems*, p. 143. [28] *Works*, 1: 183.

ing the insufficient conception of love held by the men and women in Morris's poems, Yeats writes, "They do not seek in love that ecstasy which Shelley's nightingale called death, that extremity of life in which life seems to pass away like the phoenix in flame of its own lighting, but rather a gentle self-surrender."[29] Of the many nightingales in Shelley's poetry, Yeats probably was remembering the one in *Rosalind and Helen,* for in the essay on Shelley he quotes a description of a nightingale by the dying Lionel which accords with the remark on Morris:

> Heardst thou not sweet words among
> That heaven-resounding minstrelsy?
> Heardst thou not, that those who die
> Awake in a world of ecstasy?
> That love, when limbs are interwoven,
> And sleep, when the night of life is cloven,
> And thought, to the world's dim boundaries clinging,
> And music, when one beloved is singing,
> Is death? Let us drain right joyously
> The cup which the sweet bird fills for me.[30]

In Yeats's view of *Rosalind and Helen* and *Epipsychidion,* death signifies the ecstatic intensity of the imagination uniting with the object of the soul's love. Yeats picks up Shelley's phrase "a world of ecstasy" and, as the essay on Morris shows, considers it to be the essential creation of love. Caught up in the world of ecstasy, of love in its fullest imaginative development, the lover participates in life and death but reverses the meaning of each. Death, the ecstatic manifestation of imaginative union, signifies not the end but rather "the extremity of life," in Yeats's phrase. Just as Lionel dies at his moment of greatest love, so does the poet of *Epipsychidion* pant, sink, tremble, and, finally, expire.

The use of death in Yeats's poetry reflects his reading of Shelley. The lover in "The Heart of the Woman" is "no more with life and death"[31] because the ecstatic union Yeats thought represented in the song of Lionel's nightingale has transported her to that

29 *E & I,* p. 57.

30 *E & I,* p. 72. The lines are 1121–30 of *Rosalind and Helen.* The nightingale is an appropriate image for the affinity of the loving and the poetic forms of the imagination. In the *Defence* (*Shelley's Prose,* p. 282) Shelley says, "A poet is a nightingale."

31 *Variorum Poems,* p. 152.

realm of ecstatic imagination metaphorically referred to as death. In addition, her abandonment of childish prayer and domestic conventionality for her lover's sake accords with the framework of *Rosalind and Helen* and with the adolescent Yeats's conception of Cythna as the archetype of "lawless women without homes and without children."[32]

Making death into a metaphor for union freed Yeats from representing that union within his poetry. The metaphor implies the death of the imperfect self and the consequent participation of the perfected self in a higher plane of being, for which the lover carried the potentiality even before purification. Shelley, we have seen, represented in his poetry the quest for love and the instant before completion, but not the transfigured union. As in *Epipsychidion*, the lover must either die or sink back into his earlier state. The poet cannot follow both the sympathetic and the creative imaginations if the object of each is the ideal. That is why Shelley has his "characters" describe union in the past or in the future, but not achieve it in the present. For the same reason Yeats in his early lyrics either envisions *future* union or contents himself with the world of creative imagination. His attempts to show the completion of a Shelleyan quest for love within his poetry reach their culmination in *The Shadowy Waters*, which, like *Epipsychidion*, ends with the metaphorical death of the lover.

The Shadowy Waters

Yeats provides his fullest treatment of Shelleyan love in *The Shadowy Waters*, which claimed a significant portion of his creative efforts from the early nineties until 1907.[33] This discus-

[32] *Autobiography*, p. 64.

[33] Joseph Hone reports that Yeats had "already imagined" the poem in 1883, at the age of eighteen (*W. B. Yeats 1865–1939*, p. 39). Cornelius Weygandt in 1913 (*Irish Plays and Playwrights*, p. 57): "Mr. Yeats has written that he has been brooding over 'The Shadowy Waters' ever since he was a boy, and he told me, when I asked him once which writing of his he cared most for, 'That I was last working at, and then "The Shadowy Waters."' " Yeats first mentions the work in his published correspondence in November, 1894, when he tells his father that he is "doing nothing except the play *The Shadowy Waters* which will I think be good. It is however giving me a devil of a job." (*Yeats's Letters*, p. 236). The work was finally published in 1900, although Yeats radically revised it for the 1906 edition (the one used here) and made more alterations, mostly excisions, for the "acting version" of 1907.

sion supplements others[34] by demonstrating the importance of Shelleyan love to a proper reading of the work. Describing the play to George Russell (AE), Yeats wrote, "I may be getting the whole story of the relation of man and woman in symbol—all that makes the subject of *The Shadowy Waters*."[35] The "whole story" elaborated the masculine quest for completion through feminine love. Russell reported his discussions with Yeats to Sean O'Faolain, to whom he wrote:

> His hero was a world wanderer trying to *escape from himself*. He surprises a galley in the waters. There is a beautiful woman there. He thinks through love he can escape from himself. He casts a magical spell on Dectora. Then in the original version he found the love created by a spell was an empty echo, a shadow of himself, and he unrolled the spell seeking alone for the world of the immortals [italics Russell's].[36]

The notion of escaping from oneself by love agrees with Shelley's view in both idea and phrasing. Shelley develops that concept in "On Love," and in the *Defence* he holds that the "sacred emotions" of love can "lift" us out of "the little world of self."[37] Unlike Shelley's lovers, however, Forgael finds not an idealized soul but a mere "shadow of himself" in his beloved. Yeats could envision the epipsyche, but even this early the Shelleyan problem of union with it was apparent to him. He eventually revised the ending and had Forgael and Dectora drift off in a boat together in a scene reminiscent of the nautical image from *Alastor* which had fired his imagination since boyhood. The play itself embodies five of the Shelleyan characteristics found in the lyric poetry of the same period: it depicts a love resulting in ecstatic union and in separation from the world, symbolized by death, and effected by the imagination. Let us consider each of those points in order.

[34] See particularly Richard Ellmann, *The Identity of Yeats*, pp. 80–84; Leonard E. Nathan, *The Tragic Drama of William Butler Yeats: Figures in a Dance*, pp. 41–81; S. B. Bushrui, *Yeats's Verse Plays: The Revisions 1900–1910*, pp. 1–38. Nathan (p. 66) makes a brief, illuminating comparison of the play to *The Revolt of Islam* in terms of the quest for a "soulmate." Bushrui (pp. 4–6) briefly mentions Shelleyan imagery.

[35] *Yeats's Letters*, p. 324.

[36] Quoted by Ellmann, *Yeats: The Man and the Masks*, p. 78.

[37] *Shelley's Prose*, p. 289.

Forgael himself announces that the object of his quest is love. He tells Aibric, "For it is love that I am seeking for, / But of a beautiful, unheard-of kind / That is not in the world."[38] In seeking a love which in its beauty surpasses that found in the world, he verges on the attitude toward Intellectual Beauty which Yeats in 1900 took to be the essence of Shelley's position. A passage from the first version of the poem, published the same year as the essay on Shelley, reinforces the relevance of Shelley to an understanding of Yeats at this period. In Dectora's concluding speech Yeats employs one of Shelley's favorite techniques by presenting a series of alternate metaphors for the same subject, which here is Dectora's conception of her lover. Among the flower, bird, silver fish, and white fawn we find the image, "O morning star."[39] In the essay Yeats identified the morning star as "the most important, the most precise of all Shelley's symbols, the one he uses with the fullest knowledge of its meaning."[40] Since Yeats devoted a considerable portion of the essay to explicating Shelley's association of the star with love and reiterated the connection in two essays written at the same time as the revisions of *The Shadowy Waters*,[41] his inclusion of the image in Dectora's list suggests that he had Shelley's "idea of perfect love" in mind.

The second characteristic is the goal of ecstatic union for the lovers. Forgael mentions ecstasy specifically in describing his quest:

> Where the world ends
> The mind is made unchanging, for it finds
> Miracle, ecstasy, the impossible hope,
> The flagstone under all, the fire of fires,
> The roots of the world.[42]

The union leads to a Shelleyan transcendence of the mutable human world; here, the mind becomes "unchanging." Again like Shelley, Yeats construes the union in spiritual terms, although

[38] *Variorum Poems*, p. 228. [39] 1900 version, ibid., p. 769.

[40] *E & I*, p. 88.

[41] "Religious Belief Necessary to Religious Art" and "Personality and the Intellectual Essences," *E & I*, pp. 294, 267.

[42] *Variorum Poems*, p. 227. Subsequent references are to this text and are identified by page numbers in parentheses after the quotations.

neither poet denies the physical union. When Dectora accuses Forgael of planning to use magic "Until my body give you kiss for kiss," he corrects her by saying, "Your soul shall give the kiss" (238).

The union of the lovers implies a separation from the world. In the Shelleyan manner Dectora fancies "some island" (249) where the lovers can enjoy each other without interference. She later makes the point more explicit by exhorting Forgael to "Bend lower, that I may cover you with my hair, / For we will gaze upon this world no longer" (251). Like Laon and Cythna, Prometheus and Asia, and the poet of *Epipsychidion* and Emily, Yeats' lovers mingle their souls in retreats isolated from the busy world of human affairs.

Since for both Yeats and Shelley the world of love depends upon the soul or spirit and thus constitutes a superior level of reality, entrance into it can be symbolized by a death to the old order. The purified reality compares with the normal one as the epipsyche does with the psyche. As Forgael explains, "It's not a dream, / But the reality that makes our passion / As a lamp shadow—no—no lamp, the sun. / What the world's million lips are thirsting for / Must be substantial somewhere" (229). The somewhere might lie on the other side of the grave, however. Yeats construed the death sung about by Lionel's nightingale as a Shelleyan metaphor for the completion of love. Yet union appears as death only to those who have not yet experienced it. Yeats linked death to a "mysterious transformation of the flesh, an embodiment of every lover's dream" in his own summary of the 1906 version, which also mentioned the magic harp of the imagination:

> Forgael, a Sea-King of ancient Ireland, was promised by certain human-headed birds love of a supernatural intensity. These birds were the souls of the dead, and he followed them over seas towards the sunset, where their final rest is. By means of a magic harp, he could call them about him when he would and listen to their speech. His friend Aibric, and the sailors of his ship, thought him mad, or that this mysterious happiness could come after death only, and that he and they were being lured to destruction. Presently they captured a ship, and found a beautiful woman upon it, and Forgael subdued her and his own rebellious sailors by the sound of his harp. The sailors

> fled upon the other ship, and Forgael and the woman drifted on alone following the birds, awaiting death and what comes after, or some mysterious transformation of the flesh, an embodiment of every lover's dream.[43]

The birds who are souls of the dead lead the lovers beyond clock time. They are the delivered selves whom Yeats elsewhere described as "those spirits Shelley imagined in his *Adonais* as visiting the inspired and the innocent."[44] Death appropriately symbolizes the annihilation of time for which every lover yearns. To the timorous Aibric death is only literal: he warns Forgael, "It's certain they are leading you to death. / None but the dead, or those that never lived, / Can know that ecstasy" (231). Forgael remains more optimistic. For him literal death is possible but not "for certain" (249); he allows for its symbolic implication of a victory over time. At the beginning he perceives that "the movement of time / Is shaken in these seas" (237). By the end of the play he has grown more certain of winning, for he tells Dectora that "we grow immortal" (252). In growing immortal he forsakes the world of mutability for the perfected sphere of Yeats's Intellectual vision. In the introductory poem Yeats asked, "Is Eden out of time and out of space?" (218). The play answers that question affirmatively. The lovers, like Adonais, have now become one of those stars of love which serve as a beacon "from the abode where the Eternal are." Yeats and Shelley both recognized the appropriateness of death as a metaphor for such transcendence.

The creative imagination effects the transcendence. Forgael's harp functions as the symbol for the imagination. He explains that the spirits "have promised / I shall have love in their immortal fashion; / And for this end they gave me my old harp / That is more mighty than the sun and moon" (237). Because of its link with the eternal realm of love the imagination becomes the essential aspect of the lover, insofar as only it survives the change into the higher realm. Dectora indicates awareness of that process when she tells Forgael that he has become "a burning sod / In the imagination and intellect" (245). Yeats revised those lines in a manner which echoes Shelley, for in the 1907 edition the "burn-

43 Quoted by Ellmann, *The Identity of Yeats*, pp. 80–81.
44 *E & I*, p. 483.

ing sod" became a "burning coal."[45] The metaphor suggests Shelley's famous image of the fading coal, which Yeats quoted in his essay. In *The Shadowy Waters* the wind of spiritual influence has blown the fading coal into a burning one.

Forgael's harp of the imagination indicates that Yeats had run into the inevitable poetic dilemma of Shelleyan love. The harp represents only the creative imagination, which shapes the epipsyche and expresses it through art, not the sympathetic imagination which allows for final union. Union is impossible, the play suggests, because the lovers are different and lack the means to comprehend each other. The creative imagination effects only a semblance of union, based on deception. Just as in the prose description Yeats had Forgael find only a shadow of himself in Dectora, so does she find only a shadow of her ideal archetype in him. He has tricked her into believing he is "golden-armed Iollan" (242 f.), when he is really only Forgael. "I have deceived you utterly," he admits (245). He has deceived her not into thinking of him as an ideal (he can raise himself to the level of an ideal Forgael) but into thinking of him as a different sort of ideal than he really is.

Forgael had no real choice in deceiving Dectora. His creative imagination has imaged forth an ideal vision with which, like "Alastor," he could not help desiring to unite. "Being driven on by voices and by dreams / That were clear messages from the Ever-living, / I have done right. What could I but obey?" (243) he argues. He lacks the means to complete an irresistible quest but must embark on it: the Shelleyan something within him thirsts after its own likeness and so impels him onward. He deceives Dectora in the desperate hope of completing the quest. Yeats can solve the dramatic problem only by having the lovers drift off in their private boat over the sea of generation to, again, a *future* union. Not fear of the censor but rather his own concept of the imagination as creative but not sympathetic kept Yeats from representing the final union on the stage.

After 1907 Yeats gave up all but minor tinkering with the play that had occupied so much of his time for over a dozen years. The attempt to get "the whole story of the relation of man and woman" had failed, but at least it had led to a new realization of

45 *Variorum Plays*, p. 335.

what the relation was. In his lyrics and plays after *The Shadowy Waters* Yeats abjured the whole Shelleyan notion of loving, secluded union of part with counterpart which had fit so well with his early, Intellectual vision.

The Mask

"Love is war, and there is hatred in it," cries Forgael to Dectora (244). That cry comes not just from Forgael but from Yeats himself, who had gradually lost belief in Shelley's ideal of the psyche's loving union with its epipsyche. The mature Yeats thinks of lovers not as counterparts but as warring opposites, and he brings them not into eternal union but into eternal reciprocal relationship. By abjuring union Yeats could abjure the sympathetic imagination and so free himself from the poetic contradictions of Shelleyan love: he could now stay within the limits of creative imagination and, hence, of poetry. This section first examines the nascent doctrine of the mask in Yeats's lyrical poems and then uses its explicit development in *A Vision* to explicate Yeats's most extensive treatment of love in his late period, *A Full Moon in March*. The late Yeats abstains from portraying the union of mortal lovers but readmits the struggle for union into his poetry as a part of his antinomial vision of life. The mask gains a fresh significance when seen as an alternative to the Shelleyan Intellectual vision of his early work and related to his new view of "Alastor" and Athanase as antiselves.

Three years before the final revisions of *The Shadowy Waters* Yeats published his first Cuchulain play, *On Baile's Strand*, which adumbrates the central tenet of his later theory of the mask—that lovers are contending opposites, not cooperating counterparts. Characteristically, Yeats gives the traditional metaphor of the *bellum amoris* its literal meaning, so that he both reinterprets and gives a fresh authority to the conceit. Cuchulain fights with Aoife not only in love but on the battlefield: in their youth he overcomes her, and in old age she vanquishes him. War becomes not analogous but identical to love. Cuchulain reflects:

> I never have known love but as a kiss
> In the mid-battle, and a difficult truce
> Of oil and water, candles and dark night,
> Hillside and hollow, the hot-footed sun

And the cold, sliding, slippery-footed moon—
A brief forgiveness between opposites
That have been hatreds.[46]

Cuchulain prefers the warring separation of the lovers to the loving union of Prometheus and Asia or Laon and Cythna. Perhaps reflecting his passion for Maud Gonne, Yeats preferred the warlike Cythna to the tender lover of Laon. He had Cuchulain invert Conchubar's condemnation of Aoife as a "fierce woman of the camp" into praise,[47] for only out of separation and opposition come beauty and nobility. Love depends not on similarity but on difference. Cuchulain's metaphors of immiscible opposites—oil and water, light and dark, sun and moon—combine Shelleyan form (a listing of alternate images) with very un-Shelleyan notions and prefigure Yeats's more deliberate development of symbolic contrasts in *A Vision.*

Yeats soon found that he could express the conflicts of love through the doctrine of the mask. Just as the poet could "complete" his personality by assuming a mask, as Shelley did with Athanase, so could the lover assume a mask to bring his desire to its fullest development, even if not to its satisfaction. Like the masking of poetry, the masking of love depended upon the deliberate cultivation of the antiself, not in the Shelleyan sense of the highest development of the self but in the Yeatsian meaning of the opposite of the self. "What I have called 'the Mask'," wrote Yeats, "is an emotional antithesis to all that comes out of their [subjective men's] internal nature."[48] His own mask, or Image, was "the opposite of all that I am in my daily life."[49]

Love involves a double masking: both the lover and his lady assume masks. Just as a poet could assume the mask of a Shelleyan wanderer, so could he assume the mask of a lover. He could then, as Yeats in fact did, portray the mask in his poetry as well as in his life. Conversely, the beloved also assumes a mask; and her mask—not her self—inspires her lover's passion. The Yeatsian lover thus responds not to his lady's psyche (or his epipsyche) but to a mask she deliberately maintains to inspire his passion. As early as 1899 Yeats came to think of "the desire of the man

[46] *Variorum Plays,* p. 489. The text is that of the final version.
[47] Ibid., p. 487.
[48] *Autobiography,* p. 189. [49] Ibid., p. 274.

'which is for the woman,' and 'the desire of the woman which is for the desire of the man.' "[50]

Yeats first fused his new concepts of desire and warfare with the icon of the mask in a poem called, simply, "The Mask," which first appeared in 1910:

"Put off that mask of burning gold
With emerald eyes."
"O no, my dear, you make so bold
To find if hearts be wild and wise,
And yet not cold."

"I would but find what's there to find,
Love or deceit."
"It was the mask engaged your mind,
And after set your heart to beat,
Not what's behind."

"But lest you are my enemy,
I must enquire."
"O no, my dear, let all that be;
What matter, so there is but fire
In you, in me?"[51]

The stanza by stanza progression of this poem first posits the central doctrine of the masks and then subsumes into it two ideas which Yeats explored in earlier plays. In the first stanza the lady's mask frustrates her lover's desire to know her truly. Like Britomart in *The Faerie Queene* he must be bold but not "so bold" as to know his lady's self rather than her mask. Yeats makes the mask into the limit of the lover's knowledge. The second stanza couples love and deceit, the two qualities whose conjunction distressed Forgael in *The Shadowy Waters.* The proscription of union makes deceit irrelevant; the beloved should assume that mask which creates the greatest passion in her lover. Finally, the poem presents the notion of the lover as enemy, which received literal development in the Cuchulain plays. Like the desire to discover

[50] *Variorum Poems*, p. 807.

[51] Ibid., p. 263. The first statement in each stanza is made by the (male) lover, not—as is sometimes thought—by the (female) beloved. In *The Player Queen* Decima introduces the first stanza with the comment, "The man speaks first" (*Variorum Plays*, p. 738). "The Hero, the Girl, and the Fool" is a later catechism of Yeats's full development of the mask theory, with its relegation of union to the postmortal transcendence of generation. (*Variorum Poems*, pp. 447–49).

the lady's heart (stanza 1) or her emotions (stanza 2), the desire to discover if she is an enemy also becomes irrelevant in stanza 3. The poem constitutes a catechism of Yeats's new doctrine of love, in which the creation of passion replaces the hope of union. Yeats in effect instructs himself in the repudiation of his earlier, Shelleyan view of love by showing its basic irrelevance to his new position.

From emphasizing his own disappointment in the quest of love in *In the Seven Woods* Yeats turned to emphasizing his beloved in *The Green Helmet* and *Responsibilities*. She wears the mask of Helen of Troy, who occurs repeatedly in Yeats's mature lyrics. Following his principle that the lyric poet must assume a traditional pose, Yeats here speaks through the persona of a lover. His lover desires not so much to unite with his lady as to express his desire for her. In "A Woman Homer Sung" the lover declares his goal:

> I dream that I have brought
> To such a pitch my thought
> That coming time can say,
> "He shadowed in a glass
> What thing her body was."[52]

The lover brings his thought to the required pitch by his imagination. In "The Tower" (1929) Yeats asked, "Does the imagination dwell the most / Upon a woman won or a woman lost?"[53] His own lyrics reply that Yeats's imagination dwelt the most upon a woman lost. He had explicitly answered the question nineteen years earlier, in a lyric called "The Words," which appears between two of the poems about Helen. After describing his continuing failure to make his "darling" understand himself and his work, he concludes:

> That had she done so who can say
> What would have shaken from the sieve?
> I might have thrown poor words away
> And been content to live.[54]

Since the lady's insensibility to the lover's desires precludes union, he turns his imagination upon his poetry, through which he seeks to reveal his passion. Had his quest been successful, he

[52] *Variorum Poems*, p. 255. [53] Ibid., p. 413. [54] Ibid., p. 256.

would have abandoned the world of creative imagination. Only by dwelling on the mask of inaccessible desire can he rouse his imagination to create a kind of countermask in poetry. The impossibility of union insures that he will not face the Shelleyan dilemma of the contradictory claims of the sympathetic and the creative faculties. He will always be able to remain within the myth of his poem. The danger is that the poem itself, rather than the mask it celebrates, may claim his allegiance. Yeats describes his temporary surrender to that possibility in "The Circus Animals' Desertion." Fear that political activity would destroy Maud's soul led him to make her mask immortal in his poetry; unexpectedly, he came to love the mask of the poetry better than the mask of the woman. He writes:

> I thought my dear must her own soul destroy,
> So did fanaticism and hate enslave it,
> And this brought forth a dream and soon enough
> This dream itself had all my thought and love.[55]

Yeats noted his abandonment of the sympathetic imagination in the same section of "The Tower" where he posed the riddle of the woman won or the woman lost. He writes:

> If on the lost, admit you turned aside
> From a great labyrinth out of pride,
> Cowardice, some silly over-subtle thought
> Or anything called conscience once.

The previous stanza makes clear that the "labyrinth" is that "of another's being," through which only the thread of the sympathetic imagination serves as guide. Yeats turned aside from it not just out of pride[56] or cowardice or oversubtlety or conscience but out of the necessity to avoid just that union which Shelley had found impossible to portray in *Epipsychidion.* To enter the labyrinth of another's being by means of the sympathetic imagination is to leave the labyrinth of the poem, which is constructed by the creative imagination. Yet "The Tower" reflects Yeats's persistent doubts about his decision. Through the complicated

[55] Ibid., p. 630.

[56] "Pride" in this context may have a special meaning. In "All Soul's Night" (the epilogue to *A Vision*) Yeats mentions "that sweet extremity of pride / That's called platonic love." See *Variorum Poems*, p. 471.

psychology of *A Vision* he sought to resolve the question of "The Tower" and to find some artistic place for the woman won as well as the woman lost.

Yeats brought the mask and the imagination together in the complicated theories of *A Vision*, which, we saw in chapter 5, depended upon the interactions of the four "Faculties"—Will, Mask, Creative Mind, and Body of Fate. Men of phase seventeen, like Shelley and Yeats, find their mask in phase three. There are really two masks—one assumed by the poet, and one representing that which he seeks. The latter mask is also called the Image, and represents the mask of the beloved sought by the poet after he has donned (in his poetry) his own mask of the desiring lover. Yeats describes the relation between the lover's mask and its Image (the beloved's mask): "This *Mask* may represent intellectual or sexual passion; seem some Ahasuerus or Athanase; be the gaunt Dante of the *Divine Comedy;* its corresponding Image may be Shelley's Venus Urania, Dante's Beatrice."[57]

The lover's creative imagination both creates the Image (the mask of the beloved) and strives to protect it against the pressure of reality, which continually menaces the lovers. Yeats writes that the "being, through the intellect, selects some object of desire for a representation of the *Mask* as Image, some woman perhaps, and the *Body of Fate* snatches away the object."[58] If the Creative Mind, which for phase seventeen is the imagination, fails to defend the Image against the Body of Fate, it then must select a new Image. After the initial frustration "the intellect (*Creative Mind*), which in the most *antithetical* phases were better described as imagination, must substitute some new image of desire." The imagination, that is, constantly strives to isolate from the flux of everyday events that object which corresponds to the mind and its antiself; mask and Image may be thought of "as chosen forms or as conceptions of the mind."

In an intricate way Yeats has circled back upon the Shelleyan position. In Shelley the imagination sought for its archetypal epipsyche in the external world; when it found the woman who closely resembled the archetype, it "filled up the interstices" to make the Image a true epipsyche. Should one attempt fail—for in

57 *A Vision*, p. 141.
58 All quotations in this paragraph are from *A Vision*, p. 142.

Shelley, too, the Body of Fate foils the lover—the imagination could always begin again with another subject. The apparatus of *A Vision* presents the process of masculine fulfillment by a complementary female principle in a new framework. Yeats differs from Shelley in that he conceives of the Image or mask as the opposite of the self, not as the idealized version of the highest part of the self. Furthermore, he accepts the lady's mask as the ultimate limit of the lover's knowledge; Yeats's singing school teaches man to rejoice in that tragic sundering, whereas Shelley's school—whose master is equally aware of love's limits—laments the division and hymns the effort to overcome it.

Secure in the psychological underpinning of conflict in love, Yeats could also circle partway back on his earlier notion of possible union. This time he approached union not from the direction of the attraction between psyche and epipsyche but from the "enforced attraction between Opposites."[59] Believing that "all things fall into a series of antinomies in human experience,"[60] he still limited his art to expression of the antinomies of love, mask, and Image. But he now wondered if art could not *suggest* some union of the antinomies (Shelley's example had proved that art could not *express* it). "Passionate love," he pondered, "is from the *Daimon* which seeks by union with some other *Daimon* to reconstruct above the antinomies its own true nature."[61] The context of that remark—a discussion of the soul after death—suggests that Yeats assigned the union to a realm beyond that of life and poetry. The transcendence of antinomies depends not upon sympathetic imagination, but upon the fullest possible use of the creative faculty. While keeping within the bounds of creative imagination and immiscible opposites, Yeats tried to suggest in the Sheba poems and *A Full Moon in March* the possibility of eventual union. Significantly, he did not try to express that union in his art and thus avoided the confession of poetry's inadequacy to which Shelley is brought in *Epipsychidion.*

The Solomon and Sheba poems of *The Wild Swans at Coole* and *Michael Robartes and the Dancer* maintain the separation of

[59] *A Vision*, p. 93. [60] Ibid., p. 193. [61] Ibid., p. 238.

opposing antinomies and the failure of their attempt at union. Yeats retreats from the first person narrator of the Rose lyrics (who sought union) and the mask lyrics (who abjured it) and instead appears to describe historical figures whom he manipulates for his own ends. He is no longer willing to approach the problems of union directly through too personal a mode of expression. The two lovers represent archetypal masks: the lover is a sage, like Ahasuerus or someone such as Athanase would have become, and the lady a beautiful woman, like Helen of Troy. Yeats thinks of union in apocalyptic terms, signifying the end of the world and comparable in importance to the Fall. He writes:

> Maybe the bride-bed brings despair,
> For each an imagined image brings
> And finds a real image there;
> Yet the world ends when these two things,
> Though several, are a single light,
> When oil and wick are burned in one.[62]

The disparity between the "imagined image" and the "real image" ordinarily precludes union. The speaker hopes that the union has taken place: "Therefore a blessed moon last night / Gave Sheba to her Solomon." The hope is premature, however, for "the world stays." Sheba concludes with an exhortation to a new attempt: "O! Solomon! Let us try again." Yeats does not try to present the union, but stays within the myth of the poem and the power of creative imagination. Like Shelley, he in effect exhorts man toward an ideal, but does so by presenting the nobleness of struggle toward it rather than by attempting a vision of the final goal. Yeats's metaphor for the goal in this poem, the moon, anticipates his fuller development of lunar symbolism in *A Full Moon in March.*

In *A Full Moon in March* Yeats brought the masks of the lovers into a final relation. This ersatz union—not of the self but of the mask—constitutes the only triumph possible to the Yeatsian lover. By applying the doctrine of the mask to the erotic aspects of the play, we shall arrive at a new interpretation of the swineherd and the queen, and their respective relations to the full

62 *Variorum Poems*, p. 388.

moon.[63] Only when disguised as a swineherd could "Alastor" reenter Yeats's art, as part of the quest for antiself and Image.

The male figure in the play, the swineherd, corresponds to the proper mask for a man of phase seventeen, like Shelley or Yeats. He resembles the wanderers of Shelley, whom Yeats gave as examples of that mask, in the simplicity and intensity of his passion for the queen. Just as Yeats thought of Shelley masking himself as Athanase or "Alastor," so can we think of Yeats masking himself as the swineherd. Yeats confusingly calls a mask of this type by the same term as the mask of the beloved, an Image, because like the beloved's Image this mask represents a purified antiself. "Seen by lyrical poets, of whom so many have belonged to the fantastic Phase 17," wrote Yeats, "the man of this phase [three] becomes an Image."[64]

The female principle, the queen, combines elements of phases fourteen and sixteen, the two phases to which Yeats assigned beautiful women (phase fifteen, complete subjectivity and beauty, has no representative in Yeats's system). Her "virgin cruelty"[65] comes from phase sixteen, whose women are consciously cruel and "walk like queens, and seem to carry upon their backs a quiver of arrows."[66] That suggestion of the virgin huntress Diana reinforces the connection between this phase and the queen. But Yeats's favorite queen, to whom he most often compared the lady in his lyrics, was Helen of Troy. He cites her as an example of phase fourteen, with its renunciation of responsibility. Her true mask is serenity, a quality which the queen displays in condemning her former lovers to death. Like the *Eternal Idol* of Rodin, such a woman remains unmoved by

[63] T. R. Henn reads the play in sexual terms as the ultimate male victory over the virgin cruelty of the female (*The Lonely Tower: Studies in the Poetry of W. B. Yeats*, pp. 286–88). Frank Kermode sees the swineherd as a poet maudit and the queen as the Image he seeks (*Romantic Image*, pp. 80–82). F. A. C. Wilson stresses Neoplatonic and theological elements (*W. B. Yeats and Tradition*, pp. 53–94). Finally, Helen Vendler reads the play in terms of *A Vision* but emphasizes the nature of art rather than the relation between man and woman (*Yeats's Vision and the Later Plays*, pp. 139–67). My reading is intended to supplement, not to supplant, theirs.

[64] *A Vision*, pp. 108–9.

[65] *Variorum Plays*, p. 987. Page numbers of subsequent quotations are given in parentheses within the text.

[66] *A Vision*, p. 139.

the devotion of her kneeling lover. The description of Helen in *A Vision* also applies to the queen: she "serves nothing, while alone seeming of service."[67] They are not psyche and epipsyche but rather two antinomies, alike to the "Crown of gold" and "dung of swine" of the play's first song (979).

Whereas the swineherd represents Yeats's aesthetic mask, the queen represents his erotic mask, also called the Image. She is the Image of Yeats's swineherd-mask, just as Yeats thought Venus Urania was the Image of Shelley's Athanase-mask. She is to Yeats's mature theory of love what Venus Urania was to Shelley's: the archetype of the ideally desirable. Although inappropriate to the heavenly Venus, her cruelty and egotism form part of Yeats's notion of absolute feminine desirability. She is the ideal Image, which Shelley called "unattainable." For Yeats, too, she is unattainable, at least during the lover's life.

Genuine knowledge of the beloved is as irrelevant in *A Full Moon in March* as in the earlier mask lyrics. The lady in "The Mask" maintains that "what's behind" the mask does not matter, "so there is but fire / In you, in me." Likewise, when the swineherd remarks, "The beggars of my country say that he / That sings you best shall take you for a wife," the queen corrects him: "He that best sings his passion" (980). The doctrine of the mask denies the relevance of the sympathetic imagination (whose goal is real knowledge of the beloved) and instead holds the arousal of passion, and its expression by the creative imagination, to be the sole purpose of love.

The lovers establish their final relation at the full moon. Although in "The Philosophy of Shelley's Poetry" Yeats had associated the moon with the changefulness of love, by the thirties he came to regard the lunar cycle as a symbol not of inconstant desire but of the inevitable periodicity of human relationships. The full moon thus represented the instant of maximum fulfillment of love. The swineherd knows that the queen "must be won / At a full moon in March" (981–82). Likewise, the woman of phase fourteen wanders alone "as though she consciously meditated her masterpiece that shall be at the full moon."[68] In *A Vision* Yeats describes phase fifteen, the period of full subjectivity and beauty symbolized by the full moon:

[67] Ibid., p. 133. [68] *A Vision*, p. 132.

> The *Creative Mind* [imagination] . . . has more and more confined its contemplation of actual things to those that resemble images of the mind [i.e., masks] desired by the Will. The being has selected, moulded and remoulded. . . . Now contemplation and desire, united into one, inhabit a world where every beloved image has bodily form, and every bodily form is loved. This love knows nothing of desire, for desire implies effort, and though there is still separation from the loved object, love accepts the separation as necessary to its own existence.[69]

A Full Moon in March fits all the terms of the prose passage. In a Shelleyan manner the imagination searches in the world for the woman who corresponds to the archetype in the lover's mind and then fills up the interstices—selects, molds, and remolds—until it makes her into the ideal Image. But Yeats then departs from Shelley by continuing solely according to the creative faculty rather than the sympathetic. "Contemplation and desire" are united into one because the poet has finally portrayed his mask, and the corresponding "mask as Image" in his art. He has finally united her mask, the "beloved image," with "bodily form." Since desire must cease, the play does not end until after the satisfaction of desire represented by the queen's kiss. As in the lyrics, the lovers are separated, for Yeats rejected the notion of Shelleyan union. For him love constitutes a relation between separate entities who maintain their individuation; love demands acceptance of the separation. The lovers can unite only through their masks—either through imaginative art or through the intensity of their creative imaginations in their lives.

In articulating a concept of love based solely on the creative imagination, Yeats preserved one element of his earlier, Shelleyan view—death as a symbol of the lover's completion of his quest. We saw above that Yeats noticed the same Platonic use of the star as symbol of those who find final rest and love that Shelley employed in the conclusion of *Adonais*. Yeats includes both symbols in the song of the severed head:

> I sing a song of Jack and Jill.
> Jill had murdered Jack;
> *The moon shone brightly;*
> Ran up the hill, and round the hill,

[69] Ibid., pp. 135–36.

Round the hill and back.
A full moon in March.

Jack had a hollow heart, for Jill
Had hung his heart on high;
The moon shone brightly;
Had hung his heart beyond the hill,
A-twinkle in the sky.
A full moon in March.

By inspiring her lover's imaginative love of her mask, the queen has driven him to create his own mask in his poetry and so to become eternal. Now, like Adonais, he shines "A-twinkle in the sky." The song does not complain of separation from the beloved but simply sings its own triumph, for under the full moon the lovers have been brought into a final relation by means of their masks. It is toward that relation, and not toward the Shelleyan goal of union, that Yeats's art tended after 1907.

The mature Yeats replaced Shelley's vision of the *pax amoris* with his own version of the *bellum amoris*. Sharing Shelley's frustration at love's limits, he abandoned his earlier, Shelleyan notion of similar lovers striving for union; instead, he posited the lovers' dissimilarity and sought to make their antagonism into an eternal reciprocal relation. The doctrine of the masks solved the Shelleyan dilemma by stressing creative imagination and precluding mutual, sympathetic understanding. Concomitantly, Yeats managed to suggest a possible postmortal transcendence of antinomies by continuing Shelley's use of death to symbolize erotic fulfillment. The war of the lovers becomes a ritual combat through which each creates the spiritual form so beloved to the other. Through the slit eyes of a mask, Yeats's psyche gazes forever upon his epipsyche.

7 Athens and Byzantium: History as Revelation

"Meanwhile, the need of a model of the nation, of some moral diagram, is as great as in the early nineteenth century."

—*Yeats,* Autobiography (Estrangement)

Yeats and Shelley approach history not as chroniclers but as imaginative artists. They make history into a kind of visionary poetry which not only preserves the past but, more importantly, reveals an ideal which can shape both the present and the future. Yeats classifies the historian who can "reason and compare and argue only" with "those who record and not those who reveal."[1] Shelley practices the revelatory mode of history in his essay on the Athenians, in which he emphasizes not "the history of titles" but "that perfection to which human society is impelled."[2] For him not just the philosopher but also the historian is a poet insofar as his work presents an image of the good.

Each poet embodies his ideal in a city which once formed the center of a civilization. Shelley chooses Athens and Yeats Byzantium. To a greater extent in Yeats than in Shelley, their

1 "Irish National Literature" (2), *Bookman,* 8 (August 1895): 138. Compare Shelley's distinction between a story and a poem in the *Defence.* His own attitude toward history is certainly that of the poet and not the story writer. The relevant passage, quoted in part by Yeats (see above, chapter 3, part 3) reads:

> A Poem is the very image of life expressed in its eternal truth. There is this difference between a story and a poem, that a story is a catalogue of detached facts, which have no other bond of connexion than time, place, circumstance, cause and effect; the other is the creation of actions according to the unchangeable forms of human nature, the image of all other minds. [*Shelley's Prose,* p. 281.]

Shelley adds in the next paragraph that "all the great historians, Herodotus, Plutarch, Livy, were poets."

2 "A Discourse on the Manners of the Ancient Greeks Relative to the Subject of Love," *Shelley's Prose,* p. 219.

creative imaginations shape the historical cities into icons of the highest human development, which they conceive as a unity both created by art and expressed in it. Yet Shelley's Athens represents a social ideal which depends upon nature, whereas Yeats's Byzantium (at least in his poetry) emphasizes the individual in his struggle against nature. This chapter discusses, first, the ideals of Athens and Byzantium in the thought of the two poets, and, second, the way in which Yeats's antinomial vision led him to fit his ideal city into a scheme of history quite different from Shelley's. By studying the two cities, visions of the fair, we shall be able in the next chapter to evaluate better Yeats's charge that Shelley's poetry lacked a counterbalancing vision of the foul and that his own did not.

Athens

Athens does not assume its full significance in Shelley's poetry and prose until after his establishment in Italy in 1818. Although he does mention it in his earlier writings, often with enthusiasm, Athens there lacks its later profundity and centrality. In *Alastor* Athens is merely one of the "awful ruins"—like Tyre, Jerusalem, and Babylon—passed by the poet in his wanderings.[3] Shelley early thought of the city in terms broader than those of Yeats's despised recorder of history. Even in *Queen Mab* the moral power of Athens assumes prominence: "Where Athens, Rome, and Sparta stood, / There is a moral desert now."[4] The most important of the fifteen references to the city in the poetry appears in the "Ode to Liberty," in which Shelley devotes the fifth and sixth stanzas to his vision of Athens. The fullest treatment in the prose also appears after the move to Italy, in "A Discourse on the Manners of the Ancient Greeks Relative to the Subject of Love." We shall concentrate here upon the essay and the ode.

Shelley selected the zenith of Athenian civilization as his ideal. That was the "period which intervened between the birth of Pericles and the death of Aristotle." The years from 490 to 322 B.C. were "the most memorable in the history of the world." He habitually thinks of that period in terms of the achievement it-

[3] *Works*, 1: 180. [4] *Works*, 2: 79–80.

self and its historical significance. At the beginning of the essay on the Athenians he declares that Athens was important "whether considered in itself, or with reference to the effects which it had produced upon the subsequent destinies of civilized man."[5]

Unity is the dominant characteristic of Shelley's city. He calls it "harmony," whose achievement depended upon a proper relationship to nature and an adherence to a moral and social ideal. Greek art expressed and encouraged unity with nature on the one hand and with society on the other. In contrast to the individual's transcendence of nature in Yeats's Byzantium, Shelley's Athens represents man's self-perfection within the natural and social order.

In his essay on the Athenians Shelley at once announces his intention to examine "the combination of moral and political circumstances which produced so unparalleled a progress during that period in literature and the arts."[6] That statement indicates not simple determinism but rather Shelley's conception of an organic society in which each aspect informs the others. He finds harmony to be the characteristic quality of Athenian civilization and in the remainder of the essay elucidates the kind of harmony achieved by the Greeks in art and morality.

Shelley devotes more attention to the achievement of harmony in poetry than in the other arts. He recognizes that "all the inventive arts maintain, as it were, a sympathetic connection between each other" and even concedes that Greek poetry does not maintain "so disproportionate a rank" with subsequent poetry as the other arts do with later developments.[7] Yet, being a poet himself, his main interest is in Greek poetry, a subject he was to treat in greater detail in the *Defence*.

Comparing Homer with Shakespeare, Dante, and Petrarch, Shelley finds that, whatever the individual superiority of the later poets, Homer occupies a generally higher place. That is because the harmony of his poetry embodies that of his society. Although Shakespeare's "variety and comprehension" make him the "greatest individual mind" of which we have record, Homer excels him in "the truth, the harmony, the sustained grandeur, the satisfying completeness of his images." Homer, though of

[5] *Shelley's Prose*, p. 217. [6] Ibid. [7] Ibid.

course much earlier than the Athenian city-state, is an individual example of the general superiority of Greek culture. "How superior," he exclaims, "was the spirit and system of their poetry to that of any other period!" All the poetry of these two centuries is "as harmonious and perfect as possible."[8] These reflections lead Shelley back to the "moral and political circumstances" to which he earlier attributed the excellence of Greek art.

He estimates the "worth" of a social system by two criteria—intellect and happiness—and maintains that a "summary idea may be formed of the worth of any political and religious system by observing the comparative degree of happiness and of intellect produced under its influences."[9] Greek art provides a measurement of intellectual accomplishment; Greek social structure and morality offer a measurement of the "degree of happiness." The insistence upon both criteria reflects Shelley's movement during this period away from Godwin and utilitarianism and toward that concept of liberty which Yeats found identical with Intellectual Beauty.

Although Yeats rejected interpretations of Shelley which emphasized Godwinism, he had earlier detected the importance of Godwin to Shelley's thought. Nowhere does Godwin assume greater importance for the comparison of Shelley and Yeats than in their attitudes toward history. In 1892 Yeats wrote to John O'Leary:

> The mystical life is the centre of all that I do and all that I think and all that I write. It holds to my work the same relation that the philosophy of Godwin held to the work of Shelley and I have always considered myself a voice of what I believe to be a greater renaissance—the revolt of the soul against the intellect—now beginning in the world.[10]

Yeats rightly perceives a recurrent insistence in Shelley upon such utilitarian notions as the production of the greatest happiness for the greatest number. In his view of history Shelley does emphasize philosophy and the intellect, whereas Yeats by his own admission prefers mysticism and the soul.

The Greeks achieved the harmony which underlies art and happiness by their attention to morals, which Shelley credits them

[8] Ibid., pp. 217–18. [9] Ibid., p. 218. [10] *Yeats's Letters*, p. 211.

with founding as a philosophical discipline. They initiated the "science of morals, or the voluntary conduct of men in relation to themselves or others."[11] Although condemning "personal slavery and the inferiority of women," Shelley approves of the other aspects and institutions of Athenian society. He praises the Greeks for establishing a morality based upon love and a political system based upon liberty.

In the essay on the Athenians Shelley defines love as "the universal thirst for a communion not merely of the senses, but of our whole nature."[12] Although their notions of the inferiority of women precluded the Greeks from finding that love in personal relationships that were not homosexual, they extended the concept (in Shelley's view) to the whole of society. In the *Defence* Shelley himself considers love "the great secret of morals." That love manifests itself in politics as democracy. In *The Revolt of Islam* the tyrant bribes dishonest judges to proclaim that "glorious Athens in her splendour fell, / Because her sons were free."[13] This is, of course, the opposite of Shelley's own belief that liberty caused the rise, not the fall, of Athens. Only the "moral freedom and refinement of the people" could lead to their choosing the wisest men as leaders.[14]

The final component of Greek harmony is unity with nature. Shelley develops the point at length in a letter to Peacock describing his visit to Pompeii in January 1819. Enigmatically declaring that Pompeii was "a Greek city,"[15] Shelley says that its inhabitants "lived in harmony with nature." He finds the bond with nature to underlie all Greek harmony and in effect supplements his earlier essay when he tells his friend:

> I now understand why the Greeks were such great Poets, & above all I can account, it seems to me, for the harmony the

[11] *Shelley's Prose*, p. 218. [12] Ibid., p. 220.
[13] *Works*, 1: 368. [14] *Shelley's Prose*, p. 336.
[15] Pompeii was not, strictly speaking, a Greek city but instead belonged, successively, to the Oscans, Etruscans and Pelasgians, Samnites, and Romans. Shelley may be referring to the Hellenistic architecture which became dominant in Pompeii in the third and second centuries B.C., during which the Foro Triangolare, for example, was rebuilt on the model of a Greek gymnasium to serve as a cultural center for the town. Shelley may also be remembering the Greek legend of the founding of both Pompeii and nearby Herculaneum by Hercules. In any case, his discussion of art and architecture at Pompeii as Greek seems valid.

> unity the perfection the uniform excellence of all their works of art. They lived in a perpetual commerce with external nature and nourished themselves upon the spirit of its forms.[16]

The artist can reach a beauty which in some sense transcends nature not by rejecting the natural but by being supremely faithful to it in his work. Shelley writes that the panels in a chapel at Pompeii "are Egyptian subjects executed by a Greek artist who has harmonized all the *un*natural extravagance of their original conception into the *super*natural loveliness of his country's genius."[17] In contrast to Yeats's Byzantium, which is "out of nature," Shelley's Athens exists in harmonious relationship with nature.

"What the Greeks were, was a reality, not a promise," declared Shelley.[18] Although he makes Athens into a visionary ideal in the "Ode to Liberty," Shelley elsewhere is far more historically accurate than Yeats. His ideal actually existed within the course of history and did not have to be created primarily out of the artist's imagination. "Of no other epoch in the history of our species," he wrote in the *Defence*, "have we records and fragments stamped so visibly with the image of the divinity in man."[19] The reality of the Greek achievement did not prevent Shelley from recognizing "how far the most admirable community ever formed was removed from that perfection to which human society is impelled."[20]

In his poetry Shelley makes Athens into a visionary ideal beyond the actual city described in the prose. The transfiguration accords with his definition of the workings of the imagination. He describes love in the Athenian essay in this way: "the mind . . . fills up the interstices of the imperfect image in the same manner that the imagination molds and completes." Likewise, in the letter to Peacock he says that the "interstices" of Greek columns "were portals as it were to admit the spirit of beauty."[21] In the "Ode to Liberty" Shelley's poetic imagination has allowed his mind to fill up the interstices of the admirable yet still imperfect city he describes in his prose. He writes:

[16] *Shelley's Letters,* 2: 73–74. [17] Ibid., 2: 73. Italics Shelley's.
[18] *Shelley's Prose,* p. 219. [19] Ibid., p. 283.
[20] Ibid., p. 219. [21] Ibid., p. 220.

Athens arose: a city such as vision
  Builds from the purple crags and silver towers
Of battlemented cloud, as in derision
  Of kingliest masonry: the ocean-floors
Pave it; the evening sky pavilions it;
    Its portals are inhabited
    By thunder-zoned winds, each head
Within its cloudy wings with sun-fire garlanded,—
  A divine work: Athens, diviner yet,
    Gleamed with its crest of columns, on the will
  Of man, as on a mount of diamonds, set;
    For thou wert, and thine all-creative skill
Peopled, with forms that mock the eternal dead
  In marble immortality, that hill
  Which was thine earliest throne and latest oracle.[22]

The stanza contains three major sections—the vision of a city (1–8), the superiority of Athens to the vision (9–11), and immortality through artistic expression (12–15). The first eight lines present not a description of Athens but an extended metaphor for it. Athens is not a city that vision has built; it is a city "such as" vision builds. Shelley's vision finds its building materials in nature: it makes the city out of clouds, the paving from "ocean floors," and the covering from the sky. The winds (or spirits) inhabit it. Yeats, who read the poem in terms of Intellectual Beauty, must have delighted in the conjunction of towers and water in the second and fourth lines, respectively. The metaphor closes with Shelley's characteristic notion of secular divinity: the envisioned city is a "divine work."

Divine though the vision is, Athens was "diviner yet." The remainder of the stanza propounds the reasons for the superiority of Athens: man and art. The imagery relates the city to nature and suggests the underlying harmony of the whole. Athens surpasses the vision because it rests on the will of man, for which the hardest substance in nature—diamond—is a fit analogy. He does not reject nature but uses it as the aptest source of metaphor for the revelation of secular divinity, much as the eighteenth-century Deists and others used it as a metaphor for the revelation of re-

[22] *Works,* 2: 308 (stanza 5). Shelley likens Athens to a city vision builds out of clouds, the same material to which he compares the imaginative process in the essay on the Athenians (*Shelley's Prose,* p. 220).

ligious divinity. As Shelley told Peacock, the Greek ideal was supernatural, not unnatural.

Finally, he returns, as he always does when treating the Athenians, to art. Here he mentions only sculpture ("marble immortality"), although his view holds true for the other arts as well. The marble forms, presumably those of the Parthenon, "mock" the eternal dead through their own eternal life. The antithesis is slightly confusing: the "eternal dead" are presumably the makers of the statues. Ordinarily, the immortality of their works would constitute their triumph and enable them to mock eternal death. Shelley, however, makes the forms mock the mortality of their own makers. His skepticism about the afterlife prevents him from allowing the sculptors of his Athens to achieve the immortality he later accorded to Adonais. His ideal city is thus "peopled" not with human beings but with art works, the same monuments of unaging intellect which inhabit Yeats's holy city.

Byzantium

Yeats's antinomial vision did not blind him to the ideal of Intellect; on the contrary, his antinomial lens sharpened the contrast between the ideal and the actual. He could, accordingly, make Byzantium into a perfect city of Intellect. He resisted not Intellect but rather an Intellectual vision which would carry him always upward out of life rather than downward upon it. He no longer distorted the actual in order to see the Intellectual manifest in it, but instead saw clearly the eternal opposition between the two orders. Only by rejecting any suggestion of one order's immanence in the other could he see either order properly. Thus, he set up Byzantium in opposition to the natural world of generation, even while dragging human fury and mire into his most visionary poems. After examining his concept of the ideal here, we shall examine in the concluding chapter his effort to get the actual into his work more clearly than he thought that Shelley had.

What are the factual characteristics of Yeats's city in comparison with Shelley's? Geographically, he located it a little over three hundred miles northeast of Athens, in Byzantium. Chronologically, he chose a period almost a millenium later than the age of Pericles, the reign of Justinian in the sixth century A.D. Politically, he preferred an aristocratic empire to a democracy. Religiously, he selected a Christian rather than a pagan ideal. Byzantium pervades his mature thought even more thoroughly than Athens did Shelley's. He developed the icon most fully in the "Dove or Swan" section of *A Vision* (completed at Capri in February 1925, and revised only slightly for the 1937 edition) and in the two poems "Sailing to Byzantium" (1926–27) and "Byzantium" (1930). In organizing history into a geometric pattern he allowed his imagination greater freedom than Shelley had, and, while affirming unity and art, he emphasized the individual rather than the social and the artificial rather than the natural.

Yeats admired Greece more than Shelley admired Byzantium. Thinking of more recent periods than the reign of Justinian, Shelley treated Byzantium as the symbol of domestic tyranny in *The Revolt of Islam* and as the foreign oppressor of Greece in *Hellas*. Although Yeats saw different values in Greek civilization than Shelley did, he deliberately chose a Byzantine era when he could legitimately think of the city as partly Greek. Early drafts of "Sailing to Byzantium" associate the city with the same Phidian sculpture[23] which Yeats later praised in "The Statues," with its disciplined form and measurement.

Yeats did reject the Athenian achievements which most attracted his predecessor: what Shelley called their "models of ideal truth and beauty."[24] Yeats instead admired Oedipus, whom he associated with the concrete and earthly, and saw him "altogether separated from Plato's Athens, from all that talk of the Good and the One, from all that cabinet of perfection."[25] Yeats objected not so much to Plato's talking of the Good and the One, as to his talking *only* of them, to the exclusion of the evil and the many—in short, to Plato's Intellectual vision. Justinian's clos-

[23] See Curtis Bradford's commentary and invaluable transcription of the early drafts of both Byzantium poems, "Yeats's Byzantium Poems: A Study of Their Development," which originally appeared in *PMLA*, 75 (March 1960): 110–25, and has been reprinted with revisions in *Yeats: A Collection of Critical Essays*, ed. John Unterecker, pp. 93–130. The reference to Phidias is on p. 100 of the revised version, hereafter cited as Bradford. For additional information on manuscript versions see Jon Stallworthy, *Between the Lines: Yeats's Poetry in the Making*, pp. 87–136.

[24] *Shelley's Prose*, p. 217. [25] *A Vision*, p. 28.

ing of the Academy thus assumes more than its apparently casual significance in Yeats's description of Byzantium. He stood ready to admire the abstract discipline of Greek civilization but not its morality and Platonic vision of perfection.

Yeats's continuing belief in the opposition between the worlds of Intellect and generation led him to a view of history more frankly visionary than Shelley's. Whereas the earlier poet had asserted that the historians Herodotus, Plutarch, and Livy were visionary poets, the self-proclaimed last romantic announced that visionaries like Swedenborg and Blake were really historians who chronicled the history of the soul. For Yeats the history of the soul was its descent from the Intellectual down into generation and then back to the Intellectual again. He sought in history both a stimulus to his visionary imagination and the raw material for its operation. In the dedication to the first edition of *A Vision* he explained:

> I had a practical object. I wished for a system of thought that would leave my imagination free to create as it chose and yet make all that it created, or could create, part of the one history, and that the soul's. The Greeks certainly had such a system, and Dante . . . and I think no man since. . . . What I have found is indeed nothing new, for I will show presently that Swedenborg and Blake and many before them knew that all things had their gyres; but Swedenborg and Blake preferred to explain them figuratively, and so I am the first to substitute for Biblical or mythological figures, historical movements and actual men and women.[26]

Yeats designed his "system" to embrace all human experience, of which history is the record, in order to free the creative power of his imagination. Although in poems like "Easter, 1916" he fulfills the Shelleyan duty of perceiving and expressing the spiritual achievement of "actual men and women," in the Byzantine poems he as much creates the ideal as perceives it. Like Blake, he expresses an imaginative spiritual system of his own making, but unlike Blake he substitutes "historical movements" and "actual" persons for mythological and biblical ones. The difference between Shelley and Yeats as historians is that Shelley perceives and elevates an actual historical event, whereas Yeats recreates the event in terms of his own system.

[26] *A Vision* (1925), pp. xi–xii.

Like Shelley, Yeats valued the unity of life in his idealized city. He called it "Unity of Being" in the individual and "Unity of Culture" in the society, and used Unity of Being synonymously with Shelley's term, harmony.[27] Yeats described Byzantine unity in a famous passage from *A Vision:*

> I think if I could be given a month of Antiquity and leave to spend it where I chose, I would spend it in Byzantium a little before Justinian opened St. Sophia and closed the Academy of Plato. I think I could find in some little wine-shop some philosophical worker in mosaic who could answer all my questions, the supernatural descending nearer to him than to Plotinus even, for the pride of his delicate skill would make what was an instrument of power to princes and clerics, a murderous madness in the mob, show as a lovely flexible presence like that of a perfect human body.
>
> I think that in early Byzantium, maybe never before or since in recorded history, religious, aesthetic and practical life were one, that architect and artificers—though not, it may be, poets . . . —spoke to the multitude and the few alike.[28]

Byzantium's union of "religious, aesthetic and practical" life enabled Yeats to resolve his earlier doubts about Shelley while adhering to an ideal in some ways Shelleyan. In the nineties he had eschewed "the multitude" and sought only "the few" for his audience. Following Hallam, he associated that position with Shelley. His new ideal allowed him to speak both to the multitude and to the few, and thus to escape from the impasse to which his earlier admiration for Shelley had led.

In his poetry Yeats, like Shelley, transformed his city into an ideal beyond that of the prose works. Specifically, he made Byzantium into a city of Intellect which, like the Intellectual Beauty he had associated with Shelley in the nineties, lies beyond mutability. In a cancelled passage from a BBC reading of his poetry he wrote:

> Now I am trying to write about the state of my soul, for it is right for an old man to make his soul, and some of my thoughts on that subject I have put into a poem called "Sailing to Byzantium." . . . Byzantium was the center of European civilization and the source of its spiritual philosophy, so I symbolize the search for the spiritual life by a journey to that city.[29]

[27] *A Vision*, p. 214. [28] Ibid., p. 279. [29] Bradford, p. 95.

The opening stanza of "Sailing to Byzantium" announces the rejection of the natural world of generation ("Whatever is begotten, born, and dies") for the Intellectual world of Byzantium, with its unaging monuments. The natural world is "no country for old men," since the business of old men is to make their souls. That was the business of Yeats even as a young man, for in 1897 he wrote of the value of Intellectual art: "In our time we are agreed that we 'make our souls' out of some one of the great poets of ancient times, or out of Shelley [and others]."[30] In the final stanza of the poem the poet speaks of his escape from nature into art:

> Once out of nature I shall never take
> My bodily form from any natural thing,
> But such a form as Grecian goldsmiths make
> Of hammered gold and gold enamelling.[31]

Unlike Shelley's Athenians, who achieve artistic supremacy by harmony with nature, Yeats's Byzantines do so by escaping from nature. An earlier draft makes the contrast between nature and Byzantium more emphatic: "I fly from nature to Byzantium."[32] Representing the Intellectual against the generative, Byzantium also champions artifice against nature. Even eternity, since it exists apart from generation, becomes an "artifice." "I use it," said Yeats of the golden bird, "as a symbol of the intellectual joy of eternity, as contrasted with the instinctive joy of human life."[33]

Art for Yeats was always beyond nature, and that premise is nowhere more operative than in the Byzantium poems. As early as 1901 he quoted what became one of his favorite maxims, Goethe's remark that "art is art because it is not nature."[34] For Yeats art was "unnatural" not just in its flawlessness and changelessness, but in its real participation in the eternal instead of the temporal: its images, as Shelley perhaps less literally noted in the *Defence*, participate in the life of truth. The expression of that idea in poetry is difficult, for the poet's images come from nature but in fact represent nature's antagonist, eternity. In "Sailing to Byzantium" Yeats wants to take his bodily form not from "any natural thing" but from a Grecian goldsmith's artifact, which is,

[30] *E & I*, p. 111. [31] *Variorum Poems*, p. 408. [32] Bradford, p. 99.
[33] Bradford, p. 95. [34] *E & I*, p. 101.

however, an artificer's imitation of something natural, though superior to it in being both flawless and changeless.

Yeats recognized the ambiguity, or the inconsistency, of his earlier poem by writing "Byzantium" as a gloss on it. Sturge Moore raised objections similar to ours, and Yeats conceded their validity. He told Moore: "The poem originates from a criticism of yours. You objected to the last verse of *Sailing to Byzantium* because a bird made by a goldsmith was just as natural as anything else. That showed me that the idea needed further exposition."[35]

Yeats provides the further exposition in the third stanza of "Byzantium,"[36] where he elaborates the distinction between a golden and a natural bird. The bird is now more than nature because it is art, and more than a mere handiwork because it is revelatory rather than mimetic art: "more miracle than bird or handiwork." Its "changeless metal" indicates its status in the eternity of Byzantium and its consequent superiority to "common bird or petal." Yeats finds the fittest analogue not in nature but in "the cocks of Hades," deliberately supernatural symbols which announce rebirth into eternity and which Yeats later associated with Shelley's Witch of Atlas in the first quatrain of "Under Ben Bulben." He insists that the golden bird can represent the repudiation of nature and, hence, of "all complexities of mire and blood." To adapt Goethe's maxim, the bird is art because it is not nature.

The bird speaks in the same language with which Hassan described Ahasuerus's visionary ability in *Hellas*. Just as the bird sings

> Of what is past, or passing, or to come,

so, too, did Ahasuerus speak

> The Present, and the Past, and the To-come.

An earlier draft of "Sailing to Byzantium" preserves the parallel to *Hellas* even more strongly:

> Of present past and future to come.[37]

[35] *W. B. Yeats and T. Sturge Moore: Their Correspondence, 1901–1937*, ed. Ursula Bridge, p. 164.

[36] *Variorum Poems*, pp. 497–98.

[37] See *Hellas*, line 148, and Bradford, p. 102.

The bird and Ahasuerus are equally out of nature, for both are Yeatsian images of the antiself. Their wisdom is irreconcilable with generation, and comes only to those who have put off their normal selves and united with the mask of the antiself, a union symbolized by death. In addition, while the sages standing in the holy fire clearly refer to the mosaics of the Hagia Sophia, Yeats may have associated them with Shelley's sage as well. Shelley not only made Ahasuerus an Asiatic sage but located his cavern specifically in the Sea of Marmora, by Byzantium on the northwest coast of Turkey. But whether or not Yeats associated Ahasuerus with the Byzantine sages, he clearly associated him with the visionary golden bird, as the borrowed line shows.

Paradoxically, Yeats's Shelleyan metaphor for perfection, death, leads him away from Shelley's affirmation of life. Shelley sees Athens as the perfection of earthly life. Yeats sees Byzantium as the eternal abode of the soul after its death to earth and generation. The early drafts of "Sailing to Byzantium" show that Yeats was thinking of the journey of "souls to paradise," and the later "Byzantium" treats death and rebirth more specifically. The poem plays on the same Neoplatonic doctrines we examined in chapter 4, and Yeats still uses water, here the sea, to symbolize generation. Byzantium is more a Yeatsian redaction of *Adonais* than of the "Ode to Liberty," although he dispenses with what he called "all that talk of the Good and the One." Although for Shelley (as the letter about Pompeii shows) the supernatural was not unnatural, for Yeats it was, and he found in death an appropriate symbol of the antithesis.

Yeats preserved some of the religious suggestiveness of Byzantium, for he had learned from studying Shelley that the absence of the miraculous could vitiate the force of Intellectual symbolism. Byzantium itself was the center not only of the Eastern Roman Empire but also of the Greek Orthodox church. In "Sailing to Byzantium" the speaker (whom in the early drafts Yeats described as "a poet of the Middle Ages") beseeches the "sages standing in God's holy fire" to assist his "soul." Although Yeats reduced the religious emphasis of the early drafts by changing "saints" to "sages" and by eliminating an entire stanza about an infant God asleep on his mother's lap, he kept enough of the original conception to infuse his city with more religious symbolism than Shelley's Athens. Earlier, he had criticized Shelley for restricting the wide appeal of Prince Athanase through making him too secular: "I would have had Shelley a sectary that his revelation might display the only sufficient evidence of religion, miracle . . . there are many who are not moved as they would be by that solitary light burning in the tower of Prince Athanase, because it has not entered into men's prayers nor lighted any through the sacred dark of religious contemplation."[38] Yeats made certain that the same charge could not be made against the fires of his Byzantium.

Although he insists on both unity and art, Yeats differs from Shelley not only about nature but also about society. The social unity ascribed to Byzantium in *A Vision* does not carry over into the poetry. The poems treat the relationship of the individual soul to the holy city, not the interrelationship of its inhabitants. Whereas Shelley speaks of "they," Yeats speaks of "I." Although the dolphins carry "spirit after spirit" to the city, Yeats considers only the individual relation of each to Byzantium and to generation, and not their social relation to each other. The poems neglect the "moral and political circumstances" so important to Shelley.

Whereas Shelley postulates an ideal persisting through a certain span of time. Yeats emphasizes the continuous creation of the ideal by the artist. His holy city exists—or at least can be represented—not by itself but only in relation to "sensual music" and the "fury and the mire." In creating Byzantium Yeats did not reject the unholy rag-and-bone shop of the heart, for he defined the ideal city in terms of normal imperfections. The "unpurged images of day" may "recede" from the city but they remain within the framework of the poem. Even here Yeats maintains that fair needs foul. The "golden smithies" of the emperor forge perfection out of the very mire which their monuments mock. Like Yeats, they create Byzantium out of the "dolphin-torn, that gong-tormented sea" of life.

Athenian harmony and Byzantine unity both depend upon art, but they do so in different ways. For Shelley, art expresses a natural and social ideal which can be realized on earth; for Yeats,

[38] *E & I*, p. 294.

art expresses an individual, antinatural ideal which can never become wholly incarnate in the world of generation. Creating his ideal more out of his own imagination than out of actual events, and keeping antinomies always distinct, Yeats saw history in terms radically different from those of his predecessor. That difference forms our next subject.

Time's Cyclic Poem

In the *Defence* Shelley called the institutions of the Roman republic "episodes of that cyclic poem written by Time upon the memories of men."[39] Both Shelley and Yeats saw history as cyclical, but whereas Shelley measured the cycles by an ideal which history could at certain periods incarnate, Yeats measured them by an ideal never fully realizable in the world of generation. Yeats stood indebted to his predecessor's theory of history not as speculative thinker but as practicing poet, and he echoed Shelley's verse even while presenting his own very different historical system. We can understand the relation between the two first by examining the place they allotted to Athens and Byzantium in the cyclic poem of time, and then by comparing specific passages from Shelley with Yeats's reworking of them to fit his own antinomial vision.

Shelley relates Athens to subsequent history in the sixth stanza of the "Ode to Liberty," in which, immediately after his vision of the city in its splendor, he writes:

Within the surface of Time's fleeting river
  Its wrinkled image lies, as then it lay
Immovably unquiet, and for ever
  It trembles, but it cannot pass away!
The voices of thy bards and sages thunder
    With an earth-awakening blast
    Through caverns of the past:
(Religion veils her eyes; Oppression shrinks aghast:)
    A winged sound of joy, and love, and wonder,
    Which soars where Expectation never flew,
  Rendering the veil of space and time asunder!
    One ocean feeds the clouds, and streams, and dew;
One Sun illumines Heaven; one Spirit vast
  With life and love makes chaos ever new,
  As Athens doth the world with thy delight renew.[40]

[39] *Shelley's Prose*, p. 287. [40] *Works*, 2: 308.

The stanza has a tripartite structure in which the first four lines, the middle seven, and the final four each develop a central idea and a central image. In the first four lines we discover that the image of Athens which we see is distorted by the river of time; yet, however wrinkled the image is, we can still perceive something of the outline. Time can only distort Athens, not erase it. The next seven lines indicate the means by which we perceive the city and by which it affects subsequent history—the voices of its "bards and sages." Their voices rend asunder that veil of time and space which otherwise would obscure Athens from our view (in terms of the earlier metaphor, they calm the convulsed waters of time). Unlike Yeats's "sages standing in God's holy fire," Shelley's figures are secular and even anti-religious; furthermore, they purify not the individual soul but the temporal social order, which has been corrupted by religion and oppression.

The concluding section expands upon the earlier two by making Athens the source of the earth's renewal with the delight of liberty. The verb "renew" implies a cyclical rise and fall in history; but unlike Yeats's cycles, Shelley's have a goal. Shelley early abandoned the naïve optimism which led him to declare in 1812 that "we are in a continually progressive state of improvement,"[41] and he became painfully aware that mankind could move away from an ideal as well as toward one. Nevertheless, by measuring events according to the standard of Athens, Shelley was able to impose a pattern of progress and regression upon history which rendered it more meaningful than Yeats's conception of endlessly repeating gyres.

For Shelley approval of the Greek ideal meant the rejection of other civilizations, particularly those which replaced Greece in European history. The Roman Empire, for example, was a "vast and successful scheme for the enslaving [of] the most civilized portion of mankind."[42] That enslavement derived from the Roman destruction of the Greek power of beauty, which led to disaster both politically and artistically. Shelley brings the same charges against Christianity. Christianity did more than destroy "the graceful religion of the Greeks"; more importantly, "It

[41] *Shelley's Prose*, p. 230. [42] Ibid.

seems to have been one of the first effects of the Christian religion to destroy the power of producing beauty in art."[43] (As his admiration for Dante, Tasso, Raphael, Spenser, and others shows, Shelley does not mean to condemn all Christian art, but only early medieval art, which to him presented pernicious doctrine gracelessly.) History might contain many such defeats for mankind, but there was a goal—the "harmony" of art, nature, and society—and Athens represented that goal.

Yeats maintains no such exclusiveness about his ideal. "I, upon the other hand, must think all civilisations equal at their best," he declares.[44] Yeats directs his criticism against the naïvely optimistic historian who conceives of every age as "in something or other an advance" from the previous one. Shelley certainly does not fit such a classification, nor does Yeats place him there. Yet in championing one standard of historical evaluation and one particular ideal, Shelley represents a position equally distant from both Yeats and the naïve historian. Yeats's elaborate theories about historical gyres and cones lead to an acceptance of diversity in social systems and spiritual ideals. His goals are Unity of Being and Unity of Culture, which depend more on the stage of development of a particular individual or society than upon the actual nature of the society itself. Byzantium represents a particularly clear and attractive form of the ideal, but—unlike Shelly's Athens—it is only one such form.

The crucial stage of a civilization's development is for Yeats phase fifteen, the period of balance between its subjective and objective components. In terms of the historical cones, that phase represents the intersection of the antithetical (subjective) cone with the primary (objective) one. One such point in Western history occurs at A.D. 560, the approximate date of Yeats's Byzantium. Yeats remained unsure of the exact meaning of the gyres and his freedom to manipulate them but did state that "If I were left to myself I would make Phase 15 coincide with Justinian's reign, that great age of building in which one may conclude that Byzantine art was perfected."[45]

The equipoise between subjective and objective led to a kind

[43] *Shelley's Letters*, 2: 230, 360. [44] *A Vision*, p. 206. [45] Ibid., p. 281.

of apotheosis for which Yeats used eternity (which he had early associated with Shelley) as a symbol. He speaks of "that eternal instant where the antinomy is resolved."[46] He also mentions eternity in discussing another apotheosis—that of *Prometheus Unbound*. There he associates Demogorgon with "the Thirteenth Cycle or *Thirteenth Cone*," which has the power to "deliver us from the twelve cycles of time and space." The moment when eternity is achieved, also called the "phaseless" or "Thirteenth" sphere, delivers us from the otherwise endless cycles of history. Yeats speculates, "When Shelley's Demogorgon—eternity—comes from the center of the earth it may so come because Shelley substituted the earth for such a sphere."[47] Byzantium is one, but only one, symbol for such a moment.

The location of his ideal outside the "cycles of time and space" impelled Yeats to reject Shelleyan notions, or even Shelleyan hopes, of earthly regeneration. In contrast to Athens, which locates an ideal in a definite nexus of time and space, Byzantium represents only the conditions which make each man's individual realization of the ideal possible. Yeats's ideal itself does not exist in time and space and, accordingly, is symbolized by eternity. Terrestrial events are for him only a record of generation, which is without significance, and history thus has meaning only insofar as it can be made to show the Intellectual imperfectly mirrored in the generative.

In the opening song of *The Resurrection* Yeats parodies Shelley's vision of earthly regeneration in the final chorus of *Hellas*. The similarity of diction in the two passages has become a commonplace in Yeats scholarship, but their exact relation has not been adequately examined. Both passages present the end of one civilization and the coming of a new age. Shelley writes:

> A loftier Argo cleaves the main,
> Fraught with a later prize;
> Another Orpheus sings again . . .
> Oh, write no more the tale of Troy.[48]

[46] Ibid., p. 214.

[47] Ibid., pp. 210–11. See act 3, scene 1, in which Demogorgon describes himself as "Eternity. Demand no direr name" (*Works*, 2: 228).

[48] *Works*, 3: 53.

Yeats uses similar terms:

> Another Troy must rise and set,
> Another lineage feed the crow,
> Another Argo's painted prow
> Drive to a flashier bauble yet.[49]

Both poets envision a future age in which events of ancient Greece repeat themselves. They emphasize the quest of Jason and the Argonauts for the Golden Fleece. The future becomes a repetition of the events of the past. Yet, despite the similarity in phrasing, the differences between the two passages strike the reader more forcefully than the similarities. While preserving the basic metaphor of the Argo, Yeats has given it a new diction, tone, and context, and hence a new meaning.

Shelley's passage appears in the final, visionary song of the chorus in *Hellas*. Although the Turks, aided by the English, have temporarily defeated the Greeks, the chorus hymns the eventual triumph of the Greek cause, liberty. They celebrate a new Golden Age, much like that of the fourth act of *Prometheus Unbound*. "The world's great age begins anew," declares the first line of the hymn. Shelley characteristically links the great age with his favorite ideal: the "brighter Hellas" of the seventh line becomes "Another Athens" three stanzas later. A consciously elevated diction accompanies the eulogistic tone: a "loftier" Argo "cleaves the main," "fraught" with the prize. This Argo will be even greater than its predecessor. Shelley introduces a qualification similar to the warning at the close of *Prometheus Unbound;* "hate and death" may return at any time. But he urges the reader to "drain not to its dregs the urn / Of bitter prophecy" and to rest content on the prospect of general renewal.

Yeats's song appears in a radically different context—it opens a play about the resurrection of Christ. He reprinted the poem separately as the first of the "Two Songs From a Play" in *The Tower* (1928). Even the limited context of the rest of the poem indicates how far Yeats's Argo is from Shelley's. The poet includes the dying civilization (Greece and its Dionysian religion)

[49] *Variorum Plays,* p. 903. Shelley and Yeats both build upon Virgil's earlier treatment of the new Argo in his fourth eclogue.

as well as the Roman Empire (now at its zenith but soon to decay) and the birth of the new order (Christianity). The endless repetition demanded by the gyres of history undermines the significance of the new Argo. For Yeats, repetition of classical antiquity means not the coming of a new Golden Age but the repetition of the same imperfections. The Golden Fleece implicitly becomes a mere bauble, and the goal of the new Argonauts "a flashier bauble yet." Whereas Shelley fears the possible return of death, Yeats includes "feed the crow" as an integral part of the new cycle. His bitterness encompasses the entire pattern of history. The lyricism of "And then did all the Muses sing / Of Magnus Annus at the spring" succumbs to the undercutting irony of "As though God's death were but a play." (Yeats in fact does make God's death the subject of his play.) For him man can never incarnate the ideal within actual history, which becomes an endless record of the travail of generation. Compared to the history of the soul's journey from the Intellectual through generation and back to the Intellectual, the events of generation become meaningless, and their repetition a source of bitterness. Antinomially, history is bunk.

The difference between the two views of history includes not only the coming order but also the moment of the transformation itself. Yeats early associated *Prometheus Unbound* with a final battle which would usher in the coming transformation of the world. In his first essay on Shelley he wrote:

> I have re-read his *Prometheus Unbound* for the first time for many years, in the woods of Drim-na-Rod, among the Echtge hills, and sometimes I have looked towards Slieve ná nOg where the country people say the last battle of the world shall be fought till the third day, when a priest shall lift a chalice, and the thousand years of peace begin. And I think this mysterious song utters a faith as simple and as ancient as the faith of those country people, in a form suited to a new age.[50]

By the time of the composition of "The Second Coming" Yeats no longer believed that the terror of a last battle would herald "the world's great age" of *Hellas* or of the fourth act of *Prometheus Unbound*. The last battle now inaugurates not the thousand years of peace but rather the millennium of the Antichrist. Ap-

[50] *E & I*, pp. 77–78.

propriately, Yeats's poem echoes the words of the last Fury, who represents Shelley's Anti-Prometheus, Jupiter. The Fury tells Prometheus:

> *In each human heart terror survives*
> The ravin it has gorged: the loftiest fear
> All that they would disdain to think were true:
> Hypocrisy and custom make their minds
> The fanes of many a worship, now outworn.
> They dare not devise good for man's estate,
> And yet they know not that they do not dare.
> *The good want power*, but to weep barren tears.
> *The powerful goodness want:* worse need for them.
> The wise want love; and those who love want wisdom;
> *And all best things are thus confused to ill.*
> Many are strong and rich, and would be just,
> But live among their suffering fellow-men
> As if none felt: they know not what they do.[51]
> [Italics mine]

Yeats describes the present evil which precedes a coming apocalypse in these terms:

> Things fall apart; the centre cannot hold;
> Mere anarchy is loosed upon the world,
> The blood-dimmed tide is loosed, and everywhere
> The ceremony of innocence is drowned;
> The best lack all conviction, while the worst
> Are full of passionate intensity.[52]

Shelley and Yeats include both the abstract and the human within their panoramas. In Shelley the "best things are thus confused to ill," and in Yeats "Things fall apart." Each poet refuses to remain with such abstract statements and sketches their meaning for human society. The effect is the same: the best men are reduced to inaction and their inferiors rule. Although Yeats substitutes the more Nietzschean adjectives "best" and "worst" for Shelley's more moral "good," the lines carry the same general import.

As in the Argo passages, the difference between Yeats's lines and Shelley's lies not in the basic action but in its context and in the

[51] *Works,* 2: 198–99.

[52] *Variorum Poems,* p. 402. Donald Weeks has explored Yeats's persistent association of *Prometheus Unbound* with the idea of a second coming in "Image and Idea in Yeats' *The Second Coming,*" pp. 281–92.

poet's attitude toward it. In both poems the evil already existing prefigures a possible triumph of demonic forces. Yet Shelley recoils in horror from that prospect, whereas Yeats apparently exults in its imminence. Shelley's belief in the ultimate origin of evil in the perverted will of man enables him to replace the Fury's vision with the paradise effected by the purification of Prometheus. Yeats's belief in the inevitability of the historic gyres precludes transformation of the vision; the new order must and will come, independently of human will. Furthermore, Shelley's belief in human will leads him to concentrate upon human events: thirteen of the fourteen lines concern not impersonal "things" but men. Yeats reverses that emphasis and reduces the lines dealing with mankind to two in order to emphasize the impersonality of the forces at work. Likewise, in "Leda and the Swan," even if Leda does take on Zeus's knowledge with his power, she does so only for an instant.

The poets' attitudes toward order shape their attitudes toward the coming disruption. Both view order as central to civilization. In his prose Shelley repeatedly insists on the "radical reform of institutions" without the "utter overthrow" that leads to "anarchy."[53] Although Yeats endows civilizations with wills of their own to a certain extent, he generally accords with Shelley's position. "A civilisation is a struggle to keep self-control," he declares in *A Vision*.[54] But his particular cyclical theory of history leads Yeats to welcome violence on occasion, for only such violence can throw off the restrictive husk of a dying civilization and permit the coming incarnation of energy within a new framework. He embraces the anarchy Shelley fears. In the *Defence* Shelley asserts that the poet's imagination can save the state from "the Scylla and Charybdis of anarchy and despotism."[55] Yeats's historical vortex includes the whirlpool of anarchy. He can refer to "mere anarchy," a phrase impossible to Shelley, for whom anarchy represents one extremity of moral evil. Yeats wants not a framework of order for progress toward the new Athens but rather one of cyclical disorder and reversal to allow for innumerable new Byzantiums.

[53] *Shelley's Letters*, 1: 513.
[54] *A Vision*, p. 268.
[55] *Shelley's Prose*, p. 292.

The different patterns of history in which the two poets place Athens and Byzantium accord with the difference between the ideals themselves. Athens achieved greatness through the will of men and it can be made to return whenever they again purify their aspirations. Byzantium achieved greatness because of the equipoise of universal forces, which were as much cause as effect of the minds of her inhabitants and will return whenever those forces are again in balance. Shelley is cautiously optimistic, Yeats recklessly tragic.

Yet the differences in ideals should not obscure the kinship between Shelley and Yeats. Both reject a materialistic interpretation of history. In its place they maintain systems based upon bringing human life to its fullest possible perfection. History for them reveals the striving of the human spirit toward its ideal and thus becomes a mode of visionary poetry. They and their works are themselves a part of that history. Neither Shelley nor the mature Yeats espouses that isolation from humanity which the young Yeats associated with his romantic idol. They both reveal and belong to what Shelley called "that cyclic poem written by Time upon the memories of men."

8 The Metaphysics of Vision: Yeats's Final View of Shelley

"Young men know nothing of this sort,
Observant old men know it well."
—*Yeats, "Why Should Not Old Men Be Mad?"*

"He lacked the Vision of Evil, could not conceive of the world as a continual conflict, so, though great poet he certainly was, he was not of the greatest kind," wrote Yeats of Shelley in *A Vision*.[1] That statement differs from Yeats's earlier estimation of Shelley in its conclusion rather than in its methodology, for he always evaluated Shelley more in regard to metaphysics than to poetic craft. He early recognized Shelley as a model for the poet whose art depended upon a world view which informs the poetry yet stands independent of it. In his essay on "The Philosophy of Shelley's Poetry" he undertook to prove that Shelley was a "subtle" rather than a "vague" thinker by explicating "the system of belief that lay behind" his poems.[2] Based upon Intellectual Beauty, that system found favor with the young Yeats, who had been writing poetry on the same subject partly in conscious imitation of Shelley for the previous decade. Agreement with Shelley's metaphysics prompted a high opinion of his poetry during the nineties.

After 1914 Yeats posited an antinomial metaphysical system far different from that of his youth and, accordingly, altered his view of Shelley. Previously, Yeats had treated evil in his works only tangentially, emphasizing instead the conflict between spirit and matter. Now he recognized that spirit was not synonymous with goodness, for it could be either good or evil. Although Yeats still occasionally identified matter untransformed by the imagination as evil, he articulated the central conflict of his work

[1] *A Vision*, p. 144. [2] *E & I*, p. 66.

in specific terms of good and evil. That conflict found its metaphysical underpinning in *A Vision*. Yeats described the purpose of his new system succinctly: it "helped me to hold in a single thought reality and justice."[3] By reality Yeats meant the evil which actually exists; by justice he meant the goodness which potentially exists. For Yeats Shelley represented only half the antinomies of life—those connected with justice. His new disagreement with Shelley's metaphysics as he understood it caused Yeats to adopt a still favorable but considerably more critical view of his predecessor. Possessing only an Intellectual vision of goodness, Yeats's Shelley was still "a great poet" but no longer "of the greatest kind."

The distinction between the historical Shelley and the Shelley seen by Yeats grows widest between the early twenties and the middle thirties. Yeats merged Shelley with his own earlier career, so that his discussions of Shelley pertain more to the Yeats-Shelley devotee of Intellectual Beauty during the nineties than to the actual romantic poet. To note Yeats's increasingly idiosyncratic interpretations of Shelley is not to disparage his knowledge of his sometime model, which was both wide and profound. Yeats himself recognized and stated the enormous influence of Shelley on his own career during the nineties. Emphasizing the place of love in Shelley's metaphysics, he wrote:

> The orthodox religion . . . found a substitute in Shelley. He had shared our curiosities, our political problems, our conviction that, despite all experience to the contrary, love is enough; and unlike Blake, isolated by an arbitrary symbolism, he seemed to sum up all that was metaphysical in English poetry. When in middle life I looked back I found that he and not Blake, whom I had studied more and with more approval, had shaped my life.[4]

"Shelley. . . . had shaped my life." Only by rejecting the Shelley who shaped his youth could Yeats affirm his own mature identity. Specifically, he had to repudiate the metaphysics of the Rose period, which emphasized only goodness, in favor of the new metaphysics which allowed equal place to both good and evil. He attributed to Shelley the mistaken notions of his own youth. Earlier concentration upon a regenerated world had broken his

[3] *A Vision*, p. 25. [4] *E & I*, p. 424.

Unity of Being and replaced his Vision of Evil with what he called automatonism. He now embraced the continual and unresolved conflict between good and evil in order to mend both his personality and his art. In order to be Yeats he had to repudiate Shelley, and he repudiated not so much his actual predecessor as the "Alastor"-Yeats hybrid of the nineties.

This chapter takes Yeats's effort "to hold in a single thought reality and justice" as the basis of his metaphysical system and, consequently, of his evaluation of Shelley during the twenties and thirties. His mature poetry presents not an Intellectual vision of the good but an antinomial vision of both good and evil. After battering Shelley badly in *A Vision* and the essay "*Prometheus Unbound*," Yeats—as the pilgrimage to Field Place in 1938 shows—finally made peace with him at the close of his life. We shall explore, first, his contention that Shelley did not provide an adequate treatment of evil; second, the effects of that alleged inadequacy upon Shelley's personality; and, finally, Yeats's evaluation of Shelley in terms of a visionary tradition in Western poetry stemming principally from Dante.

Ideas of Good and Evil

Yeats insisted upon capitalizing the phrase Vision of Evil in order to distinguish it from a mere vision of evil. Although he does not define the phrase precisely, the closest approach to definition occurs in the lengthy discussion of Shelley as a representative of phase seventeen (Yeats's own phase) in *A Vision*. There Yeats uses "lacked the Vision of Evil" synonymously with "could not conceive of the world as a continual conflict." The context makes clear that the "continual conflict" is between good and evil. Following Yeats's own usage, we may here use the term Vision of Evil to signify a vision of good and evil in which the two maintain a continual and unresolved conflict. Although Yeats uses the corresponding term, Vision of Good, only once, it apparently fits both Shelley's poetry and his own early work by its implication of the eventual triumph of goodness over evil. The difference between Yeats and Shelley on this point is that Shelley—who was at least as aware as Yeats of the prevalence and reality of evil in the world—thought it the poet's duty to celebrate the Vision of Good as an ideal for human aspiration, whereas Yeats—who also upheld the good as an ideal—thought that any vision of the triumph of the good, undertaken for any reason whatsoever, involved a misrepresentation of evil and consequent falsification of the good. Both poets approach the same problem: how to teach man goodness and inspire him to attain it. They represent opposing answers to the same question, one Intellectual and the other antinomial, and differ not in their conception of the problem, but in their conception of the solution.

Yeats saw in Shelley's poetry not a deliberate elevation of good over evil but simply an inadequate treatment of evil. Unable himself to hold reality and justice (evil and good) in a single thought except by imagining them in continual conflict, Yeats refused to admit the possibility that Shelley had done so. He writes that Shelley

> creates *The Cenci* that he may give to Beatrice Cenci her incredible father. His political enemies are monstrous, meaningless images. And unlike Byron, who is two phases later, he can never see anything that opposes him as it really is. . . . The justice of *Prometheus Unbound* is a vague propagandist emotion and the women that await its coming are but clouds. . . . Being out of phase so far as his practical reason was concerned, he was subject to an *automatonism* which he mistook for poetical invention, especially in his longer poems. *Antithetical* men (Phase 15 once passed) use this *automatonism* to evade hatred, or rather to hide it from their own eyes; perhaps all at some time or other, in moments of fatigue, give themselves up to fantastic, constructed images, or to an almost mechanical laughter.[5]

According to these remarks Shelley's inability to conceive of the world as continual conflict caused him to misrepresent evil in his works and, therefore, to falsify the triumph of goodness over it. Yeats advances *The Cenci* as an illustration of the misrepresentation of evil and his former "sacred book," *Prometheus Unbound*, as a presentation of an unrealistic triumph of justice. He holds that both works reveal Shelley's surrender to "automatonism," the faculty that hides hatred and constructs "fantastic images." The extent to which Yeats's discussion of evil, justice, and automatonism fits both Shelley's work and his own earlier poetry demands our closer attention.

[5] *A Vision*, pp. 143–44.

Throughout his life Yeats said very little about *The Cenci.* In 1933 he recalled that over forty years earlier he had urged John Todhunter to avoid the examples of Shelley's *Cenci* and Tennyson's *Beckett* because their authors "had tried to escape their characteristics, had thought of the theatre as something outside the general movement of literature."[6] Although Yeats openly emulated Shelley in his poetry before 1903, he never mentions him during his immersion in drama between 1903 and 1917. His silence about the chief dramatic work of his professed poetic model suggests not merely a waning general enthusiasm for Shelley but, in addition, a particular indifference to the dramatic and metaphysical principles of *The Cenci.*

Although he apparently disagreed with it, Yeats would have known Shelley's discussion of the problem of evil in the preface to *The Cenci,* included in nearly all editions. There Shelley announces his intention of "teaching the human heart, through its sympathies and antipathies, the knowledge of itself."[7] Although the historical facts were "fearful and monstrous" enough to oblige the author to "increase the ideal and diminish the actual horror of the events," such idealization did not mean falsification of character and incident. Shelley wished "to represent the characters as they probably were," and "sought to avoid the error of making them actuated by my own conceptions of right or wrong, false or true; thus under a thin veil converting names and actions of the sixteenth century into cold impersonations of my own mind."

Yeats rejected Shelley's estimate of both his work and his intentions. For him the idealization of horror resulted in just what Shelley hoped to avoid: the conversion of the sixteenth-century story into a representation of the author's mind. Although both the play and Shelley's preface and letters emphasize his preoccupation with Beatrice,[8] Yeats found the sole purpose of the play to be to "give to Beatrice Cenci her incredible father." In the essay "*Prometheus Unbound*" Yeats calls the count "an artificial

[6] *Letters to the New Island,* ed. Horace Reynolds, p. ix.

[7] All quotations in this paragraph are from the preface to *The Cenci* in *Shelley's Prose,* pp. 322–25.

[8] The letters reveal Shelley's persistent interest in the portrait of Beatrice; see *Shelley's Letters,* 2: 103, 107, 159.

character, the scapegoat of his [Shelley's] unconscious hatred" who makes the play "unendurable" in spite of its otherwise "magnificent construction."[9] Shelley locates the center of the play in Beatrice and explores the phenomenon whereby the best lose all conviction. Yeats insists that the count forms the true center of interest in a false portrayal of the worst being full of passionate intensity.

Yeats's work during the nineties presents a much less adequate treatment of evil than does Shelley's play. In general Yeats seeks during that period to solve the problem of evil by eliminating it from his work. He creates his own world of peace and Intellectual Beauty, and he tolerates melancholy but not outright evil in it. There are no Count Cencis on the lake isle of Innisfree. When Yeats does present evil he embodies it in images far more simplistic than those of Shelley. In *The Countess Cathleen*, for example, Yeats presents the antagonists to the heroine as quite literally devils. Since the demons are also merchants, the play renders a physical presentation of Shelley's metaphor that poetry and gold are the God and Mammon of the world.

Yeats's reaction against the lack of evil in his early work suggests an explanation for his insistence that Count Cenci stands at the center of the play. Himself intent upon getting evil into his poetry, he naturally concentrated upon the clearest image of evil in the play—the count. He took the count not on Shelley's terms—as the external spur to Beatrice's internal corruption—but in terms of his own need to present an image of evil. His own artistic needs dictated his view of the play. The count may have been just such an image as the younger Yeats would have sought had he written at length about evil, but his totally evil nature had no attraction for the later Yeats, who confined his images of evil to his poetry and presented more ambiguous figures in his plays.

Having indicted Shelley for inadequate treatment of reality in *The Cenci*, Yeats further accuses him of inadequate treatment of justice in *Prometheus*. He finds that the poem presents only "a vague propagandist emotion" awaited by cloudy women. To Yeats, presentation of the ultimate triumph of the good necessarily falsifies it into something "miraculous" or "superhuman."

[9] *E & I*, p. 421.

For him the good can be exhibited only in terms of its perpetual conflict with evil. From his point of view Shelley is twice wrong: he misrepresents both good and evil because he cannot hold reality and justice in a single thought. Before we can understand the aesthetic and metaphysical implications of Yeats's rejection of Shelley, we must first look at Shelley's presentation of justice in its own terms rather than in those of Yeats.

Shelley understood well the connection between good and evil, justice and reality. In the *Essay on Christianity*, for example, he remarks, "Good and evil subsist in so intimate an union that few situations of human affairs can be affirmed to contain either of the two principles in an unconnected state."[10] Sure of the mixture of reality and justice in the world, Shelley was less sure of the origin of evil and the possibility of its permanent eradication. In insisting upon the morality of Shelley's work to nineteenth-century readers, Mary Shelley may have unwittingly furnished a weapon to those twentieth-century readers eager to dismiss Shelley for excessive, facile morality. Yeats, for example, apparently took at face value her note to *Prometheus Unbound:*

> The prominent feature of Shelley's theory of the destiny of the human species was, that evil is not inherent in the system of the creation, but an accident that might be expelled. . . . Shelley believed that mankind had only to will that there should be no evil, and there would be none. . . . That man could be so perfectionized as to be able to expel evil from his own nature, and from the greater part of the creation, was the cardinal point of his system.[11]

Mary's statements about the origin and future of evil do not accord with the main body of Shelley's mature work. Although Shelley did derive the external evil of institutions from the internal evil of man's mind, he remained unsure about the origin of that internal evil. In one of Yeats's favorite works, *Hellas*, Shelley writes in a note: "Let it not be supposed that I mean to dogmatize upon a subject concerning which all men are equally ignorant, or that I think the Gordian knot of the origin of evil can be disentangled by that or any similar assertions."[12]

The future of evil remained nearly as uncertain as its origin. After his early hopes for an earthly paradise Shelley veered toward

[10] *Shelley's Prose,* p. 198. [11] *Works,* 2: 269. [12] *Works,* 3: 56.

Manicheanism in *The Revolt of Islam*, partly under the influence of Peacock.[13] Prompted by the struggle between the eagle and the serpent, the visionary woman tells the mystified poet:

> Know then, that from the depth of ages old,
> Two Powers o'er mortal things dominion hold
> Ruling the world with a divided lot,
> Immortal, all-pervading, manifold,
> Twin Genii, equal Gods—[14]

Although holding to the view of twin genii of good and evil, the mature Shelley passed beyond the simple dualism of *The Revolt*. In *Prometheus Unbound* he again envisioned the triumph of good, but the triumph is neither easy nor necessarily permanent. Demogorgon's speech at the conclusion of *Prometheus Unbound* reflects a creed other than what Yeats called "propagandist emotion" and transformation "in the twinkling of an eye":

> Gentleness, Virtue, Wisdom, and Endurance,
> These are the seals of that most firm assurance
>   Which bars the pit over Destruction's strength;
> And if, with infirm hand, Eternity,
> Mother of many acts and hours, should free
>   The serpent that would clasp her with his length;
> These are the spells by which to reassume
> An empire o'er the disentangled doom.
>
> To suffer woes which Hope thinks infinite;
> To forgive wrongs darker than death or night;
>   To defy Power, which seems omnipotent;
> To love, and bear; to hope till Hope creates
> From its own wreck the thing it contemplates;
>   Neither to change, nor falter, nor repent;
> This, like thy glory, Titan! is to be
> Good, great and joyous, beautiful and free;
> This is alone Life, Joy, Empire, and Victory.[15]

Demogorgon's speech makes clear that the triumph of justice, or the good, is not necessarily permanent. Shelley thought the poet had a duty to encourage mankind in the struggle against evil, even if final victory was impossible. Such visions of regeneration as that in *Prometheus Unbound* provided an ideal for hu-

[13] The influence of Peacock on *The Revolt* has been examined in detail by Carlos Baker, *Shelley's Major Poetry: the Fabric of a Vision*, pp. 61–86.
[14] *Works*, 1: 264. [15] *Works*, 2: 262.

man aspiration, and Shelley eloquently defended their utility. In a note to the chorus of *Hellas* which Yeats parodied in *The Resurrection* Shelley declares:

> Prophecies of wars and rumours of war, &c., may safely be made by poet or prophet in any age; but to anticipate, however darkly, a period of regeneration and happiness, is a more hazardous exercise of the faculty which bards possess or feign. It will remind the reader "magno nec proximus intervallo" of Isaiah and Virgil, whose ardent spirits overleaping the actual reign of evil which we endure and bewail, already saw the possible and perhaps approaching state of society in which the "*lion shall lie down with the lamb*," and "omnis feret omnia tellus." Let these great names be my authority and my excuse.[16]

Shelley provides his own framework for handling justice and reality. Reality he calls "the actual reign of evil which we endure and bewail"; justice is "the possible and perhaps approaching state of society." Although Yeats advocates holding both reality and justice in a single thought, Shelley favors portraying the potential triumph of justice over reality and cites Isaiah and Virgil as his authorities. The central proposition of this chapter again becomes obvious: Shelley and Yeats conceive of the problem of good and evil in similar terms but advance fundamentally irreconcilable solutions to it. Seen by Yeats, Shelley's work lacks an adequate treatment of evil. If Shelley could have seen Yeats's work, he might well have retorted as he did to Medwin: "Perhaps you belong to the tribe of the hopeless & nothing shocks or surprises you in politics."[17]

For Shelley escape from the problem of good and evil was impossible. He told Byron, "We are damned to the knowledge of good and evil."[18] His hope for human regeneration was not the facile desire imputed to him by Yeats; rather, it was a duty at once imperative and awesome. Shelley approvingly quoted Coleridge's remark, "Hope is a most awful duty, the nurse of all other virtues."[19]

If Yeats's argument about Shelley's handling of justice does not fit *Prometheus Unbound*, what does it fit? It fits Yeats's own work during the nineties, although in his zeal to free himself from his earlier work and attitudes Yeats judges his former

[16] *Works*, 3: 57. [17] *Shelley's Letters*, 2: 169.
[18] Ibid., 2: 358. [19] Ibid., 1: 504.

achievement more harshly than an impartial observer might. Concerned in the Rose poetry with justice and Intellectual Beauty, Yeats banishes the actual world of reality and evil from his own private cosmos. His lovers leave actuality behind and journey to justice; Forgael and Dectora in *The Shadowy Waters* disappear on a ship into the mist. The poems do not evince a Vision of Evil, for they anticipate and sometimes even depict the final triumph of the ideal world. When actuality and evil intrude —as in "The Lover Tells of the Rose in His Heart"—the speaker "hunger[s] to build them anew."[20] Far from accepting continual conflict as the basic condition of imaginative life, Yeats here desires just that triumph of the ideal which he later condemns Shelley for seeking to celebrate.

The desire to remake the world in the image of one's imagination brings us to the third and final accusation which Yeats derives from Shelley's alleged lack of a Vision of Evil—submission to what he called "automatonism."[21] Another term not defined

[20] *Variorum Poems*, p. 143.

[21] In his *Autobiography* Yeats extends the consequences of Shelley's lack of a Vision of Evil beyond the concerns of this chapter by charging Shelley with inadequate treatment of sexuality and suffering. In "The Tragic Generation" Yeats advocates the physical as a balance to the spiritual: "Donne could be as metaphysical as he pleased, and yet never seemed unhuman and hysterical as Shelley often does, because he could be as physical as he pleased; and besides, who will thirst for the metaphysical, who have a parched tongue, if we cannot recover the Vision of Evil?" (p. 326).

For all the differences between the lovers in "The Exstasie" and the Crazy Jane poems, they both subsume bodily urges into their spiritualized world view in a way that, say, Prometheus and Asia do not. Yeats feels that the sexuality of Donne's poems and his own enables them to include the realm of metaphysics and spirit without seeming "unhuman." He includes the body as one of the contending elements in his antinomial vision. Unlike the allegedly cloudy women of Shelley, Crazy Jane declares to the Bishop, "Fair and foul are near of kin, / And fair needs foul." With her, Yeats has moved about as far as he can from his early conception of women as like either Cythna or the *Alastor* maid.

Finally, Yeats includes suffering as an essential part of a Vision of Evil. In "If I were Four-and-Twenty" he associates evil with suffering and declares that a man comes to believe in it only unwillingly. Once he does, the resultant Vision gives his work "strength and weight." With the exception of the suffering arising from "personal feeling," Yeats misses in Shelley's work the inevitability of suffering embraced by both Dante and Balzac. For Shelley, he maintains, "human nature has lost its antagonist" (*Explorations*, pp. 275–77).

precisely, automatonism is a mechanical, automatic faculty of invention which can sometimes replace genuine creativity in the artist. Yeats favors the sparing use of automatonism as a rest from the continual conflict of life.[22] He charges Shelley with using automatonism not as a rest but as a refusal of conflict and accuses him of inability to distinguish true creativity from its mechanical substitute:

> He was subject to an automatonism which he mistook for poetical invention, especially in his longer poems. *Antithetical* men (Phase 15 once passed) use this *automatonism* to evade hatred, or rather to hide it from their own eyes; perhaps all at some time or other, in moments of fatigue, give themselves up to fantastic, constructed images, or to an almost mechanical laughter.[23]

According to Yeats's argument, Shelley's automatonism precluded an adequate treatment of justice and reality in his works. He holds that instead of confronting the conflict between good and evil Shelley retreated from it. Retreat led in *Prometheus* to the triumph of a "propagandist" justice over a "fantastic, constructed" image of evil. We have already examined the significance of Yeats's misrepresentation of Shelley's concept of justice in *Prometheus* and of evil in *The Cenci*. Like that misrepresentation, the charge of automatonism derives from Yeats's reading of Shelley in terms of his own solution, rather than Shelley's, to the problem of evil. He associates automatonism with two major topics—the role of Demogorgon and the range of mysticism in Shelley's works.

Yeats advances a unique interpretation of Demogorgon. The uniqueness results from the same determination to find an embodiment of evil and make that embodiment the center of a literary analysis which shaped Yeats's reading of *The Cenci*. Earlier, he admired and imitated *Prometheus Unbound*. But in the essay "*Prometheus Unbound*" (1932) his interpretation of Demogorgon drastically reduces his previous admiration. Yeats finds Demogorgon a nightmare figure of evil and argues that Shelley needed such a monster as a balance against "the object of desire conceived as miraculous and superhuman."[24] Demogor-

[22] *A Vision*, p. 95. [23] Ibid., p. 144. [24] *E & I*, p. 420.

gon exemplifies to him Shelley's inability to portray "whatever seemed dark, destructive, indefinite"[25] except as a fantastic, mechanical bogeyman. If one grants Yeats his interpretation, one can concede that Demogorgon does indeed make the "plot incoherent, its interpretation impossible."[26]

But one cannot grant the validity of Yeats's interpretation. Whereas in the nineties he read his own work in terms of Shelley's, he now wants to reverse the process and read Shelley's work in terms of his own. Had Shelley, like the mature Yeats, tried in his poetry to hold reality and justice in a single thought, and had he further identified Demogorgon with evil or reality, then Yeats's charges would be true. But in his poetry Shelley tried instead to present the (possibly temporary) triumph of justice over reality; for his purposes, Jupiter adequately represented evil. Nor is Jupiter's evil merely external, as Yeats would have it; his evil is the internal one of the mind which Yeats seeks to locate in Demogorgon. Seen in Shelley's terms, Demogorgon becomes necessity, or the agent of the inevitable overthrow of evil once justice has triumphed in the mind of Prometheus. Yeats's interpretation reflects his antinomial vision of the continual conflict between good and evil rather than Shelley's Intellectual vision of regeneration brought about by "beautiful idealisms of moral excellence."[27]

Why does Yeats condemn Demogorgon but not his own rough beast in "The Second Coming"? Both, after all, represent to him the "dark, destructive, and indefinite" forces of apocalyptic upheaval. The distinction lies in the attitude of the author toward the apocalypse; more specifically, it lies in his attitude toward the possibility of an apocalypse that will end the reign of evil and institute the golden age of justice. Yeats accuses Shelley both of fearing the Day of Judgment and of expecting a miraculous transformation of reality into justice. On the one hand he rhetorically asks, "Why is Shelley terrified of the Last Day like a Victorian child?" and adds that that day was "not terrible to Blake."[28] On the other hand he reverses his earlier defense of Shelley's vision of liberty and now contends that "Shelley the political revolutionary expected miracle, the Kingdom of God in

[25] *E & I*, p. 421. [26] *E & I*, p. 420. [27] *Works*, 2: 174. [28] *E & I*, p. 420.

the twinkling of an eye, like some Christian of the first century."[29]

Both those statements derive from Yeats's ascription of his own historical view to Shelley. We saw in the previous chapter that Yeats emphasizes apocalyptic reversals in the course of history, whereas Shelley, though keenly aware of reversals, emphasizes the possibility of eventual development toward an ideal. The poet's function was to encourage men toward that ideal by providing a vision of it in his art. Yeats, not Shelley, expects transformations in "the twinkling of an eye," but his conception of continual conflict between reality and justice preserves him from the terror of a permanent victory of evil or the naïveté of expecting a simple victory of good. To him, any triumph of the good, whether in his own work or in Shelley's, meant the expectation of miracle. In a note to "The Second Coming" he substitutes the phrase "lightning flash" for "twinkling of an eye":

> The revelation which approaches will however take its character from the contrary movement of the interior gyre. All our scientific, democratic, fact-accumulating, heterogeneous civilization belongs to the outward gyre and prepares not the continuance of itself but the revelation as in a lightning flash, though in a flash that will not strike only in one place, and will for a time be constantly repeated, of the civilization that must slowly take its place.[30]

Yeats completes his metaphysical evaluation of Shelley by concluding that he "was not a mystic."[31] If one denies that automatonism is the alternative to mysticism, the statement seems fair enough. Yeats finds that his former idol's "system of thought was constructed by his logical faculty to satisfy desire, not a symbolical revelation received after the suspension of all desire." Yeats was always on shaky ground in his association of Shelley with such mystics as Plotinus and Swedenborg, while his first essay on Shelley considerably overstated the romantic poet's knowledge of Porphyry and affinity for him. The close identification of Yeats's self-image in the nineties with Shelley suggests that Yeats was also uncomfortable about the validity of his own mysticism in the Rose poems.

Yeats's judgment derives from his determination to accept the metaphysical antinomies of good and evil as the basis of his system

[29] *E & I*, p. 419. [30] *Variorum Poems*, p. 825. [31] *E & I*, p. 421.

of belief. He finds that Shelley could "neither say with Dante, 'His will is our peace,' nor with Finn in the Irish story, 'The best music is what happens.' "[32] But Shelley's refusal to acquiesce in the eternal order of events reflects not his inability but rather his refusal to portray human destiny in his poetry without envisioning the potential triumph of justice. Determined to accept the conflict between justice and reality, Yeats saw Shelley's refusal to do likewise as a contradiction of mysticism as he understood it. Before his sharp divergence from Shelley became apparent to him, he advanced Shelley's "vehement vision" as a corrective against the espousal of any cause. His statement clearly demonstrates the distinction between his and Shelley's manner of presenting reality in poetry. If Shelley would have made Yeats a chieftain of "the tribe of the hopeless," Yeats came to see Shelley in the same light as the "zealous Irishman" to whom he argues:

> Even if what one defends be true, an attitude of defence, a continual apology, whatever the cause, makes the mind barren because it kills intellectual innocence; the delight in what is unforeseen, and in the mere spectacle of the world, the mere drifting hither and thither that must come before all true thought and emotion.[33]

Seen in its proper context, Yeats's contention that Shelley lacked a Vision of Evil pertains not so much to the way in which the two poets conceive of the metaphysics of justice and reality as it does to their different methods of presenting evil in their works. Both recognize the reality and probable continuation of evil in the world; they disagree about its role in art. Shelley holds that the artist must present a vision of the triumph of justice in order to inspire mankind toward that ideal, even if the ideal will never be achieved permanently. In contrast, Yeats insists that only by presenting justice and reality, good and evil, in continual conflict can the artist bring mankind to an adequate understanding of either. To Yeats, Shelley abrogated his poetic responsibility by his "constant resolution to dwell upon good only."[34]

Dwelling upon evil as well as on good does not mean that the poet must become morbid or morose. On the contrary, in poems like "Lapis Lazuli" Yeats assumes a gaiety notably absent from

[32] *E & I*, p. 422. [33] *E & I*, p. 314. [34] *Explorations*, p. 275.

his posturing as "Alastor" in the nineties. By seeing evil as it is he demythologizes it. Through accepting all of life rather than rejecting part of it he can reduce both the Battle of the Boyne and German air raids to King Billy pitching in his bomb-balls. In this poem he wears a mask like the faces of the aged Chinamen, who by seeing human tragedy as art can both accept and transcend the antinomies. Only in that way can he make his Vision of Evil fulfill the poet's proper task, to "bring the soul of man to God."[35]

Ultimately, both Shelley and Yeats affirm the power of the human mind, not to conquer reality but to attain a vision of justice. For Shelley that power is hope, which, says Demogorgon, "creates / From its own wreck the thing it contemplates." Even when subject to reality man can affirm his vision of justice. Yeats locates the visionary power not in hope but in acceptance. Acceptance of both reality and justice frees a man to create a unified vision (or receive a mystic one) during life and to enter after death a world of justice which he in some sense creates. Yeats affirms that "being dead, we rise / Dream and so create / Translunar Paradise."[36]

From Metaphysics to Psychology

In Shelley's life Yeats saw the same discrepancy between reality and justice that he saw in his work. His biographical observations have a post hoc character; one senses that Yeats sought to portray the psychological condition of a typical artist who lacked a Vision of Evil rather than the actual state of mind of the romantic poet. Yeats said little about Shelley's life, nor did he interest himself in biographical details except insofar as they supported his metaphysical and psychological theories. He argued that Shelley's refusal to come to terms with evil resulted in a loss of Unity of Being, comparable on the biographical level to loss of a Vision of Evil on the literary. We have explained this misconception of Shelley's actual attitude toward evil. Our concern here is with the psychological conclusions Yeats drew from his metaphysics and the extent to which Shelley serves as a hapless tool for his explication of them. The subject has three main

35 "Under Ben Bulben," *Variorum Poems*, p. 638.
36 *Variorum Poems*, p. 415.

facets—the connection between personality and literature, the psychological implications of a Vision of Evil, and Yeats's idiosyncratic biographical interpretation of Shelley.

For Yeats personality was inseparable from literature. As early as 1888 he maintained that he was "no idle poetaster" because he had "broken my life in a mortar" in order to make poetry out of it.[37] In 1905 he declared that "All art is founded upon personal vision" and added that "impersonal types and images" could lead only to "bad art."[38] Yeats never wavered in his association of literature with personal life, although the doctrine of the mask—with its principle of the poet's rebirth as the psychological type opposite to his normal self—led to a more complex formulation of it. In 1937 he could still open his essay "A General Introduction for My Work" with the statement, "A poet writes always out of his personal life."[39]

The connection between a poet's personality and his art did not lead Yeats into an easy equation of the poet and the man. He held that during periods of composition the poet achieved exceptional sensitivity and unity which lifted him above his normal self. Significantly, Yeats chose Shelley to illustrate his point:

> even when the poet seems most himself, when he is . . . like Shelley "a nerve o'er which do creep the else unfelt oppressions of this earth" . . . he is never the bundle of accident and incoherence that sits down to breakfast; he has been reborn as an idea, something intended, complete.[40]

Shelley provides an apt example, for he himself made a similar distinction between the poet and his ordinary self. In a letter to the Gisbornes he states the dichotomy even more extremely than Yeats: "The poet & the man are two different natures; though they exist together they may be unconscious of each other, & incapable of deciding upon each other's powers & effects by any reflex act."[41] Although distinguishing the poet from the man, Shelley elsewhere posits a relationship between them substantially consistent with that later detected by Yeats. The poet

[37] *Yeats's Letters*, p. 84. [38] *Explorations*, p. 194. [39] *E & I*, p. 509.

[40] Ibid. Yeats here quotes from the maniac's speech in *Julian and Maddalo*, lines 449–50.

[41] *Shelley's Letters*, 2: 310.

represents the rebirth and perfection of the man. In the *Defence* Shelley defines poetry as "the record of the best and happiest moments of the happiest and best minds."[42] At such moments "the interpenetration of a diviner nature" through his own completes and perfects the poet's normal self. Shelley and Yeats, then, both connect poetry with personality, although they elevate a writer's poetic nature above his normal one.

Yeats's indictment of Shelley's poetic self is easier to accept, even if only because harder to verify, than his interpretation of Shelley's normal self. Although the longest discussion of Shelley's lack of a Vision of Evil appears in *A Vision* in the 1937 edition, deleted sections from the text of 1925 provide a fuller psychological analysis of the subject. There Yeats chooses not reality and justice but the "light" and "dark" powers of the mind as his basic antinomies. The power of light does pertain to the vision of justice and the good, and the power of darkness to the vision of reality and evil, but one must resist a simple equation of the two sets of opposing principles. Undoubtedly, the pair that assumes dominance later—reality and justice—grows out of the earlier opposition of dark and light, but the pairs function differently. Justice and reality pertain to the final *product* of perception and vision, light and dark to the *process* of perceiving and envisioning. In discussing the first version of *A Vision*, adherence to the terminology of the earlier set of antinomies preserves us from misrepresenting Yeats's thought by imposing a false coherence upon it.

In a manner reminiscent of Freud's suggestion that suppression of the id limits and warps the personality, Yeats emphasizes the necessity of accommodating the "daimon," which possesses "the entire dark of the mind." Refusal to accommodate the daimon destroys the possibility of achieving Unity of Being, for the daimon then wars on the part of the mind dedicated to light and seeks to "quench" it. In contrast, acceptance of the dark power of the daimon strengthens a man's imaginative intuition by infusing daimonic power into his perception of the events of his life. In Yeats's phrasing he "apprehends the truth" by a faculty "analogous" to the senses, "though without organs." Such a man will then be free to struggle within "his fate and destiny"

[42] *Shelley's Prose*, p. 294.

(themselves in a sense determined by his mind) rather than condemned to waste his energy by an internal psychic struggle.[43] In freeing his own imagination to create rough beasts as well as circus animals, Yeats avoided that shrill hysteria which destroyed Pentheus in *The Bacchae*.

Acceptance of conflict connects Unity of Being with the Vision of Evil. Yeats declares, "He who attains Unity of Being is some man who, while struggling with his fate and his destiny until every energy of his being has been roused, is content that he should so struggle with no final conquest."[44] Acceptance of struggle without conquest repeats in a man's life the same effect it has in his work. Recognizing conflict as the basic condition of life, the poet can then bring "all that happens . . . into an emotional or intellectual synthesis and so to possess not the Vision of Good only but [also] that of Evil."[45]

Yeats carries the importance of the daimon over into the final version of *A Vision*, where he calls the man of phase seventeen "the *Daimonic* man because Unity of Being, and consequent expression of Daimonic thought, is now more easy than at any other phase."[46] The key word is "consequent," because it indicates the connection between the early antinomies of light and dark and the later ones of justice and reality. Accommodation of the daimonic power of darkness during moments of creativity necessarily produces an art which includes reality as well as justice. Here as elsewhere Yeats discusses only those artists who already have an adequate visionary power of light and consequent vision of justice in their works. Again, one must point out that the dark power of the mind is not the same thing as evil: the daimonic is not the demonic.

Yeats works deductively in imputing a lack of Unity of Being to Shelley's poetic self. For him the absence of a Vision of Evil (not a vision of evil) in the poetry implies a lack of it in the mind of the poet. The argument is solid if one grants Yeats's initial premise about Shelley's approach to the problem of evil. We saw above that that premise involved an evaluation of Shelley not according to his solution of the problem of evil but rather according

[43] *A Vision* (1925), p. 28. [44] Ibid., p. 28.
[45] Ibid., p. 29. [46] *A Vision*, p. 141.

to Yeats's. Shelley did see the connection between reality and justice but deliberately chose to elevate justice above reality in his art. The psychological evaluation, then, accords perfectly with Yeats's literary one, but not with a more accurate literary interpretation. The lack of Unity of Being during moments of creativity, then, does not follow from applying Yeats's psychological principles to Shelley's work. Yeats's terminology makes it difficult to see what would follow from Shelley's poetry, unless that Shelley deliberately excluded daimonic power not from his mind but from his poetry except insofar as it strengthened his power of presenting justice.

Yeats holds that Shelley the man achieved even less unity than Shelley the poet, although "even as poet unity was but in part attained." In the biographical sketch in *A Vision* he makes the following observations:

> Shelley out of phase writes pamphlets, and dreams of converting the world, or of turning man of affairs and upsetting governments . . . how subject he is to nightmare! He sees the devil leaning against a tree, is attacked by imaginary assassins . . . he can never see anything that opposes him as it really is. . . . [He] found compensation for his "loss," for the taking away of his children, for his quarrel with his first wife, for later sexual disappointment, for his exile, for his obloquy—there were but some three or four persons, he said, who did not consider him a monster of iniquity—in his hopes for the future of mankind. . . . This is in part because the age in which Shelley lived was in itself so broken that true Unity of Being was almost impossible.[47]

All these remarks contain a common premise: Shelley's hopes for the future of mankind manifest not a true vision of justice based upon an acceptance of reality but rather an artificial vision based upon compensation for it. Yeats here replaces his earlier approval of Shelley's millenarianism because it represented Intellectual Beauty with disapproval because it eliminated Unity of Being and the Vision of Evil. Yeats himself hammered his thoughts into unity, or at least tried so to hammer them. Because Shelley's political aspirations contradicted Yeats's metaphysical principles, he thought that Shelley had never forged such a union.

[47] Ibid., pp. 143–44.

Yeats's own biography illustrates a successful application of his metaphysics better than Shelley's does an unsuccessful one. After the period of identification with Shelley in the nineties, Yeats moved outward into public life. Appointment as a senator of the Irish Free State and winning the Nobel prize followed two decades of involvement with the Abbey Theatre and other enterprises. Being simultaneously a poet and a public man, he found a metaphysics which not only allowed for the rivalry of reality and justice but also exploited that rivalry as the raw material for poetry. The condemnation of Shelley's life provides a biographical equivalent of the denunciation of his work: both imply a repudiation more of the Shelley-Yeats figure of the nineties than of the actual romantic poet.

Brothers of a Company

Yeats considered Shelley not just in isolation but also as part of a visionary tradition in Western poetry. In the nineties Yeats argued that the best Irish artists had celebrated the same Intellectual Beauty he praised in his own Rose poems; consequently, he pleaded for recognition as a "true brother of a company" of visionary Irishmen.[48] By the twenties and thirties Yeats had consciously remade his art into a more generally European poetry which still preserved a distinctive Irish quality. The company he now desired to join included not just Davis, Mangan, and Ferguson but some of the greatest European visionary poets, chief among them Dante. A change from Intellectual to antinomial vision accompanied the change in models: Yeats now appreciated not the vision of justice alone but that of reality and justice in a working fusion. This new dialectic allowed not only for Dante but also for Villon; furthermore, it provided a framework for classifying the varieties of modern fragmented visions. Seen in Yeats's terms, Shelley's vision became a fragment of Dante's, Burns's a fragment of Villon's. Only Blake among the moderns approached the unified vision of his great predecessors. Yeats himself yearned to unite the antinomies once again, to become the Dante of the modern age.

To an extent both Shelley and Yeats remake Dante in their own images. Shelley sees Dante's vision as the triumph of justice,

[48] *Variorum Poems*, p. 137.

or of love and the good; Yeats sees it as the continual conflict between justice and reality, good and evil. Disagreeing about the essential nature of Dante's vision, the two poets nevertheless agree about many of its other qualities. Both value the intensity and unity of his work and recognize its intimate relation to fourteenth-century Italy. Their interpretations of Dante provide an illuminating comparison of the contrasts and similarities in their own personal visions.

Shelley commended Dante to Leigh Hunt because of his "energy and simplicity, and unity of idea."[49] Because their works showed "the vigour of the infancy of a new nation," Dante, Petrarch, and Boccaccio surpass Ariosto and Tasso, who were "the children of a later and of a colder day." Yeats was later to take up the concept of a later and colder time in comparing Shelley himself to Dante. Shelley holds that the era not only inspired Dante to vigor but also permeated his productions. Such perfect correspondence between the work and the age was one evidence of greatness. In the *Defence* Shelley ranks Dante immediately after Homer as "the second epic poet: that is, the second poet, the series of whose creations bore a defined and intelligible relation to the knowledge and sentiment of the age in which he lived and of the ages which followed it, developing itself in correspondence with their development."[50]

Shelley's ascription to Dante of unity and of correspondence with the age finds its counterpart in Yeats's concept of Unity of Culture. Yeats believed that historical circumstances gave Dante an advantage over Shelley. Unlike the time of Dante, "the age in which Shelley lived was in itself so broken that true Unity of Being was almost impossible."[51] Lack of Unity of Culture in the modern age made achievement of Unity of Being more difficult. According to Yeats, Dante's personal and cultural unity depended upon the emergence of personality. Even though Dante lived until 1321, Yeats assigns him to the late thirteenth century, which corresponds to phase eight of the historical system of *A Vision*. Always a phase of important transition, phase eight (1250–1300) here marks the emergence of personality as the dominant political, religious, and artistic force.

[49] *Shelley's Letters*, 2: 122. [50] *Shelley's Prose*, p. 280.
[51] *A Vision*, p. 144.

Although he gives the phrase a different meaning, Yeats, like Shelley, imputes to Dante a "defined and intelligible relation" to the age. Eschewing a political or religious example in favor of a literary one, Yeats writes:

> I prefer, however, to find my example of the first victory of personality where I have more knowledge. Dante in the *Convito* mourns for solitude, lost through poverty, and writes the first sentence of modern autobiography, and in the *Divina Commedia* imposes his own personality upon a system and a phantasmagoria hitherto impersonal; the King everywhere has found his kingdom.[52]

Yeats thought himself the same psychological type as Shelley and Dante. They all belonged to the seventeenth phase of the psychological system in *A Vision*.[53] His interpretation of Dante's personality thus assumes particular importance for understanding both Yeats's own ambitions and his view of Shelley. Yeats thought that as poet Dante attained to that Unity of Being which Shelley lacked and which he himself sought to achieve. Dante's unity made him the supreme example of a school of visionary artists opposed to "the mechanical theory of life." Yeats asserted his own faith in that visionary tradition: "I was born into this faith, have lived in it, and shall die in it; my Christ, a legitimate deduction from the Creed of St. Patrick as I think, is that Unity of Being Dante compared [in the *Convivio*] to a perfectly proportioned human body."[54] Dante's personality as well as his poetry was an ideal for Yeats.

Following his conception of the two different natures of the artist, Yeats concluded that Dante achieved unity as a poet but lacked it as a man. According to Yeats, the political activity of both Dante and Shelley revealed their lack of unity. He writes that Dante "was, according to a contemporary, such a partisan,

[52] Ibid., p. 289.

[53] In 1925 Yeats included only Dante and Shelley as his examples of the phase. In 1937 he added Landor. Scholars assign Yeats to this phase on the authority of his wife. Richard Ellmann told me in conversation that Mrs. Yeats said her husband regarded himself as a man of phase seventeen.

[54] Dante treats the human body at length in the *Convivio*, especially in book 3 and to a lesser extent in book 4. Yeats was probably thinking of a passage like the opening of chapter 8, book 3, where Dante's term *concordia* has connotations similar to those of John Butler Yeats's term "harmony." See *Il Convivio*, ed. G. Bushnelli and G. Vandelli, 1: 344 f.

that if a child, or a woman, spoke against his party he would pelt this child or woman with stones."[55] For Yeats, intense political partisanship nearly always implied a distortion of personality.

In its firm grasp upon both reality and justice Dante's poetry showed that he "attained, as poet, to Unity of Being."[56] Like Shelley, he made his poetry a compensation for his life: "Dante suffering injustice and the loss of Beatrice, found divine justice and the heavenly Beatrice." Unlike Shelley, he could incorporate an antinomial vision into his poetry. According to Yeats, Dante as poet "saw all things set in order" and "was content to see both good and evil." The architectonic symmetry of *The Divine Comedy*—which balanced Bernard against Boniface, Beatrice against the Whore of Babylon, heaven against hell—made Dante a more attractive model to Yeats than was the Shelley whom he identified with his own youth.

Although they agree about the unity of Dante's art and about its close relation to its age, Shelley and Yeats disagree about the specific quality of Dante's vision. Shelley sees Dante as a great poet of justice, an ideal goodness to be achieved through love. Yeats sees Dante as a poet of both justice and reality, included in his art through an acceptance of both good and evil. Like most original modern artists Shelley and Yeats read past literature in the light of their own preoccupations and created there a tradition within which they could place their own work.

Shelley saw in the past a tradition of visionary poets celebrating justice and love. His chosen lineage in the *Defence* includes Plato in the classical world and "Ariosto, Tasso, Shakespeare, Spenser, Calderon, Rousseau, and the great writers of our own age." Despite the achievements of the Provençal troubadours and of Petrarch, the fountainhead of the modern tradition was Dante, whom Shelley "considered as the bridge thrown over the stream of time, which unites the modern and ancient world." For him Dante is the great poet of justice conceived of as love and goodness:

> Dante understood the secret things of love even more than Petrarch. His *Vita Nuova* is an inexhaustible fountain of purity of sentiment and language: it is the idealized history of that period and those intervals of his life which were dedicated

[55] *A Vision,* p. 143. [56] Ibid., p. 144.

> to love. His apotheosis of Beatrice in Paradise, and the gradations of his own love and her loveliness, by which as by steps he feigns himself to have ascended to the throne of the Supreme Cause, is the most glorious imagination of modern poetry. . . . [*The Paradiso*] is a perpetual hymn of everlasting love.[57]

Yeats finds not love but rather the Vision of Evil at the center of Dante's genius. Dante could hold in a single thought reality and justice. Yeats rejects Shelley's interpretation of Dante for the same reason that he rejects the premise of Shelley's art as he understood it: he no longer shares "the conviction that . . . love is enough."[58] For Yeats acceptance counted more than aspiration. His visionary ideal was accessible only to a sensibility like that of Dante, who "was content to see both good and evil" and therefore could "conceive of the world as a continual conflict."[59] The ideal art would include all the elements of life, transfigured by the shaping imagination of the artist but still rooted in the earth.

Yeats's comparison of Shelley to another poet, Villon, suggests his own desire to give his art the broadest possible scope. While attributing a Vision of Evil to Villon, Yeats emphasized not Villon's embrace of both good and evil but rather his union of a different set of antinomies—what Yeats called the bird and the market cart, or subtlety and common appeal. Dante showed the feasibility of including reality and justice in a single vision; Villon showed that the artist could express his vision in a popular form through the lowest levels of society. "Villon, pander, thief, and man-slayer," declared Yeats, "illustrates in the cry of his ruin as great a truth as Dante in abstract ecstasy, and touches our compassion more."[60]

Villon's whores and thieves proved that he had not surrendered to a false vision of life, and the "Ballade de la Grosse Margot" vouched that no false piety underlay "Ballade pour prier Nostre Dame." Concomitantly, they kept him close to common life and, hence, to popular appeal. Although Yeats in the nineties

[57] *Defence of Poetry*, in *Shelley's Prose*, p. 289.

[58] *E & I*, p. 424.

[59] *A Vision*, p. 144.

[60] *E & I*, p. 339. For a fuller explication of Yeats's view of Villon see George J. Bornstein and Hugh H. Witemeyer, "From *Villain* to Visionary: Pound and Yeats on Villon," pp. 308–20.

praised and adopted Hallam's assertion that spiritual art must always be unpopular, he now repudiates Hallam's view and Hallam's model, Shelley, as well. Yeats concedes that the difference between Villon's time and Shelley's accounts for part, but only part, of the difference in their art. In an essay called "Personality and the Intellectual Essences" Yeats contrasts Villon and Shelley:

> Villon the robber could have delighted these Irishmen with plays and songs, if he and they had been born to the same traditions of word and symbol, but Shelley could not; and as men came to live in towns and to read printed books and to have many specialized activities, it has become more possible to produce Shelleys and less and less possible to produce Villons.[61]

Again, Shelley appears as a fragment, as half an antinomy—in this case as spirituality. Villon embraces the whole. The mature Yeats respected and valued Shelley's half but insisted that it was only a half. Nevertheless, even that much was preferable to, say, Robert Burns. Shelley was at least an alternative to Villon; Burns was merely a debasement. Thinking of Burns's grasp of common life but lack of metaphysical subtlety, Yeats writes, "The last Villon dwindled into Robert Burns." Here Yeats fights another skirmish in his long guerrilla war against Matthew Arnold. Arnold suggested Burns's earthiness as a curative for Shelley's ethereality. Yeats repeatedly insists on Shelley's value as a visionary poet of the soul. Although himself seeking to unite the bird and the market cart, Yeats had no doubt about which was more valuable: "Shelley's Chapel of the Morning Star is better than Burns's beerhouse." Yet even Burns could be enlisted in the attack upon the materialists. Yeats declares that both Shelley and Burns surpass "that uncomfortable place where there is no beer, the machine-shop of the realists."[62]

Finally, Blake offered Yeats not only an art based on antinomies but also a conscious, philosophic defense of it. "Without Contraries is no progression," wrote Blake in a poem which by its very title suggests the antinomies of good and evil, justice and reality, heaven and hell.[63] Although "he [Shelley] and not Blake"

[61] *E & I*, p. 266. [62] *E & I*, p. 267.

[63] *The Marriage of Heaven and Hell*, in *The Complete Writings of William Blake*, ed. Geoffrey Keynes, p. 149. The relation of Blake to Yeats has been explored in detail by Hazard Adams, *Blake and Yeats: the*

shaped Yeats's vision of Intellectual Beauty in the Rose poems, Blake's antinomial system supplants Shelley's emphasis on justice in its closeness to the mature verse. Studying Blake "more, and with more approval" ultimately led to his assigning Blake a higher place in the visionary tradition.

The drive toward a wider art encompassed even moral statement, against which Yeats had recoiled in the nineties. Moral statement provided one means of introducing art into the mainstream of society, just as Villon's scenes of lowlife provided another. Recalling his earlier devotion to the principles of Hallam, Yeats wrote: "I now see that the literary element in painting, the moral element in poetry, are the means whereby the two arts are accepted into the social order and become a part of life and not things of the study and the exhibition."[64] Yeats could now praise Shelley not only for his pure sensitivity but also for having, like Tennyson and Wordsworth, "moral values that were not aesthetic values."[65] The aim was vastness in art. In 1936 Yeats revealed Shelley's partial return to grace by grouping him with the two greatest English poets in illustration of a remedy for one defect of contemporary poetry. He told Dorothy Wellesley that "we need, like Milton, Shakespeare, Shelley, vast sentiments, generalizations supported by tradition."[66]

Throughout his life Yeats admired Shelley as a fellow chronicler of "the one history—and that the soul's." In the nineties his admiration reached its zenith and he composed poems about the same Intellectual Beauty praised by Shelley. His "one unshakeable belief" during that period was that "whatever of philosophy has been made poetry is alone permanent." Later, Shelley came to represent one half of the antinomies out of which Yeats made his own poetry. Art, like personality, should include all the antinomies of life, earth and sky, market cart and bird, lust and love, foul and fair, all the manifestations of the actual and the ideal. Although he might rail at Shelley's failure to embody

---

Contrary Vision and Margaret Rudd, *Divided Image*. Harold Bloom and I have independently come to similar conclusions about the changing relation of Blake and Shelley to Yeats: see his recent article, "Yeats and the Romantics," in *Modern Poetry: Essays in Criticism,* ed. John Hollander, pp. 501–20.

[64] *Autobiography*, p. 490. [65] Ibid., p. 313. [66] *Yeats's Letters*, p. 853.

the whole of experience, he did not waver in his appreciation of Shelley's achievement as a visionary poet. At the end of his career as the beginning, Yeats could still

> Swear by what the sages spoke
> Round the Mareotic Lake
> That the Witch of Atlas knew,
> Spoke and set the cocks a-crow.[67]

[67] *Variorum Poems*, pp. 636–37.

BIBLIOGRAPHY OF WORKS CITED

SHELLEY

Works by Shelley

Address to the Irish People. Edited by T. W. Rolleston. London, 1890.

Essays and Letters of Shelley. Edited by Ernest Rhys. London, 1886.

The Letters of Percy Bysshe Shelley. Edited by Frederick L. Jones. 2 vols. Oxford, 1964.

A Philosophical View of Reform. Edited by T. W. Rolleston. London and New York, 1920.

Poems from Shelley. Edited by Stopford Brooke. London, 1880.

The Poetical Works of Percy Bysshe Shelley. Edited by W. M. Rossetti. 2 vols. London, 1870.

The Shelley Correspondence in the Bodleian Library. Edited by R. H. Hill. Oxford, 1926.

Shelley's Prose; or, the Trumpet of a Prophecy. Edited by David Lee Clark. Albuquerque, 1954.

The Works of Percy Bysshe Shelley. Edited by Roger Ingpen and Walter Peck. 10 vols. London and New York, 1927–30.

Works about Shelley

Baker, Carlos. *Shelley's Major Poetry: the Fabric of a Vision*. Princeton, 1948.

Bloom, Harold. *Shelley's Mythmaking*. New Haven, 1959.

Brooke, Stopford. "Some Thoughts on Shelley." *Macmillan's Magazine* 42 (1880): 124–35.

Browning, Robert. *An Essay on Percy Bysshe Shelley*. Edited by W. Tyas Harden. London: Shelley Society, 1888.

Grabo, Carl. *Prometheus Unbound: An Interpretation*. Chapel Hill, N.C., 1935.

Hogg, Thomas Jefferson. *The Life of Percy Bysshe Shelley*. 4 vols. London, 1858.

Jones F. L. "*Alastor* Foreshadowed in St. Irvyne." *PMLA* 69 (September 1934): 969–71.

Notopoulos, James A. *The Platonism of Shelley*. Durham, 1949.

———. "Shelley and Thomas Taylor." *PMLA* 51 (1936): 502–17.

Rogers, Neville. *Shelley at Work*. Oxford, 1967.

Santayana, George. "Shelley." In *The Winds of Doctrine*. New York and London, 1913.

Sharp, William. *The Life of Percy Bysshe Shelley*. London, 1887.

Todhunter, John. *Notes on Shelley's Unfinished Poem "The Triumph of Life*." London, 1887.

———. *Shelley and the Marriage Question*. London, 1889.

———. *A Study of Shelley*. London, 1880.

White, Newman Ivey, ed. *The Unextinguished Hearth*. Durham, N.C., 1938.

Woodman, Ross Grieg. *The Apocalyptic Vision in the Poetry of Shelley*. Toronto, 1964.

YEATS

Works by Yeats

Autobiographies. London, 1966.

"A Bundle of Poets." *The Speaker* 8 (22 July 1893): 81.

"Discoveries: Second Series." *Massachusetts Review* 5 (Winter 1964): 297–306.

Essays and Introductions. New York, 1961.

Explorations. New York, 1962.

"A First Rough Draft of Memories" (facsimile). MS, Houghton Library.

Ideas of Good and Evil. New York, 1903.

Irish Fairy and Folk Tales. Edited by W. B. Yeats. London, 1888.

"John Todhunter." *The Magazine of Poetry* (Buffalo), vol. 1, no. 2 (1889), pp. 143–44.

The Letters of W. B. Yeats. Edited by Allan Wade. New York, 1955.

Letters on Poetry from W. B. Yeats to Dorothy Wellesley. New York, 1940.

Letters to the New Island. Edited by Horace Reynolds. Cambridge, Mass., 1934.

Mythologies. London, 1959.

"Nationalism and Literature." MS 12148 of the National Library, Dublin.

Plays in Prose and Verse. London, 1922.

Poems. London and Boston, 1895.

The Poems of Spenser. Edited by W. B. Yeats. Edinburgh, 1906.

"Rosa Alchemica." *The Savoy*, no. 2 (April 1896), pp. 56–70.

The Secret Rose. London, 1897.

Seven Poems and a Fragment. Dundrum: Cuala Press, 1922.

The Variorum Edition of the Plays of W. B. Yeats. Edited by Russell Alspach. New York, 1966.

The Variorum Edition of the Poems of W. B. Yeats. Edited by Peter Allt and Russell K. Alspach. New York, 1957.

A Vision. London, 1925.

A Vision. Rev. ed. New York, 1956.

W. B. Yeats and T. Sturge Moore: Their Correspondence, 1901–1937. Edited by Ursula Bridge. London, 1953.

W. B. Yeats: Letters to Katharine Tynan. Edited by Roger McHugh. Dublin, 1953.

Yeats, W. B., Eglinton, John, AE, and Larminie, W. *Literary Ideals in Ireland*. London, 1899.

Works about Yeats

Adams, Hazard. *Blake and Yeats: The Contrary Vision*. Ithaca, N.Y., 1955.

Bloom, Harold. "Yeats and the Romantics." In *Modern Poetry: Essays in Criticism*. Edited by John Hollander. New York, 1968, pp. 501–20.

Bornstein, George J., and Witemeyer, Hugh H. "From *Villain* to Visionary: Pound and Yeats on Villon." *Comparative Literature* 19 (Fall 1967): 308–20.

Bushrui, S. B. *Yeats's Verse Plays: The Revisions 1900–1910*. Oxford, 1965.

Colum, Padraic. "Reminiscences of Yeats." *Tri-Quarterly*, no. 4, pp. 71–76.

Ellmann, Richard. *The Identity of Yeats*. New York, 1954.

———. *Yeats: The Man and the Masks*. New York, 1948.

Engelberg, Edward. *The Vast Design: Patterns in W. B. Yeats's Aesthetic*. Toronto, 1965.

Henn, T. R. *The Lonely Tower: Studies in the Poetry of W. B. Yeats*. Rev. ed. London, 1965.

Hone, Joseph. *W. B. Yeats: 1865–1939*. Rev. ed. London, 1962.

Jeffares, A. Norman. "Thoor, Ballylee." *English Studies* 28 (December 1947): 161–68.

———. *W. B. Yeats: Man and Poet*. Corrected ed. London, 1962.

———. "Yeats's 'The Gyres': Sources and Symbolism." *Huntington Library Quarterly* vol. 15, no. 1 (1951), pp. 87–97.

Jeffares, A. Norman, and Cross, K. G. W., eds. *In Excited Reverie: A Centenary Tribute to William Butler Yeats 1865–1939*. New York, 1965.

Kermode, Frank. *Romantic Image*. New York, 1957.

Lentricchia, Frank. *The Gaiety of Language: An Essay on the Radical Poetics of W. B. Yeats and Wallace Stevens*. Berkeley and Los Angeles, 1968.

Nathan, Leonard E. *The Tragic Drama of William Butler Yeats: Figures in a Dance*. New York and London, 1965.

Parkinson, Thomas. *W. B. Yeats, Self-Critic*. Berkeley and Los Angeles, 1951.

Ronsley, Joseph. *Yeats's Autobiography: Life as Symbolic Pattern*. Cambridge, Mass., 1968.

Rudd, Margaret. *Divided Image*. London, 1953.

Stallworthy, Jon. *Between the Lines: Yeats's Poetry in the Making*. Oxford, 1963.

Torchiana, Donald T. *W. B. Yeats and Georgian Ireland*. Evanston, Ill., 1966.

Unterecker, John, ed. *Yeats: A Collection of Critical Essays*. Englewood Cliffs, N.J., 1963.

Vendler, Helen. *Yeats's Vision and the Later Plays*. Cambridge, Mass., 1963.

Weeks, Donald. "Image and Idea in Yeats's *The Second Coming*." *PMLA* 63 (March 1948): 281–92.

Wilson, F. A. C. *W. B. Yeats and Tradition*. New York, 1958.

RELATED WORKS

Abrams, Meyer. *The Mirror and the Lamp: Romantic Theory and the Critical Tradition*. New York, 1953.

Arnold, Matthew. *The Works of Matthew Arnold*. 15 vols. London, 1903.

Augustine. *Confessions*. Translated by E. B. Pusey. London and New York, 1949.

Blake, William. *The Complete Writings of William Blake*. Edited by Geoffrey Keynes. London, 1957.

Bloom, Harold, and Hilles, Frederick W., eds. *From Sensibility to Romanticism: Essays Presented to Frederick A. Pottle*. New York, 1965.

British and Irish Public Characters of 1798. Dublin, 1799.

Campbell, Mrs. Patrick. *My Life and Some Letters*. London, 1922.

Coleridge, Samuel Taylor. *Collected Letters of Samuel Taylor Coleridge*. Edited by Earl Leslie Griggs. 4 vols. Oxford, 1956.

Dante, Alighieri. *Il Convivio*. Edited by G. Bushnelli and G. Vandelli. 2 vols. Florence, 1934.

De Vere, Aubrey. *Essays, Chiefly on Poetry*. 2 vols. London, 1887.

Evans, Frank B., III. "Thomas Taylor, Platonist." *PMLA* 55 (1940): 1060–79.

Gregory, Lady Augusta. *Lady Gregory's Journals*. Edited by Lennox Robinson. New York, 1947.

Hallam, Arthur Henry. *The Poems of Arthur Henry Hallam*. Edited by Richard Le Gallienne. New York and London, 1893.

———.*The Writings of Arthur Hallam*. Edited by T. H. Vail Motter. New York and London, 1943.

Hinkson, Katharine Tynan. *Twenty-five Years: Reminiscences*. New York, 1913.

A New English Dictionary on Historical Principles. Edited by A. H. Murray et al. 10 vols. Oxford, 1888–1928.

Pausanias. *Description of Greece*. Edited and translated by Thomas Taylor. 3 vols. London, 1794.

Peacock, Thomas Love. *Works of Thomas Love Peacock*. Edited by H. F. B. Brett-Smith and C. E. Jones. 10 vols. London, 1934.

Plato. *The Cratylus, Phaedo, Parmenides and Timaeus of Plato*. Edited and translated by Thomas Taylor. London, 1793.

———. *The Republic*. Translated by Benjamin Jowett. New York: Modern Library, n.d.

———. *The Works of Plato*. Edited and translated by Thomas Taylor. 5 vols. London, 1804.

Poe, Edgar Allan. *The Complete Works of Edgar Allan Poe*. Edited by James A. Harrison. 17 vols. New York, 1902.

"The Poetry of Herbert Trench." Anon. review, *Times Literary Supplement*, 13 November 1924, p. 726.

Porphyry. *The Select Works of Porphyry*. Edited and translated by Thomas Taylor. London, 1823.

Pound, Ezra. *The Spirit of Romance*. Norfolk, Conn., 1953.

Proclus. *The Philosophical and Mathematical Commentaries*. Edited and translated by Thomas Taylor. 2 vols. London, 1788–89.

Raine, Kathleen. "The Sea of Time and Space." *Journal of the Warburg and Courtauld Institutes* 20 (1957): 318–37.

———. "Thomas Taylor, Plato and the English Romantic Movement." *British Journal of Aesthetics* 8 (April 1968): 99–123.

Raine, Kathleen, and Harper, George Mills, eds. *Thomas Taylor the Platonist: Selected Writings*. Princeton, 1969.

Schiller, Friedrich. *Werke*. Edited by F. H. Ehmcke. 2 vols. Zurich and Munich, 1957.

Seward, Barbara. *The Symbolic Rose*. New York, 1960.

Southey, Robert. *New Letters of Robert Southey*. Edited by Kenneth Curry. 2 vols. New York and London, 1965.

———. *Selections from the Letters of Robert Southey*. Edited by John Wood Warter. 4 vols. London, 1856.

Symons, Arthur. *The Romantic Movement in English Poetry*. New York, 1909.

Taylor, Thomas. *A Dissertation on the Eleusinian and Bacchic Mysteries*. Amsterdam, 1790.

"Taylor's Plato." Anon. review. *The Edinburgh Review* 14 (April 1809): 187–211.

Thompson, Francis. *The Real Robert Louis Stevenson*. Edited by Terence L. Connolly. New York, 1959.

Thompson, William I. *The Imagination of an Insurrection: Dublin, Easter 1916*. New York, 1967.

Weygandt, Cornelius. *Irish Plays and Playwrights*. Boston and New York, 1913.

Yeats, John Butler. *Letters of John Butler Yeats*. Edited by Joseph Hone. New York, 1946.

———. *Further Letters of John Butler Yeats*. Edited by Lennox Robinson. Churchtown, Dundrum: Cuala Press, 1920.

INDEX

NOTE: For works by Shelley or Yeats *see* Shelley, works of; Yeats, works of.